UNDER SIEGE

MY FAMILY'S FIGHT TO
SAVE OUR NATION

ERIC F. TRUMP

THRESHOLD EDITIONS

New York   Amsterdam/Antwerp   London
Toronto   Sydney/Melbourne   New Delhi

Threshold Editions
An Imprint of Simon & Schuster, LLC
1230 Avenue of the Americas
New York, NY 10020

First Threshold Editions hardcover edition October 2025

THRESHOLD EDITIONS and colophon are trademarks of Simon & Schuster, LLC

Simon & Schuster strongly believes in freedom of expression and stands against censorship in all its forms. For more information, visit BooksBelong.com.

For information about special discounts for bulk purchases, please contact Simon & Schuster Special Sales at 1-866-506-1949 or business@simonandschuster.com.

The Simon & Schuster Speakers Bureau can bring authors to your live event. For more information or to book an event, contact the Simon & Schuster Speakers Bureau at 1-866-248-3049 or visit our website at www.simonspeakers.com.

Manufactured in the United States of America

10 9 8 7 6 5 4 3 2 1

Library of Congress Cataloging-in-Publication Data has been applied for.

ISBN 978-1-6682-0587-7
ISBN 978-1-6682-0589-1 (ebook)

To my incredible children, Luke and Carolina—

You are my greatest blessings, my daily inspiration, and the future I fight for. Watching you grow reminds me of the power of love, the importance of family, and the responsibility we all have to leave the world better than we found it.

One day, you will read about these times in your history textbooks. When you do, I hope this book stands as a testament to the truth— and a lesson I hope to pass on. In life, hold fast to your integrity, stay resilient, and always have the courage to stand for what's right. Never stop dreaming, never stop fighting for what matters, and always remember how deeply you are loved.

Dad

CONTENTS

Foreword by President Donald J. Trump   ix

Foreword by Lara Trump   xi

Introduction: Under Siege   1

PART ONE: BEFORE THE SIEGE

CHAPTER 1: My Father the Fighter   11

CHAPTER 2: Family Business   21

CHAPTER 3: The Apprentices   36

CHAPTER 4: 2016   53

PART TWO: UNDER SIEGE

CHAPTER 5: Separation of Company and State   77

CHAPTER 6: Welcome to Washington   88

CHAPTER 7: No Good Deed   107

CHAPTER 8: Defeat by a Thousand Cuts   118

CHAPTER 9: Show Me the Crime   139

CHAPTER 10: It's All Connected   158

CHAPTER 11: Not Sending Our Best   178

PART THREE: CRUSHING THE SIEGE

CHAPTER 12: Proud of the Fight   191

CHAPTER 13: Fight, Fight, Fight   209

CHAPTER 14: Success as Revenge   224

EPILOGUE: So Much Winning   238

Acknowledgments   244

Notes   249

FOREWORD

President Donald J. Trump

When Eric left for college at Georgetown University, it wasn't settled whether he would come back to work at the Trump Organization. He was smart, tough, and talented, and the opportunities were limitless. But one day he came to me and said, "Dad, I'm in"—and he has been, 100 PERCENT, since day one.

From making deals in the office and the boardroom, to building, beautifying, and managing our award-winning properties, vetting candidates on *The Celebrity Apprentice*, and campaigning for me in three historic presidential elections, Eric has always been there for me, our family, and our country.

Eric is not one to chase the spotlight. He just works, fights, and WINS. He is calm under pressure, strong, focused, and unshakably loyal. When I first became president, I needed someone I could trust, who was "rock solid," who could lead thousands of employees and oversee the best skyscrapers, golf courses, clubs, hotels, and vineyards, anywhere in the world. Eric was only thirty-three at the time, but I didn't doubt him for an instant. He became my true "apprentice," running the Trump Organization in my absence, and doing an INCREDIBLE job. Many people have said to me, "Sir, Eric might be working even harder than you." He is a WINNER at everything he sets his mind to, and has delivered amazing results, all the while being UNDER SIEGE.

Eric Trump may be the most subpoenaed human being in the history of our country (besides ME!). When the deep state, the hoaxes, and the witch hunts were unleashed on me and my family, and many other brave people, Eric never flinched. He is the kind of person you want with you "in the trenches." Eric never once left my side, but stood tall, unshaken, unbroken. He is a phenomenal son, a devoted husband, a loving, hands-on father, and a great patriot!

This book gives you a look inside our world, the battles we have faced (and won!) together, and what it means to fight on the front lines of a family, company, and country UNDER SIEGE. You will see what we have overcome, but, more importantly, you will see what keeps Eric going—his love of God, family, and the USA.

I am proud of you, Eric!

—**Donald J. Trump**
45th and 47th President of the United States

FOREWORD

Lara Trump

Life is funny. Often, I look back and realize that the times of frustration, failure, or irritation are the very times that have shaped my life for the better. And, no different, on a night I was prepared to enjoy a movie in a comfy set of sweats, my first New York City roommate, Marielle, had other plans. She had a friend in town and desperately wanted me to help entertain for the evening. As irritated as I was in the moment, without that pleading, I certainly would not have ended up meeting my husband.

I noticed a very tall guy, and he noticed me. I'm quite the tall drink of water at five foot eleven, and when I put on heels it's more like six three. Eric is six five. I'll admit, my first thought was, *This guy's taller than me, and I'm in heels. This might just work out. . . .*

Turns out, it did. But I still had some questions. I'll confess I had preconceived ideas about what someone with Eric's background would be like. And those expectations weren't all that good.

I never expected to even *like* Eric Trump, let alone love him. But every day since we met, I've liked—and loved—him more (okay, on average, anyway!). I didn't anticipate he would be genuinely humble and caring and charming. Honestly, I never anticipated *any* of this wild ride we've been on, but here we are.

After dating for about two months, I invited Eric to join me on a weekend trip back home to North Carolina. I had just graduated culinary school and was ready for a relaxing break with friends and family. *What would he be like with my parents and other "normal" people?*

I plugged him into *my* world in my hometown, Wrightsville Beach, in my home state, North Carolina (which would become so consequential to us later in life), without a second thought. And not for a moment did he seem out of place. He just fit in so well, and was so gracious to both my parents. Eric surprised me. He was *normal*. Would I have said "yes" if he'd asked me to marry him that weekend? Maybe not, but that trip was a big deal for me.

A few weeks later, I learned something else about Eric that I didn't expect. We had talked about getting together that week and he mentioned he had plans on Thursday. On Friday morning I found out all about it—on social media.

"Were you at some event last night?" I asked.

He was clearly embarrassed and uncomfortable. "Yeah, I was at a charity event."

It was like pulling teeth, but I soon learned that he had recently started a foundation to help fund the kids at St. Jude Children's Research Hospital, and the event had raised hundreds of thousands of dollars.

When I asked him why he hadn't told me about this, Eric said he didn't want to seem like he was bragging about it. He poured his heart and soul into helping those children, and he still does. As hard as he negotiates in business, he's ten times tougher when it brings extra funds to St. Jude—a mission that became one of the biggest of his life.

Years later, I can't tell you how often I wake up in the middle of the night and look over to find my husband wide awake, staring at the ceiling. "What's going on?" I'll ask. "Are you okay?"

Then he'll tell me about some horrible media lie, one of dozens of subpoenas that were arriving on a weekly basis, or one of the unrelenting court cases he shouldered. He worried about how every attack could affect the thousands of employees, the contractors, the housekeepers, the tenants, and the restaurant staff. During COVID lockdowns, he was focused on people keeping their jobs—especially the many who have been with the company for decades.

When the company sold the Old Post Office hotel, the Trump International Hotel Washington, D.C., one of the conditions Eric insisted on was that the current staff would keep their jobs for a guaranteed period of time. That's rare in this business—and any business, really. It says a lot about this family.

A month before our wedding, I broke my wrists while riding a horse. I couldn't go to work, so I stayed home and tried to follow doctor's orders. One day I heard a knock at the door, which startled both me and our dog, Charlie. I peeked out the window and couldn't believe who was standing there. Sure enough, it was my future father-in-law, Donald Trump.

"I just wanted to see how you were doing. Can I bring you anything?"

Surprised again. It might not sound like much, but that moment meant the world to me.

First, I realized Eric Trump was normal. Then I realized he was anything but normal—in a good way. And so is his family. I hope you'll see it in these pages.

UNDER SIEGE

INTRODUCTION

UNDER SIEGE

> "Every single day we get another subpoena
> and they do it for one reason: because they don't want
> Donald Trump to run and win again in 2024."
> —ME, AUGUST 8, 2022[1]

Good morning, Eric. The FBI is here at Mar-a-Lago with a search warrant. . . . There must be thirty agents."

That's how August 8, 2022, started for me—and my family. I got the phone call in my office. I was surprised, but I wasn't alarmed. Interacting with wonderful people in law enforcement was part of my daily life, from local police to the U.S. Secret Service and everyone in between. There was no reason to believe the FBI was there for anything more than a security sweep.

After all, *if this was a big deal, my father's Secret Service detail at the property certainly would have received plenty of notice, right?*

But something was very wrong with this operation. The more I learned in that call, the more betrayed and furious I felt. I asked if anyone had told my father, and there was a long silence. "Okay," I said. "I'll call him now."

"You're kidding me," he sighed when I gave him the news. We were both in New York at the time, so I headed to his office in Trump Tower.[2]

On the way, I made several calls, attempting to understand what was happening. I phoned the team at Mar-a-Lago and requested that the FBI agents wait for our attorney to observe the search. "Absolutely not," they told the team. One of our attorneys lived nearby, and she arrived at Mar-a-Lago in a matter of minutes. The agents told her she was not allowed on our property and forced her to wait outside the gate.

They also demanded that we turn *off* our security cameras, which we have all across the property to safeguard our members, guests, employees, and family. *No* was my answer. We had no legal obligation to turn off our security system. Refusing to let our lawyer observe was already a red flag. But trying to block us from recording where they went, what they searched, and what they took was worse. This was private property.

Why wouldn't the FBI want anyone to see what they were doing?

My father, seated at his desk, was surprisingly calm when I walked into his office. Behind him, that priceless view of Central Park, Wollman Rink, the Plaza Hotel, the General Motors Building—all part of a skyline he transformed.

Even though we had faced many politically motivated attacks throughout the years, this situation was intensely personal for me. His *home*, our family's home, had been invaded by forces *inside* our government. Mar-a-Lago wasn't just another one of our commercial properties. As a kid, I'd spent countless days there, riding four-wheelers on soon-to-be-transformed landscaping. In a very real sense, it was *my* home.

Yet, on another level, nothing shocked us anymore. After seven years of baseless attacks and outright lies, we were numb to the legal and political lawfare. (Little did we know what would be unleashed over the coming months.)

"It's okay," he said matter-of-factly. "Let's write a statement."

People have all sorts of ideas about how Donald Trump posts on social media or writes statements. If anyone else had their home raided by the FBI, they'd be bouncing off the walls, but he was incredibly cool, collected, and confident. As I'd seen countless times before, and would see again and again, his level of calm was remarkable as he wrote these words: "These are dark times for our Nation, as my beautiful home, Mar-a-Lago in Palm Beach, Florida, is currently under siege, raided, and occupied by a large group of FBI agents."[3]

My father always says what needs to be said. Most people in similar circumstances would have a dozen lawyers in the room, debating what to say—and the pros and cons of saying anything at all. But he and I knew exactly what this raid was about. Whoever orchestrated it wanted to release *their* version to the press on their own terms.

Remember in 2019 how CNN *just happened* to have a camera crew set up at Roger Stone's home when the FBI raided it at 6 a.m.? I can relate; I often learned about an oncoming subpoena from the media—before it arrived at my office. He wasn't about to let anyone else tell this story.

"Nothing like this has ever happened to a President of the United States before. After working and cooperating with the relevant Government agencies, this unannounced raid on my home was not necessary or appropriate."

He knew not to trust the establishment or the media. This was not a statement to the press. He wrote directly to the American people.

"Such an assault could only take place in broken, Third-World Countries. Sadly, America has now become one of those Countries, corrupt at a level not seen before. They even broke into my safe!"

Transparency was, and always is, the only way to seek true justice. People needed to be reminded of the never-ending attacks and see this day in its true context.

"The political persecution of President Donald J. Trump has been going on for years, with the now fully debunked Russia, Russia, Russia Scam, Impeachment Hoax #1, Impeachment Hoax #2, and so much more, it just never ends. It is political targeting at the highest level!"

We immediately knew the *real* reason why Mar-a-Lago was being ransacked like a crime scene. And most Americans did, too, regardless of political affiliation. And we would soon learn that Joe Biden had a hobby of collecting classified documents and "willfully" sharing them with others.[4][5] The fake outrage and lawfare from the Left was another example of their projection—accusing others of what they're guilty of.[6]

"Now, as they watch my endorsed candidates win big victories, and see my dominance in all polls, they are trying to stop me, and the Republican Party, once more. The lawlessness, political persecution, and Witch Hunt must be exposed and stopped. I will continue to fight for the Great American People!"

In true Donald Trump fashion, he broke the internet with his statement that morning. The story dominated the headlines for months in 2022 and beyond, but not exactly the way the White House and Department of Justice crew hoped it would.

* * *

The first seventeen months of the Biden-Harris administration had not been going the way of the Democrats' wishful thinking. Or, to put it more directly, everything they touched was failing.

Gas prices were soaring, as were inflation, interest, and crime rates. Bidenomics went from being a hopeful slogan to a derogatory term.

Iran and China were rattling their swords as the smell of weakness from the Oval Office spread around the world. In just two years, the United States had gone from being energy independent back into energy dependency. And to add to all of this, was the botched withdrawal from Afghanistan, a year earlier, which was a national disgrace, a heartbreaking human tragedy, and a strategic scandal.

The southern border had gone from bad to worse under the absentee "border czar." Despite a coordinated cover-up by the media and the establishment, people were waking up to the fact that Hunter Biden's laptop was not some Russian hoax, and reported kickbacks to "the big guy" were ringing true to anyone who followed the money.[7]

Oh, and the midterm election was just *three months away*.

The worse Joe Biden looked (and he was looking worse every time he spoke), the better Donald J. Trump looked. And that was unacceptable to the Left. But this was about more than public perception. The more that people realized the *truth* about Biden and Trump—and saw the glaring differences in their words, actions, and outcomes—the more desperate Biden and company became. They needed to change the narrative.

The world stopped when we broke the story that morning. News helicopters hovered around Mar-a-Lago for days on end. As we watched news coverage and aerial shots, my father remarked how beautiful the property looked. I joked that the footage ran like an infomercial—the stunning landscaping, close-up aerial views of the facilities and signature tower, with water glistening on either side. The name Mar-a-Lago means "sea-to-lake" in Spanish, reflecting the fact that the estate extends from one side of Palm Beach Island to the other, touching the Atlantic Ocean on the east and the Intracoastal Waterway on the west. As usual, we managed to have some lighter moments despite this new barrage of attacks.

I soon learned that the FBI and the Biden administration were not happy about the statement. Donald J. Trump beat them to the punch and they were furious. "How dare you make this public?" they squealed.

How dare you *raid our home!!*

Despite the fact that my father's team was in communication about false claims of classified material, the FBI took passports, medical records, tax returns, and personal documents protected under attorney-client privilege. FBI agents went through Melania's closet and searched Barron's room. He was just sixteen years old at the time. No wonder they wanted our security cameras turned off. Sifting through underwear drawers was not a good look.

And it wasn't until two years later that it was revealed that the FBI had been authorized to use *deadly force* during the raid. That's right. Shoot to kill, if necessary. The FBI later said this was "standard protocol," which raises even bigger questions. There was nothing "standard" about this home invasion, so why would they keep this lethal option on the table that day?[8]

We would also learn that what was taken during the raid had been compromised—tampered with—and documents were flagged, with false "classified" cover sheets in the FBI's staged photo shoots.[9] As more details came out, our disbelief and anger exploded. On the day of the raid I posted on Twitter (now X), "We truly live in a third world country!"

Who had authorized this raid? They would never raid the Clintons' or the Obamas' home, right? Hillary had a secret email server in her home—I didn't see the FBI storm her home in Chappaqua!

I started raising obvious points, like the fact that there was no way in hell that the FBI director would authorize a raid on a former president's home without White House approval.[10] The timing of the raid was also suspect. The Secret Service knew that my father was in New York at the time. And did the Biden administration actually expect anyone to believe the raid was on behalf of the National Archives and Records Administration (NARA) as was originally stated—*a glorified public library*?

A family that has always loved and supported law enforcement had their front door "kicked in." But thousands of people came out in support that day, driving by the property and lining the street and nearby overpass, waving Trump flags and American flags. Quite the contrast to today's paid protesters on the Left.

The next day I posted, "Breaking: DonaldJTrump.com is shattering all fundraising records and I'm told has raised more money in the past 24 hours than ever before in recent history! The American people are pissed!"[11] (Two years later we'd break another fundraising record, based on one of the sham trials in New York City.) This misguided and malicious raid was, for millions of voters, absolute proof that Donald J. Trump was a political target—and that the system was corrupt.

THIS IS ABOUT YOU

As we learned during the 2016 campaign, clear-minded people can see through political attacks—and that the system was corrupt. Deep down they know these are also attacks on them, their freedoms, and their future.

Does anyone think the raid, the lawsuits, the spying, the hoaxes, made-up and paid-for dossiers, and attempts to remove a candidate from ballots are about bringing down one *man*?

These attacks were—and still are—about bringing down a *movement*. And let's be honest, the "movement" the Left is attacking is actually foundational American values and constitutional patriotism. *You* are the movement.

In February of 2024, the Biden administration confirmed that federal investigators worked with financial institutions to surveil Americans based on "politically charged search terms" like "MAGA" and "Trump."[12] According to a report by the House Judiciary Committee in March of 2024, the federal government conducted "broad" surveillance of private financial transactions based on so-called "extremism indicators," which included "the purchase of books (including religious texts)," like the Bible.[13]

But this is nothing new. Under President Obama, the IRS finally admitted it had targeted conservative groups. When Lois Lerner, the director of exempt organizations, was pressed for answers, her emails conveniently disappeared when a computer "crashed."[14] *I bet Lois and Hillary had the same IT guy.*

The raid on Mar-a-Lago was a global news story, but still has implications for today. We are under siege. Does that sound like an exaggeration? The term *siege* has two main meanings: to compel surrender, and a persistent attack.[15] That's an accurate definition of what has been done to my father, our family, and our business. The assassination attempt on July 13, 2024, wasn't the beginning—it was the culmination. A violent act in a long series of coordinated battles waged against us in courtrooms, in the media, and through the full weight of the United States government. The Left does not just disagree with us—they fear us. And in that fear, they have chosen to weaponize the very institutions meant to serve the people. Targeting law-abiding citizens is not justice—it's a betrayal of the Constitution, of the legal system, and of basic decency. The raid on Mar-a-Lago was not the first time the country I loved would break my heart. And it would not be the last. The raid was symbolic. It was about a fight for power.

Welcome to the fight. Welcome to my family.

PART ONE

BEFORE THE SIEGE

CHAPTER 1

MY FATHER THE FIGHTER

"Going against the tide is often a very clever thing to do.
While it can involve unbelievable risks, often, going in the
opposite direction can lead to the highest level of
achievement."
—DONALD TRUMP, *THE ART OF THE COMEBACK*[1]

How do I describe my father to you?

Have you ever tried to tell a friend all about your mom or dad? It's impossible, right? Now imagine describing Donald Trump. Regardless, I'm going to try. (Dad, I know these words will fall short, but I hope they show my absolute love and eternal respect.)

Donald Trump is certainly "unconventional." He is certainly not "politically correct"; he's tough, no bullshit, and beautifully ambitious. He also has a heart of gold and is the greatest father a son or daughter could ever have.

To say my father is motivated when it comes to achieving his dreams is an understatement. When I was growing up, his life was his business. He has a work ethic that is unparalleled, and he is laser-focused—which all Americans still witness today. The older I get, the more I appreciate his absolute dedication to the goals and tasks at hand. Defining skylines, building the best hotels and golf courses, acquiring properties, building a brand, becoming an icon, having the number one TV show, and achieving the ultimate success: winning the two (*three?*) general elections and becoming the 45th and 47th president of the United States.

He always set his sights high. He aimed for the moon and rarely fell short. He was and is the ultimate competitor. It's a magical combination.

Did he miss some of my school activities? Sure. Wiffle ball in the backyard every afternoon? No. But my childhood was . . . unparalleled. In the mid-to-late eighties, we flew back and forth every weekend to Atlantic City on his Super Puma helicopter as he built the East Coast's "Las Vegas." We made that trip together hundreds of times, usually with fascinating guests on board. These were the days of Mike Tyson and Don King, Michael Jackson, Axl Rose, Tony Bennett, and Barbara Walters—the biggest stars, celebrities, and businesspeople. The casinos were booming, and Atlantic City was the place to be for the biggest events. As a child, I was along for the ride of a lifetime that I'd later realize was truly incomparable.

In New York, my father was building and operating some of the most iconic buildings and properties in the world: the amazing Plaza Hotel, Trump Tower, Trump World Tower, Trump Park Avenue, the General Motors Building, Wollman Rink, 40 Wall Street—a seemingly endless skyline. I spent countless hours in his office on the twenty-sixth floor of Trump Tower building *my* buildings, with Legos, as he built his.

He was creating an empire, he was building his family, and he was shaping his son. Sure, I'd sometimes dream of sitting in that chair someday, running the company. But honestly, I was simply trying to soak it all in. That day did come, but in a way I never imagined.

THE ORIGINAL APPRENTICE

My real, and favorite, classroom was wherever my father was. If he was checking on a property on the weekend, I would often follow him through the maze of conduit, framing, and HVAC ducting, watching what he did, how he spoke, and where he was focused. He taught more by example than instruction, which was always his style. Those visits and conversations were priceless and fascinating. Yes, I went to "prestigious" schools, but watching and working with him all those years taught me far more.

Despite his pace, my father was always good at being present when it mattered, while also giving us freedom and latitude. He maintained his expectations, but did so without needing to lecture. Candidly, my biggest struggle today is finding the balance between running one of the largest private real estate empires on earth and enjoying my beautiful family. My father got that balance right. He brought us into a life that was so much larger than ourselves, but he also shielded us from that very life when it was ugly, evil, and strained.

Don, Ivanka, and I had everything we could have wanted growing up—including love and support from both our parents. We lived at some of the most iconic addresses on earth, places like Mar-a-Lago and the penthouse of Trump Tower. Even though we were at the casinos on weekends and in the best schools during the week, my parents were also fundamentally against giving us money to burn.

Our father didn't just want us to *have* money, he wanted us to *understand* money. I was raised to be motivated to work and gain skills to be successful. Donald Trump understood that success never comes in the form of a handout; it always comes in the form of work. But even work took second place to family.

My father's door was always open, and his kids were always first. And no matter who he was meeting with, as a child I was always welcomed to play on the floor and build my toy empires—as long as I did so with good manners and respect. He would always stop for his kids. *Always.*

When I called his office "1-800-Collect" from school, or immediately after a presidential debate (his adrenaline still racing), I was never told that he would call me back later. And that's true with each of my siblings: Don, Ivanka, Tiffany, and Barron. I've had him pick up the phone when he was in meetings with some of the most powerful and famous people in the world.

"Hi, Eric, I'm here with the great Mayor Giuliani. Say hello!" It didn't matter if it was Hillary Clinton, Prince Charles, or the biggest artists, singers, entertainers, and captains of industry. Today, it still holds true during conversations with congressmen, senators, and the most important heads of state.

Being the proverbial fly-on-the-wall was an education in itself, an initiation into a life that was hard to grasp at a young age, but one that I am truly blessed to have experienced.

THE TRUMP "EYE"

Donald Trump has an eye for detail unlike anyone I have ever known . . . except for maybe me, though I both inherited it and learned it from him. Even when walking briskly through a casino with an entourage, he could glance up at a thousand light fixtures and spot the single burned-out bulb. At first, as a child, I was too mesmerized by the energy of a room to notice the small details, but he was never distracted, and he expected perfection. He expected the people around him to be meticulous. His focus on "simple" excellence brought focus to our teams and instilled pride in everyone at our properties.

A burned-out bulb or drip of paint would stop our convoy in its tracks. You better believe that made a statement, and you better believe it would be fixed before he walked past the area again.

In the same way, my father always had a remarkable ability to spot talent and a remarkable willingness to give people big opportunities. Very often, these people didn't have the credentials "on paper" and might never have been given a chance in the corporate world. But once he saw that talent, he would build them up, instill confidence, empower them to succeed, and then brag to others about their abilities. He changed so many lives and helped so many people realize their true potential. I see it to this day in his role as president.

I'll never forget when, as a young child, we drove by a beautiful stone wall being built by a lone craftsman. "That's the most incredible wall I've ever seen," my father said. *"Did you see that, Eric?"* He hit the brakes on the white Rolls-Royce, backed up, and pulled over next to the man.

Oh my God, it's Donald Trump, he must have thought.

"Hi, I'm Donald Trump. What a beautiful wall!" After a few minutes discussing masonry, the benefits of bluestone versus granite, "dry-stacked" versus "wet-packed" stone walls, the art of pointing, and cement chemistry, my father said, "Give me your number. I'd like to give you my work."

Sure enough, weeks later, Frank Sanzo brought his skills to one of our projects. Before long, it was clear that not only was he a world-class mason, but he was also a man who could get anything accomplished with zero bullshit—a perfect fit for the Trump Organization.

He was a lead member of our team for decades and became a father figure to me.

Frank was an old-school Italian, in all the best ways. He would laugh if his guys—or if I—decided to wear gloves as we demolished walls, built the most beautiful patios, poured concrete, toppled trees with chainsaws, and brought Trump projects to life. Olive oil was the cure for every scrape or injury. Frank was pure steel, fueled by pots of coffee and packs of Marlboro Reds.

I worked for him for many summers, and my lungs suffered for it, but the experience was truly priceless. I endured his crew's hazing for being the prepubescent kid in a testosterone-charged group of work-hardened men but I was relentless and stubborn. I loved arriving at the jobsite every morning, and the feeling of accomplishment when I looked at what we had built that day. What I lacked in strength and skill, I made up for in hard work, regardless of making minimum wage. Along with expanding my colorful vocabulary, I earned their respect. Several of those incredible men still work with me today.

The beauty that Donald Trump spotted in that stone wall was ingrained into the culture of our company. Thanks to Frank and hundreds of people with the same dedication to excellence—from building to customer service to sales—our company stands apart.

THE GREATEST SALESMAN

A real estate development can be beautiful, but if you can't sell your product, or the vision behind it, you will fail.

My father left the world of middle-income walk-up buildings in Brooklyn and Queens, for which my grandfather had become so well known. Donald Trump was enamored by Manhattan and its energy—captivated by building the biggest and the best, the tallest and the most beautiful, and the most expensive. New York real estate was the ultimate cutthroat, high-stakes game; that's what he thought back then, anyway.

My grandfather's favorite building materials were bricks: cheap and indestructible, yet ordinary. My father's choice was glass: expensive, fragile by comparison, yet extraordinary.

Unlike the middle-income projects in the outer boroughs, in luxury real estate you were not selling to people who *needed* a product—you were selling to a person who aspired to own a certain product and live a certain lifestyle.

There was no one better at selling a vision and a lifestyle than Donald Trump. There was also no one better at executing and bringing that vision to life and I would argue this is even more true today.

People by nature are attracted to positivity and his voice carries that energy. "I'm building the greatest skyscrapers in New York," he would say. He would acquire the best location, pick the most talented architects, and set new standards. Where other developers were using small twelve-inch-by-twelve-inch tiles, he would use four-foot-by-four-foot slab marble, book-matched perfectly so the grain of the stone would continue seamlessly across a lobby. Where others would install a five-foot bathtub and a single sink in a master bathroom, he would install a six-foot-six-inch Jacuzzi, dual vanities, and a bidet. Where other developers would design nine-foot ceilings in a penthouse, he would create fifteen-foot ceilings with solid glass exterior walls and unobstructed views of the city.

But in addition to running ahead of the competition, he could also *sell* that dream.

Donald Trump could describe properties in the simplest yet most compelling terms. He was never interested in the poetic nonsense written by overpriced PR firms. His messages were, and are, always simple and strong. "Turnberry is the greatest golf course on the planet. Nothing compares." It was an easy message to carry because it was true. "I have friends who buy Monets," he would say. "Turnberry is my Monet, and it's far more beautiful."

As a company, we've built many projects from the ground up. Other times, we purchased properties where previous owners didn't have vision or couldn't execute. He was the best at turning a diamond in the rough into the most iconic properties. Time after time, previous owners would come back to our renovated properties and say, "I just never saw the potential that you saw." Often, the difference was seeing what others couldn't; other times it was simply having pride of ownership and unwavering standards.

The first time Ivanka and I toured what would become Trump Doral, we decided to have lunch in one of the restaurants. Over her shoulder, I saw an uninvited guest walk across the floor and sit down in the middle of the dining area. It was a rat. That vermin symbolized what I already knew—the then-owners and management had lost all pride, vision, and care.

Paint sticks were holding live wires apart in electrical panels that should have had circuit breakers. Everything was grimy. When we saw empty beer cans scattered in the management's office, I knew I would let them go before the ink on the contract was dry. That property became one of our most successful turnarounds. Open any door to any mechanical room and it will be spotless, well lit, organized, perfectly painted, and dust free.

Believe it or not, government can work the same way. But it takes more than words. Turnaround requires both *pride and execution*.

My father always campaigned on recapturing our nation's potential. He sold a vision. "America is the best. We are the strongest military, we have the greatest economy, and we have the most energy." He is the rare combination of a positive visionary and someone who can execute and deliver.

Passion breeds passion. Optimism breeds optimism. Results breed results. Donald Trump embodies all of the above. He is the world's best cheerleader, certainly in promoting iconic properties, but more importantly in promoting the United States of America.

Donald Trump has always seen potential—in real estate and in our nation. There's a positive vision of America that he carries in his mind, and he couldn't shake it if he tried. I feel the same way. That's why he left a business empire to Make America Great Again.

THE FIGHTER

I always say that the very quality that makes Donald Trump the most effective president is the same one that was most used against him on the campaign trail. He has always believed that if somebody punches you in the face, you punch back—harder. While past administrations, in both parties, let other nations, meddlers, and terrorist organizations walk all over our country, he punches back.

I have learned that hitting back delivers two powerful results: first, it makes your opponents far less likely to come after you again; second, it sends a clear warning that makes others think twice before even taking a swing. This is, as they say in international circles, *deterrence*. The alternative is weakness.

In the early nineties, when Donald Trump was $900 million in debt, he fought and worked relentlessly. He went to war with the banks and he came back stronger than ever. (So the saying goes "If you owe a million dollars, the bank owns you. If you owe a billion dollars, you own the bank.") He was listed in *The Guinness Book of World Records* for the "Greatest Personal Financial Recovery."[2] He always focused on solutions, not the problems, and he was willing to fight.

This country needs fighters. It needs people who will stand up for it, who can't be bought, bribed, or coerced. The past ten years have shown how important it is to have a leader who will stand up for *themselves* against unthinkable lies, fake news, distortions, slander, and the never-ending stream of "tell-all books" and interviews.

I have seen lies written by distant family members, who pretend to know us, but neither my father nor I have spent fifteen minutes with that person in the last thirty years. Then I read the catchy headlines; how that individual exposed the "dark history" of our family. Give me a break. I've connected with some Uber drivers on a deeper level than those "tell-all" authors.

Sometimes it's not easy to bite my tongue, especially when it's a relative whom you've given millions of dollars to help support. Frankly, I often take those hits more personally than my father, who might just understand the often-cruel reality of life. But that leads me to something else I've learned from my father.

He taught us not to let emotions cloud our judgment.

In the thick of the lawfare that intensified in 2024, Donald Trump was incredibly stoic. I was in the New York courtroom when they read off the thirty-four felony counts. After court was adjourned for the day, he stood up, turned around, looked me in the eye, and shook my hand. His face was no different than it was that morning in the car on the way to the courthouse—or most mornings at the office.

Some of the worst moments, when bad news and insane lies were raining down, have been the times I've seen him stay the calmest. And this includes the lawfare, the siege at Mar-a-Lago, and the brutal campaigns. His words, his calm, and his example have helped me and my family navigate these challenges as well.

THE LOYAL FRIEND

From my perspective, Donald Trump has been exponentially more loyal to friends than certain ones have been to him. The "good ones" (you know who you are) are rare. The bad ones probably know it, too, albeit they're always quick to offer fake pleasantries. None of it is lost on any of us—they're present in good times and absent in bad. They clamber to go to inaugurations, while ignoring requests to testify in court or speak up in the media, when their voice or testimony would make a difference. They voice adamant support in person, but attend fundraisers for political opponents when commercially profitable and politically expedient. I have seen it all.

There's much more I could say on the subject, but one powerful example of true friendship—although I could name many—is our friend Steve Witkoff. Steve was at the grueling trial in Manhattan almost every day, sitting on those hard, uncomfortable wooden "pews." He had zero reason to be in that courtroom except for the quiet, steadfast loyalty of being there and standing by his friend.

When my father told us in 2015 that after he entered the presidential race "we would find out who our *real* friends were," he wasn't kidding. As his son, I've learned it's all about who is there when it matters.

BEING THERE

During the trials in N.Y.C., I was in the front row virtually every day. Frankly, as a businessman, I find that *not* being in control—not being able to effectuate change or a desired outcome—is frustrating and uncomfortable.

There was nothing I could do in those courtrooms. But I was there. When the verdicts were read, when my father turned around, I was the first person he would see. We shook hands and walked out of the building together, heads held high.

Sure, the connection with my dad was built in good times, iconic projects, long talks, and unforgettable life moments. But as I think about what truly forged our bond—what stands out to me—is that it was in the toughest, lowest moments, when so few others showed up, that our connection grew strongest. And it's usually not the words, it's simply being there. It's the look in the eye. It's the feel of the handshake. It's knowing who was there next to you when it was uncomfortable, and when it mattered.

Dad, you are absolutely unconventional—and unequaled. You're a father and a fighter with unrelenting determination and conviction. I'm so grateful you went against the tide and that you still do.

The world may not fully realize what an incredible man, father, and grandfather you are—but I do, and I'm grateful every day.

CHAPTER 2

FAMILY BUSINESS

"OK, Boys, Biz Is All Yours"

—*NEW YORK POST* HEADLINE, JANUARY 12, 2017

Before *The Apprentice*, there were three real-life apprentices: Don Jr., Ivanka, and me. We didn't fully realize it in our early years, but we were in training to take the reins of the Trump Organization, and each of us would contribute in our own unique ways.

Over three decades we have built one of the most famous global brands. Our phenomenal company has some of the best properties on earth, including iconic hotels, golf courses, residential and commercial buildings, retail, hospitality, estates, vineyards, and countless other entities. Our properties have thousands of members, residences, homeowners, and customers—and we cater to hundreds of thousands of guests who come through our lobbies each and every year. Most important, we are blessed to have several thousand of the most talented and kind employees, many of whom have spent their entire careers in the company and are like members of our family.

Leading up to 2015, Don, Ivanka, and I were focused on new projects across the country and internationally. The White House was certainly not on our minds, and a life in the political arena certainly wasn't on the radar for young Tiffany or Barron.

My older brother, Don, was always my closest friend. As kids we were inseparable. He taught me to shoot, hunt, and fish—striped bass in the Long Island Sound and bluefish on a small, 11.9-foot Boston Whaler. Don is six years older than me and always had a loud voice, strong presence, and huge personality. He never cared that much for the minute details of operations, but was the perfect personality for partners, overseas deals, and marketing. He was made for the microphone and for social media. Amazingly, he thrives on both ends of the spectrum: in the serenity of the wilderness and in the chaos of politics.

During our father's first term as president, I'll never forget the Secret Service agents storming into my office in Trump Tower. These professionals are some of the most incredible people you will ever meet.

"Eric, we have a problem," the agents said. Their faces wore that classic, no-BS look, but I could tell they were concerned.

"What happened?"

"Don wants to go hunting in Turkmenistan with some buddies. Sir, do you know where that is located? It borders Iran and Afghanistan."

After ending terrorist leaders Qasem Soleimani and Abu Bakr al-Baghdadi, let's just say that part of the world was, and remains, off-limits for Westerners—especially those wearing our last name. Relieved and trying not to laugh at the distress of two agents I loved and respected, I assured them, "Guys, I'll handle it."

I walked to his office. "Don, I love you. I love your sense of adventure, but are you out of your fucking mind?!"

Suffice it to say, some mountain sheep lived to see another day, in Turkmenistan, anyway, but there are several points to this story. First, welcome to my world, which straddles business, family, politics, and international relations. Second, those agents probably would have made the trip because they are the best. Don's love for the outdoors knows no boundaries. While he might not outshoot his little brother with a shotgun or rifle, or anything else that flies through the air, Don is a modern-day Teddy Roosevelt, and I don't say that lightly.

By the way, my Secret Service code name *was* Marksman because of my love for the shooting sports. Each of our code names began with the letter *M*.

Donald J. Trump: Mogul (titan of industry)
Melania: Muse (inspirational force)
Ivanka: Marvel (wonder and amazement)
Don: Mountaineer (always looking for new adventures)
Eric: Marksman (skilled and focused on the target)

Lara: Marathon (Spartan attitude with endurance and grit)
Luke, our son: Musket (powerful, loud, and the product of a
    marksman)
Carolina, our daughter: Mermaid (Lara won that debate . . . I
    wanted Machete)

Ivanka was always a superstar in virtually every aspect of her life. She could represent any five-star brand in the world with her natural sophistication and polish. In public, she chooses her words carefully, but authentically. She is remarkably on point, with poise and elegance like few others. Like our mom, she loves design and naturally brings glamour to everything she does. She can wow a room in any setting or zoom by everyone on a ski slope, all with our mother's elegance.

When the cameras are off, she is remarkably funny. Don't let that poise fool you—she will let out a hilarious "snort" if you really get her laughing. Growing up, Ivanka would blame Don (or me) for virtually every mistake she made as a child, including the legendary destruction of a priceless chandelier with a beach ball. She threw Don under the bus but Ivanka really is a wonderful person, mother, and friend.

My personality is probably a mix of both of them—but different. I love the outdoors and have always been fascinated with construction, finance, and business. I can live in a suit or in Carhartts. People often ask if I'm a big-picture person or a details person, and my answer is *both*.

I know every detail of a property, from HVAC to carpet to design. I've always hated wasted space and inefficiency. One might call it OCD, but everything needs to be perfect, clean, and organized. I'm famous for doing property visits and beginning with the loading dock—opening every closet and setting a high bar in spaces guests would never see. But it matters. No company compares to the standards of our assets.

Once the presidential campaigns started, for security reasons we rarely entered through the main lobbies of hotels. I was always shocked at what I saw at the "big name" hotels: burned-out lights, dirty hallways, scraped-up walls, ceiling tiles missing or stained. Our properties are a reflection of all of us, our family, employees, and customers. But that ethos seems lost in the big-box brands.

So many of the properties we have acquired had solid "bones," but were poorly run. There was no one better at seeing potential than Donald Trump—buying buildings like 40 Wall Street, Mar-a-Lago, and the Old Post Office in Washington, D.C., for pennies on the dollar and turning them into crown jewels. Before the presidential campaign was even a dream, my father did an unbeatable job of being the face and leader of the Trump Organization. He also did an unbelievable job of growing us into the people we are today.

After the 2016 election, Ivanka decided to pursue opportunities to help in Washington. Alongside Jared, their family moved to Washington, D.C., weeks before my father took office.

I can't say this enough: *We were outsiders.* Our dad always joked that he had only been to D.C. ten times prior to his inauguration, and most of those visits were with us as we renovated the Old Post Office, a magnificent hotel we redeveloped at 1100 Pennsylvania Avenue. That hotel became a home away from home for our family when our father lived down the block at 1600. Having Ivanka in Washington was a gift for our entire family. First, she would be effective at anything she chose to do, and second, having us nearby would be important to a new president navigating a new world. There is a perspective that only family can bring.

While Don remained involved in the company, he also pursued his passion in the political arena, helping Republicans win elections across the country. It was a true team effort—each of us harnessing our passions, skills, talents, and ambitions and contributing in our own way. From our days on *The Celebrity Apprentice* to reshaping skylines around the world— and ultimately helping secure one of the biggest victories in U.S. history by dethroning a political dynasty—we became a truly formidable team.

With all this success and opportunity came great responsibility. As Luke 12:48 reminds us, "to whom much is given, much is required." The path ahead was ours to build or to break—but thankfully, we had some excellent guidance.

RAISING TRUMPS

Despite the unique environment we were born into, our parents did a remarkable job of keeping us out of the spotlight. Yes, we constantly accompanied them to events, parties, fights in Atlantic City, and on construction sites, but somehow, in their own way, they kept us grounded.

My mom, Ivana Marie Zelníčková, was born and raised in communist Czechoslovakia. Don, Ivanka, and I spent a significant amount of time there with my mother's parents in the summertime—even before the Berlin Wall fell and the country freed itself from the Soviet Union in 1989. At first, I was too young to fully appreciate the country's fight for freedom. But with every visit I noticed the stark differences between our countries and the shadow of communism—even after the country broke free and became the Czech Republic.

Food was simple. Items we took for granted in America weren't available. Forget video games or television. The price of gasoline dictated whether my grandparents used their car that week or not. Speaking of cars, I learned to drive a stick shift on a well-used Škoda.

As you might know, or can imagine, the country was very poor, like other former Soviet satellites. My grandparents' humble way of life was a far cry from the three-story penthouse in Trump Tower overlooking the Manhattan skyline. Our Czech playground was the woods, mowing the small yard, making bows and arrows out of string and tree branches, and target practice with a well-used BB gun. We all played cards and cooked sausages over small campfires. So pure. So innocent. So right, in many ways.

Those summers helped us understand how blessed we were in the United States, but also to appreciate the aspects of life that are most important and can't be measured in dollars or square feet. The experiences gave us understanding of life outside of our fairy-tale home and a lasting respect for the grit, hard work, and courage of those individuals in a post-communist world.

My grandmother was a telephone operator and worked in a shoe factory. My grandfather was an electrical engineer. They raised my mom, Ivana—a force of nature. She grew up in that hard, gray world that few Americans can imagine. She was a gifted athlete and contender for the Czechoslovakian National ski team, which opened up opportunities to travel and attend university. At her first victory in a ski race, she won an orange. No, that's not some kind of medal, but an *actual* orange—an exotic fruit rarely seen in that country. My mom was a professional skier by day and a fashion model by night. The only people allowed out of the country were the athletes, to train and compete. So she went to Canada, and then to New York.

She could race the best male skiers down the slopes in Colorado, then put on her stilettos and grace the most famous runways in the world. She was tough, yet elegant, fun, yet firm.

Her parenting style made my father seem like an easy mark. She expected her kids to open doors for others and finish the food on their plates—even liver, which she loved, but that tasted horrible to our little palates. When it came to discipline, more times than I can count, I felt her long fingernails on my neck. A spanking was not off-limits (they were extremely frequent); as shunned as it is in today's society, it was 100 percent effective on the three of us. As we got older, I often heard her go-to reply to our complaints: "Too fucking bad. *Deal with it.*"

And you know what? We learned to deal with it.

As she said in one of her interviews in her tough but beautiful Slavic accent:

I gave my kids enough money to be able to give their friends . . . buy the pizza or buy the hamburger, and take them out, but that was it. And then you teach your kids the value over the money. I would take the kids to Europe on the months of June and July, and months of August, they had to return back to America from age of ten. They were working on cutting the grass on the Trump golf courses. They had to go and clean up the boats in Atlantic City, which I ran because there was a shipyard, or Ivanka was working in the flower shop. . . . And they were making four to five dollars an hour, 9 a.m. to 5 p.m., and eventually, Donald Jr. was like fourteen. And he came to me and he said, "Mom, why you don't raise us from four dollars to six dollars?"

And I said, "You know why?"

"Why?"

I said, "Because you did not ask. You don't ask, you don't get."

My mom was a tough but gracious businesswoman. She could speak easily with anyone. Construction workers loved her, as did British royalty. She had a sharp sense of humor, put up with zero bullshit, and was a matchless negotiator. She would go toe-to-toe in negotiations with the biggest union guys in the city at a time when women just weren't part of those conversations. She was an iconic trailblazer.

My high school graduation happened to be on the same week as the Monte Carlo Grand Prix, which is a very big deal to Europeans. When I told her the date of my ceremony, she replied, "Eric, no frickin' way. Sorry. Every moron graduates high school. I'm not missing Monte Carlo." Don, Ivanka, and I still laugh about that moment to this day. (By the way, if this was about graduating from MIT with a PhD, I would have received the same answer.) That might sound harsh, but really, she simply spoke her mind. Her attitude gave us the backbone we would need later in life. And the truth was, we spent a lot of time together—more than I sometimes appreciated as a kid. I miss her.

I saw the world before the age of eighteen because of her adventurous spirit. We were dragged to operas, musicals, and black-tie events around the globe. I hated it at the time, but truly appreciate now how she opened our eyes to the world and gave us a different lens through which to view it. My siblings and I developed into social chameleons, in a positive sense. We were as comfortable with royalty as we were with the concrete crew.

My mother was caviar and champagne; my father is meat and potatoes. She knew every street of every European city. He knew every square inch of New York—and would own many of them. She often joked with my father, "When the kids turn eighteen, I'm done. I got them through school, took care of them, taught them to be great skiers, and showed them the world. They're good kids. Now, Donald, it's on you."

She shaped so much of our childhood, and our father shaped our entire adulthood. Sadly, in the later years of her life, she struggled with alcohol—a gene unfortunately all too pervasive in our family.

I've never talked about this publicly, but I was at Mom's townhouse just minutes after her body was found in 2022. I was in my Trump Tower office when the call came, and I beat the paramedics to her home on 64th Street, just blocks away. After they left, I sat in silence. She was gone. But I couldn't really grieve yet. Her fall down the staircase had left a gruesome trail of blood.

I sat and slowly, carefully, cleaned her blood off the stairs, in the house she called a home for many years.

I have always tried to be cleanup guy—the one who steps up when it matters most—quietly handling the hardest moments so the rest of the family doesn't have to. That day was no different.

It's true that my mom had an alcohol problem late in life, and drinking contributed to the accident that ended her life. But that's such a tiny piece of who she was. Ivana Trump was a wife, a mom, a cultural icon, and one of the top saleswomen that the Home Shopping Network and QVC ever had. Women in Middle America adored her. She embraced a movement and female empowerment with her no-bullshit "Don't get mad, get everything" line, made famous in *The First Wives Club*. My parents were *the* power couple in New York for many years. But when the studio lights went out and the haute couture came off, she was a hard-charging athlete and businesswoman. *And she loved her kids fiercely.*

I really thought she would outlive all of us. She told me a day before she passed away: "I'm going to live to be a hundred, Eric, because only the good die young."

Rest in peace, Mom. We love you.

Her funeral was almost as unique as the life she lived. When Ivana Trump passed away, her supposedly "disconnected" family came together. Her ex-husband, a former president, together with his wife, Melania, and son, Barron, all attended her funeral and burial, as did Tiffany. Everyone celebrated her life, and grieved her passing, together. I had the honor of delivering this eulogy.

> Last week, this world lost an incredible woman. Our mom was one of the most beautiful, elegant, athletic, and iconic women of our generation. It's an impossible combination to find. . . . She was a force of nature!
>
> She had a deep love for our nation, while always embracing the old-world glamour, sophistication, and elegance of her European roots. She was the embodiment of the American Dream.
>
> Our mother was one-of-a-kind. If you put Joan Rivers, Lindsey Vonn, and Claudia Schiffer in a blender, you might scratch the surface of creating another Ivana. But still, you wouldn't get completely there.
>
> She could beat any man down the slopes, any model on the runway. She had brains, beauty, and grit. She could tell the most

intimidating person to "take a hike" while also being able to captivate every woman in the United States on Home Shopping Network and QVC. She still holds all-time sales records. People adored her!

She ruled the three of us with an iron fist and a heart of gold. We are no stranger to tough parents—there is no one tougher than our father—but there were times we hid behind him to escape her old-world discipline.

Manners—you better believe it.

You knew when she was happy, mad, and when she was being sarcastic—three very distinct voices that I can hear in my head today.

She was proud of her children, and all we have accomplished as adults.

She was proud of the President. As journalists called, salivating to try and get any sensational story, she never once wavered. She supported my father with massive conviction and backbone. "That man will make a great f-ing president. You just watch."

They loved each other. Respected each other. They protected each other. He hosted her wedding—at his house. They even starred in a Pizza Hut commercial together (maybe the best of all time). Most importantly, they always acted in unison, as parents, teaching us (1) work ethic, (2) to stay away from drugs, and (3) to be unapologetic about what we believed.

And she was a great mom. She loved the "bowl-cut"—which remained on me and Don until she accidentally cut off part of my ear. That's when she put down the scissors.

She made me wear Ivanka's hand-me-downs, which consisted mostly of pink clothing. "You're growing like a weed—get over it," she would say.

No chance were we flying next to her in First Class. I can recall sitting in more smoking sections on TWA flights as we helped drag her ridiculously heavy Louis Vuitton trunks from country to country.

And don't even think about calling her grandma . . . she would kill you. "*Glam*-Ma." "Ivana-Ma." Grandma was just not her thing.

No matter where we are from, or what paths we take in our lives, we all have one common goal: to leave our footprint on this world. There is no doubt, our mother has left a lasting footprint. . . . Just look at this church.

Mom: I am here today to tell you, your legacy as a business-woman, athlete, icon, and most importantly mother will never be forgotten.

You are truly one-of-a-kind.

We love you and we will miss you. . . .

FROM THE GROUND UP

My mother's Eastern European grit balanced our New York lives. We went to the best schools and saw amazing places, but if I wanted a bike, I had to earn the money to buy it. At eleven years old, I began working at Seven Springs, a sprawling several-hundred-acre estate in Westchester, New York, which my father had recently acquired. Over a span of six years Don and I worked on that property, doing everything from demo, to electrical, plumbing, masonry, HVAC, digging lines with backhoes, cutting trees, and pouring concrete. Our lunch breaks generally consisted of an Italian sandwich and then beating the hell out of each other in some corner or on some lawn.

That kind of hard work either makes someone never want to have anything to do with real estate and construction or fall in love with it. I loved it. We earned five bucks an hour, but the experience was worth millions. Priceless, actually. We learned the value of money and what it took to earn it. But there were other benefits.

After grinding for ten hours a day, we had no interest in spending our hard-earned money on drugs, partying, or other distractions—moreover, we were usually too exhausted. I've never touched a drug in my life, but I saw many of my friends from wealthy families go down that road. Many ended up in rehab. Everything was given to them, and they never discovered purpose, never learned any tangible skills, and never learned the building blocks of an industry.

It always made me laugh when friends couldn't mount a TV on a wall, correctly hang a picture, or read the eighth or sixteenth markings on a tape measure. Forget sharpening a chainsaw, or changing hydraulic oil. A few years ago, when Lara and I bought our home, I did half the electrical work. She thought I was crazy, installing new outlets and changing high hats and light fixtures. But I have a love for tools, woodworking, machining, and seeing chips fly—either off a metal lathe or out the back of a chainsaw.

I appreciate craftsmanship. It really brings me back to those childhood days and the hard men I had the honor of working for. I'm sure I was a pain in the ass to those contractors and tradesmen. (*Seriously, this twelve-year-old kid wants to learn how to lay tile?*) But I was relentless. More than anything, it gave me an unbelievable respect for the hard work and talent of the people who built our nation and continue to do so every day.

Working alongside these men was maybe the best part of those days. Like summers with my grandparents, the time with them was just what I needed to grow up. I started to understand what being a craftsman was all about: hard work, long hours, taking pride in your craft, and going above and beyond when nobody is looking.

My father said it publicly many times: if his kids weren't good at what they did, they wouldn't have a place in the company. He was serious about this—there was too much at stake and too many people relying on us to get it right every day.

SINK OR SWIM

During my years in college, working in the family business was not a foregone conclusion.

Should I go into the Trump Organization, or should I explore other opportunities? I did investment banking work in the summers throughout my time at Georgetown University and worked at two different firms.

One of the firms did military defense banking focused on financing communication platforms and missile guidance systems. Fascinating work. Subsequently, I took an analyst role at one of the best boutique investment banking firms in New York, Houlihan Lokey. We focused on bankruptcies and restructurings of some of the biggest names in the country, including WorldCom, American Airlines, and

AT&T. I spent my time on consumer packaging, focused on then distressed companies like Anchor Glass. Construction and real estate development were on the opposite end of the spectrum from Wall Street, but both are a constant grind—one fueled by sweat and blood, the other by money, drugs, and nightlife. It was eye-opening, but I was still weighing my options.

My managing director, Derron Slonecker, was wonderful, and I learned so much from him. I'd received one of the top offers in their financial restructuring group (FRG), which is where I wanted to be. The smartest people with the most complicated, fun, and interesting jobs all went through FRG. On the other side of the coin, in 2006, the real estate world was on fire; a little too hot, as it turned out. The Trump Organization was doing great, and joining something that wore our name was hard to resist. One day, Derron offered a not-too-subtle encouragement.

"Chief," as he called me, "I'm saying this to my own detriment. You're one of the hardest workers I've ever had. I would love to work with you here, but you're an idiot if you don't join your family's company."

Derron was right, and he's still a dear friend today. In my heart, I always wanted to work alongside my family and be part of building something real. While the world of investment banking—and the challenge of fixing broken, bankrupt companies—was fascinating, it never felt tangible. It was just numbers on a screen. 10-Qs and 10-K quarterly and annual statements on Bloomberg terminals. Employees at these companies were merely commodities—entries on a spreadsheet. The polar opposite of the culture my father built, which celebrated craftsmanship, beauty, and excellence, with legends like Frank Sanzo, Vinny Stellio, and so many others.

I followed Derron's advice . . . straight into a little, windowless cubicle at the Trump Organization, doing licensing deals and other small projects. Most might assume I started in a corner office, but I had zero chance. Consistent with my childhood, there was no coddling.

Looking back, it was the best decision I ever made. It was also a decision that ultimately allowed my father to feel comfortable enough to step aside from his empire to become the 45th, and years later 47th, president of the United States.

Thanks, Derron.

The Art of the Comeback: Work with People You Like
"If you go to the office and don't find the energy in the people
you are with, it is highly unlikely that you will be energized
toward success." —DJT[1]

Even though my father has an unbelievable eye for detail, he was never a micromanager. His expectations were simple and clear. "If you're going to take on a project, do it 110%. Understand every detail. Fight to win. Love what you do." He answered questions, offered remarkable perspective, and was the greatest role model in the world. But he also gave tremendous latitude. This would be sink or swim for me.

We worked, we fought, we put our heart and soul into everything we did, every property we acquired, every project we built. The results would speak for themselves. Make no mistake, if we weren't good at our jobs there was no question he would have encouraged—and I use that word in the nicest possible way—us to do something else. I would never let him down.

In 2007, Don, Ivanka, and I were exploring a perfect piece of land in what we thought was the best location in Charlotte, North Carolina. We wanted to build a massive office building with a luxury hotel—2 million square feet and a billion-dollar budget. This would be our mark—in the company and on the world—and we were excited to begin.

As we moved closer to being under contract, our father's feedback was consistent. "Kids, it's not the right time. I've seen this economy before. Everything is getting too crazy. Believe me, this won't last."

We wanted to create the Trump Tower Charlotte. Bank of America and Wachovia were booming. The city was expanding and becoming one of the great financial hubs in the United States. Real estate was roaring. People were building. Everything was turning to gold.

"I'm telling you, kids, the world's going to come crashing down."

And it did.

A few months later, the crash of 2008 hit like a tidal wave. Had we not listened to him, we would have been committed to a billion-dollar project. But because his intuition was correct, because we had backed off when everyone was going all in, we were in an unbelievable position as a company to leverage the new real estate landscape after the crash.

While other developers were going out of business left and right with too much debt and no buyers, no long-term loans, and values falling through the floor, we saw and seized the opportunity. Whether in business or politics, it's during troubled times when my father is the calmest. He fought for his life and lived through the 1980s and 1990s, when interest rates were double digits and developers in New York were going bankrupt in droves. He was nearly a billion dollars in debt and had to fight his way out. He did not want to live those years again.

My experience restructuring deals and debt came in handy in the aftermath of 2008. Saying no to projects at the top of the market allowed us to say yes to big opportunities. We diversified. We took our company international. While most of our peers were fighting for survival, we were buying every special piece of property we could get our hands on, often for pennies on the dollar—golf course after golf course, hotel after hotel, and Trump Winery and so many others. The market downfall created some of the best opportunities we had ever seen and we went all in!

It wasn't all smooth sailing, of course. A few months after the crash, everyone who had put a deposit down on our new, sold-out condos wanted their 20 percent back. "Buyer's remorse." Every developer faced the same onslaught. As was expected, I owned every aspect of those properties—and the challenges that came with them. It was legal hell. Nothing like the lawfare that would come, but hell nonetheless. We were on the right side of those lawsuits, and we won every dispute.

At the same time, struggling golf properties were approaching us by the dozen because of our name and reputation in the golf world. I traveled the country buying some of the best golf courses, in the best zip codes, at huge discounts. These sellers loved the Trump brand. Many equity-member-owned clubs lacked the knowledge, experience, business synergies, financial wherewithal, or capability to run properties, especially during a recession. They knew we'd make world-class improvements that would be inconceivable under their bureaucratic, board-run operations. And members and future members were excited to play our other properties around the world and be part of what we were doing. Instantly, they witnessed the transformations, both physical and in service. No one did it better than our team!

In my office hangs a framed, full-page article from the *New York Post* with the headline "OK, Boys, Biz Is All Yours" and a Sharpie-penned note from my father: "Kids, you are the best in the world! Love, Dad." That was the moment I felt the shift had actually happened. I'd managed to help take the burden of the business off my father's shoulders.

In Donald Trump's letter to employees, which we wrote together, the magnitude of the role sunk in even more. He trusted me. And I was determined to make him, our family, and our team proud.

Ok, Boys, Biz Is All Yours

CHAPTER 3

THE APPRENTICES

"I continue to believe Mr. Trump will not be president. . . .
It's not hosting a talk show, or a reality show.
It's not promotion, it's not marketing.
It's hard and a lot of people count on us getting it right."
—PRESIDENT BARACK OBAMA, FEBRUARY 2016[1]

What was the most shocking, high-profile firing on *The Apprentice* and *The Celebrity Apprentice*?

I'll give you my answer by the end of this chapter. Do you remember those fourteen seasons, how they shaped television, and the fact that Donald J. Trump starred in the *top* television show for over a decade? Of course, this was all before the siege. It was a different world back then, wasn't it?

The Apprentice premiered in January of 2004 and instantly became the number one show on television, making ratings history. The first season finale had the highest ratings that year, after the Super Bowl, with 41.5 million people watching. The series would become known as one of the longest-running and most successful reality TV shows in history, earning my father a star on the Hollywood Walk of Fame.

People from every walk of life loved the show. Contestants and celebrities from all backgrounds and political persuasions lined up for an opportunity to compete. *The Celebrity Apprentice* was also a catalyst for raising tens of millions of dollars for many wonderful charities, a fact that the media would later conveniently forget.[2]

Speaking of nonprofits, NBC was struggling before *The Apprentice* launched in 2004. Over on CBS, *Survivor* was eating their lunch. One day, Mark Burnett, the producer of *Survivor*, approached my father and proposed an "urban survivor" idea. Before Mark left the office, they had the concept and a handshake deal.

Donald Trump was already well known—a celebrity entrepreneur with casinos, construction, condominiums, and hotels. But people learned about Trump the *man* on *The Apprentice*. They watched him interact with friends, strangers, staff, and competitors. His heart and soul came through—unscripted, as always. In a matter of weeks, he would add "biggest TV star in the world" to his résumé. Many would even argue that the show saved NBC. Ironic, I know.

He was no stranger to high-profile interviews, but being in front of lights and cameras every week for ten years certainly made him—along with my siblings and me—much more comfortable in the spotlight. It also made Donald Trump a household name, not only in America but around the world.

Television is ratings, ratings is business, and Donald Trump had the biggest ratings. He and Mark Burnett pioneered innovations that media companies still emulate today. The biggest companies in the world, including Budweiser, Crocs, 7UP, Pontiac, Microsoft, Burger King, Domino's Pizza, Pepsi, Levi Strauss & Co., Mattel, Sony, and dozens more, *begged*—and paid handsomely—to be part of the show. For every brand that made the cut, and cut the check, there were hundreds more who wanted to do the same.

Many might assume that my father (and later, Don, Ivanka, and I) showed up a few minutes a week to step in front of the camera or film the boardroom scene. But the show was a six-days-a-week job for everyone involved. For the contestants, the long hours, the relentless schedule, the sleepless nights, and the sheer magnitude of the pressure brought out the best and worst of the personalities.

Monday morning was "task delivery," when the contestants started work on the new challenge. Tuesday we would check on progress, do interviews, and go to the boardroom in the evening ("You're fired!"). Wednesday started the next round, with the boardroom Thursday, and repeat another round Friday to Saturday. Three episodes and three firings per week for several weeks is a lot of work, and that's one of the reasons the show became so raw—and so explosive—as it went on.

THE BOARDROOM

As the ratings rolled in, it became clear that viewers' favorite part of the show was the boardroom drama—so those scenes grew longer and longer as the series went on. It was all about the man in the center chair.

He was tough but fair, and he made wise decisions. He called balls and strikes. He wasn't always politically correct. What you saw on TV is exactly what I saw every day working with him. Zero difference. And every season he, and everyone, got better and better. When those twenty camera lights came on, he was on. We thought being in the media spotlight was challenging *before* the show premiered, but this was a whole new level. These weren't scripted episodes. There were no second or third takes. When the director yelled, "Rolling!" it was go time. Some people shine under that kind of pressure—and some crumble. In an episode of *The Celebrity Apprentice*, I witnessed the CEO of that week's sponsoring company step into the spotlight.

"Are you ready?" my father asked.

"Yes, absolutely. I'm a professional," the CEO replied.

The boardroom was full of a dozen big-name celebrities, which was intimidating enough. Each contestant had their own camera pointed at them, filming every second and every small facial expression. There were multiple cameras for the boardroom advisors, jib cameras flying overhead, plus massive arrays of lighting and countless microphones.

"Action!" Dozens of red lights on the cameras blinked on. It was the CEO's moment to shine. The poor guy froze. After some reassurance from my father, he stumbled through the segment.

It's one thing to address your own board in a room with no cameras. It's another to deliver the goods when you know millions will watch. When the spotlight is on, many people don't perform, which is also true in the political arena. It was a great lesson in pressure: some can handle it and others simply can't. Moreover, all the editing in the world can't fix stupid. (Hello, *60 Minutes*.)

THE PROVING GROUND

The Celebrity Apprentice mirrors politics in so many ways. You're on-stage and there are no do-overs. If you screw up, the media will hold it against you and recycle it for years. It was an education for the biggest job in the world.

And frankly, it gave my siblings and me the experience we appreciated years later in the first campaign. Nobody asked us if we were ready for "action." Fast-forward to 2016, when my father asked, "Hey, Eric, will you go on *Megyn Kelly* tonight and talk about immigration?"

"Sure," I answered with a smile. "But you realize I build hotels and know zero about immigration, right?"

I don't know how I would have fared in those interviews and campaign events if it hadn't been for being on and around those cameras on that iconic show and in our professional lives. The experience prepared me for the campaign trail as a surrogate, in countless rallies, on every news show imaginable, and on stages at the Republican National Convention, broadcast to hundreds of millions around the world.

I'll admit, I was sometimes a bit starstruck on the set of the show. I was young, and sure, I had scored a few life accomplishments. But everyone on *The Celebrity Apprentice* was at the top of their game, more often than not, with decades of fame and global sucess under their belts.

Beyond that, interacting with and befriending such a wildly eclectic group of people—from crew to cast—was fascinating. Where else could you see Sig Hansen, a crab fisherman, with Hollywood actors, sports legends, and celebrities? The funny thing was, they all had one thing in common—they were extremely "Type A," were accustomed to being the "boss," and they all had an unwavering drive to succeed.

That's a huge reason the show dominated the ratings—an electric mix of stars, each with an impressive résumé. But throw in the challenge of actually cooperating as a team and answering to authority, and that's when the real sparks ignited. These powerhouse personalities went from calling the shots to playing the apprentice—and the tension was undeniable.

The exposure breathed new life into the careers of many terrific people, with Joan Rivers being a prime example. After becoming a household name decades earlier, she was the first to admit her career had run out of steam. When she and her daughter, Melissa, joined *The Celebrity*

Apprentice, it reminded America of just how remarkable Joan really was. She won in 2009 and became a fixture on the show—which she parlayed into her greatest success and achievements.

Dennis Rodman was a fascinating character, and I mean that in a positive way. What are the odds that a billionaire from New York and a nose-ringed NBA superstar would actually develop a relationship with each other—and a North Korean dictator?

Country music singer John Rich's charity was St. Jude Children's Research Hospital, which is extremely close to my heart. Since I was rooting for his cause, I sometimes worried about being perceived as a partial judge—I wasn't! The celebrities were not paid to be on the show, and each played solely for their favorite charity.

Paul Teutul Sr., the fiery force behind *American Chopper*, was exactly the same guy—24/7. He refused to wear makeup. When I first met him, he was sitting quietly on a couch, a Leatherman on his belt, wearing the oil-stained tank tops that made him so famous. We became fast friends. I always loved the builders—people who use their hands to create functional beauty.

Geraldo Rivera was as you might expect. He had his convictions and his charm. In person he was always fun. Your best friend one day and a total enemy the next.

Names below are from *The Celebrity Apprentice* only

The Celebrity Apprentice, Season 1

Trace Adkins	Lennox Lewis
Carol Alt	Piers Morgan (winner)
Stephen Baldwin	Omarosa
Nadia Comăneci	Tito Ortiz (I'm a big UFC
Tiffany Fallon	fan. He's still a friend.)
Jennie Finch	Vincent Pastore
Nely Galán	Gene Simmons (Larger
Marilu Henner	than life. Truly one of a
	kind.)

The Celebrity Apprentice, Season 2

Clint Black

Andrew Dice Clay

Annie Duke

Tom Green

Natalie Gulbis

Scott Hamilton

Jesse James

Claudia Jordan

Khloé Kardashian

Brian McKnight

Joan Rivers (winner)

Melissa Rivers

Brande Roderick

Dennis Rodman

Herschel Walker (the one and only)

Tionne "T-Boz" Watkins

The Celebrity Apprentice, Season 3

Rod Blagojevich

Selita Ebanks

Bill Goldberg

Michael Johnson

Maria Kanellis

Cyndi Lauper

Carol Leifer

Bret Michaels (winner)

Sharon Osbourne

Holly Robinson Peete

Summer Sanders

Sinbad

Curtis Stone

Darryl Strawberry

The Celebrity Apprentice, Season 4

Gary Busey (#wild)

Jose Canseco

David Cassidy

Hope Dworaczyk

Richard Hatch

La Toya Jackson

Star Jones

NeNe Leakes

Lil Jon

Marlee Matlin

Mark McGrath

Meat Loaf

John Rich (winner)

Lisa Rinna

Niki Taylor

Dionne Warwick

The Celebrity Apprentice, Season 5

Clay Aiken	Penn Jillette
Michael Andretti	Lisa Lampanelli
Adam Carolla	Dayana Mendoza
Tia Carrere	Aubrey O'Day
Lou Ferrigno	Dee Snider
Debbie Gibson	George Takei
Teresa Giudice	Paul Teutul Sr.
Victoria Gotti	Cheryl Tiegs
Arsenio Hall (winner)	Patricia Velásquez

The Celebrity Apprentice, Season 6

Trace Adkins (winner)	Lil Jon
Stephen Baldwin	Bret Michaels
Gary Busey	Omarosa
Marilu Henner	Lisa Rinna
La Toya Jackson	Brande Roderick
Penn Jillette	Dennis Rodman
Claudia Jordan	Dee Snider

The Celebrity Apprentice, Season 7

Jamie Anderson	Shawn Johnson
Johnny Damon	Kevin Jonas
Vivica A. Fox	Lorenzo Lamas
Leeza Gibbons (winner)	Kenya Moore
Brandi Glanville	Terrell Owens
Kate Gosselin	Keshia Knight Pulliam
Gilbert Gottfried	Geraldo Rivera
Sig Hansen	Ian Ziering

The Art of the Comeback: Be Lucky
"You can help coax luck into your life by working hard and
being at the right place at the right time." —DJT[3]

Was my father lucky to host *The Apprentice*? I'd say he was certainly the right person, in the right place, at the right time. Beyond that, he had guts. Standing on that stage is not easy. Look at Arnold Schwarzenegger. His later version of *The Apprentice*, with the tagline "You're terminated," folded in weeks. The same with Martha Stewart. "You just don't fit in." Both were major celebrities who had made their careers in front of the camera. Donald Trump made his career behind a desk and on construction sites. He was the one on top for fourteen seasons.

They say, "If you have the ratings, you own the network. If you don't, they won't even call to say goodbye." TV is cutthroat—it demands backbone and guts. We all worked hard to master the art of television, but my father walked onto the set with charisma from day one. Was it luck that propelled the show to number one year after year? I'll let you be the judge.

REAL REALITY

No one on *The Celebrity Apprentice* was coached—not even the judges. Sure, we got briefed on the drama behind the scenes, but every question we asked in the tasks or the boardroom was off-the-cuff and unscripted. When lines are preplanned, the emotional energy is zero. It's the same in politics.

On the debate stage, establishment candidates wait for the opportunity to deliver their canned zinger—the line they rehearsed in the mirror a hundred times. It never works. People detect BS and insincerity.

Take this line from the 2019 Democrat debates, from the person who would become the last-minute 2024 Democrat nominee. "Donald Trump, in office on trade policy, you know, he reminds me of that guy in 'The Wizard of Oz,' when you pull back the curtain, it's a really small dude?"[4] George Stephanopoulos, all five foot nothing of him, was the debate moderator. My father was not impressed, and neither was the audience. As Harris would later say in her low-rated role as vice president, "It is time for us to do what we have been doing, and that time is every day."[5]

Contrast this to Donald Trump's comeback line. When Hillary said, "It's just awfully good that someone with the temperament of Donald Trump is not in charge of the law in our country," he instantly responded, "Because you'd be in jail."

And, of course, we'll never forget "Only Rosie O'Donnell."

Lines like these can't be rehearsed.

FRIENDS?

Wonderful friendships developed between the contestants and our family and it is astounding to look back on the personal dynamics before 2015. In those days, everyone, Democrat and Republican, was friendly toward my father, and there was an unending stream of celebs contacting our family to get on the show. One person stands out.

Donny Deutsch always seemed obsessed with fame. Every time I went on his CNBC show, he'd ask, "When are you gonna get me on *The Celebrity Apprentice* again?"

> "So funny to watch Little Donny Deutsch on TV with his own failing show. When I did The Apprentice, Donny would call me (along with @ErinBurnett & others) and BEG to be on that VERY successful show. He had the TV 'bug' & I would let him come on though he (& Erin) had very little TV talent."
> —DONALD J. TRUMP, 2019[6]

Of course, after the famous escalator ride, he, like so many other phonies, changed his tune completely. In fact, during the recent campaign he recommended that Joe Biden "scare the shit out of people" as a strategy to beat Donald Trump. So much for his "big ideas."[7]

Writing this chapter on *The Celebrity Apprentice* really took me back to those years. Many of the contestants became friends then— and many still are. Almost all were genuinely supportive and appreciative of my father. But as I revisited the list, it was striking—and sad—to see how some completely changed their tune. True to form, many flipped again in November 2024. People like to be on a winning team.

Being in the middle seat in the boardroom certainly prepared my father for what was to come, including taking the center podium on the chaotic debate stages in the 2016 election. There's no disputing that Donald J. Trump's presence at those first debates was undeniably a ratings magnet. When he opted out of the 2024 primary debates—because he was crushing everyone else in the polls—the ratings plummeted. He *was* the ratings, and without him, the show simply didn't exist.

YOU'RE FIRED

My father asked me to be in the meeting with Mark Burnett in 2015. It was a conversation they had on a regular basis—time to talk about renewing the show for several more seasons. The money was huge. Hundreds of millions per season, including product placement revenues, which alone were in the tens of millions per year. But I suspected something Mark didn't.

After Mark and his team made their expected pitch, I tried to act nonchalant as we waited for my father's response.

"I'm thinking about doing something else, Mark."

The room went silent. I'm sure that Mark and the production executives had been braced for a tough negotiation, but they never could have imagined him walking away from one of the most successful and lucrative shows in television history. Give anyone else the option to continue a top-rated series, which also brought positive exposure to their businesses, and they wouldn't have hesitated. Who would?

As their initial shock wore off, the NBC executives practically begged him to sign. But he said, "I really have something else on my mind. I'm going to have to get back to you." This was not a negotiation ploy. He'd made up his mind.

That day, Donald Trump told NBC, "You're fired." Ironically, *this* was the most shocking dismissal in the history of the show. Nobody fires prime-time TV. It fires you, as Martha and Arnold quickly learned.

He didn't mention running for office in that meeting, but as news spread that he wasn't signing on for future seasons, the rumors started

swirling about the presidency. Once he gave NBC the official no, produc-
ers discussed the idea of Don, Ivanka, and me continuing *The Celebrity Apprentice*. But we knew there was no way we could continue the show while supporting our father the way we wanted to. And, frankly, reality television seemed very small compared to the goal that lay ahead.

Despite what you may have heard (*or read*[8]) about *The Apprentice*, Donald J. Trump never looked back. Once he set his sights on the highest office in the world—and an opportunity to truly Make America Great Again—everything else was trivial by comparison.

When you consider the massive implications of the decision to leave the show, it's clear Donald Trump was *all in* for an incomparably greater role.

THE GAMBLE

It still astonishes me. Who walks away from the money and positivity of *The Apprentice* franchise to run against *sixteen* seasoned political candidates? Who imagines it's possible to win the presidency as their first run at elected office? Who decides to spend their own money to fund a start-up campaign and take on legacy political names with hundreds of millions of donations sitting in their war chests?

Not only did he walk away from *The Apprentice*, as a company we walked away from billions in development deals. The decision would cost us a fortune in lost revenues, plus campaign expenses and staggering legal fees. My father didn't care about the impact on our bottom line. He still doesn't.

A candidate, who had never run for any elected office, chose to turn down countless sure-thing opportunities for the slim chance he'd not only win the GOP nomination but then also defeat the heir-apparent Democrat. According to the Republican establishment, the moment was perfect for Jeb Bush to ascend to the throne—and with hundreds of millions of dollars behind him, the path seemed clear. Basic statistics would give *our* candidate a 1 percent chance to win the presidency, and there was a 100 percent chance he would be bloodied by the fight—win or lose. No billionaire on the Forbes 500 list would take that deal. Well, actually, there was one.

Am I looking for sympathy for my father and our business? *No.* Neither is anyone in my family. But consider all those politicians, appointees, and bureaucrats who go into government broke and mysteriously come out worth eight figures. For my father it was the ultimate gamble.

SOMEBODY HAS TO

"Somebody has to do it. If it were me, that would be fine. I could do it. Somebody has to help this country, and if they don't, the country—and the world—are in big trouble. Because within a short period of time, as sure as we're sitting here, there's not going to be a country, and there's not going to be a world. [. . .] Somebody has to do it. If it were me, that would be fine. I could do it."

—DONALD TRUMP IN A 1985 INTERVIEW WITH MIKE WALLACE
ON (THE NOW DISGRACED) *60 MINUTES*[9] [10]

The decision to run for president of the United States was a decades-long process. A *slow burn*, you might say. Many people have speculated that the 2011 White House Correspondents' Dinner was a pivotal moment for my father in terms of deciding to enter the arena. Those people don't know Donald Trump, and refused to believe him when he clearly stated the truth about that evening.

Here's one of the attempted digs from President Obama that night.

Obviously, we all know about your credentials and breadth of experience. For example—no, seriously, just recently, in an episode of *Celebrity Apprentice*—at the steakhouse, the men's cooking team did not impress the judges from Omaha Steaks. And there was a lot of blame to go around. But you, Mr. Trump, recognized that the real problem was a lack of leadership. And so ultimately, you didn't blame Lil Jon or Meat Loaf. You fired Gary Busey. And these are the kind of decisions that would keep me up at night. Well handled, sir. Well handled.[11]

Why would insecure jabs from a community organizer mean anything to someone like Donald Trump?

The press and the president were laughing it up while our nation was in decline. We were being invaded on the southern border, with an approving wink from President Obama, Joe Biden, and the Democrats. Our military and veterans were being neglected and disrespected. We were losing our manufacturing capacity, and jobs were being shipped around the world.

The decline of our public schools really pissed off my father. Per pupil, we were spending ten times what other nations were investing, and we were ranked close to thirtieth in the world.

The Obama-Biden administration gave *billions* of dollars to Iran while their leaders chanted, "Death to America." ISIS was terrorizing the Middle East. All the while, the Left obsessed over fears of climate change, but ignored culture change.

I saw Donald Trump become vividly angry about these issues countless times. "Are our leaders the *dumbest* people in the entire world?" he'd often say. These weren't momentary frustrations; the stupidity and ineptitude of our leaders—in both parties—simultaneously blew his mind and broke his heart.

"Why in the world would we project this weakness to the rest of the world? Who is stupid enough to allow this to happen to our military, and who in the world would showcase this to our enemies?!"[12]

The truth is, for decades our country was being run—into the ground—by amateurs. *Apprentices* is too kind of a word for the incompetence and complacency from so-called leaders in *both* parties.

In a 1988 interview with Oprah Winfrey, she asked if he would ever consider running for president. His reply? "If it got so bad, I would never want to rule it out totally."[13] It *was* bad. *So bad.* Even before he announced he was running in 2015, his name was prominent in the polls.

In June of 2015, I received a call. "Honey, bring the kids up to my office." We were on the twenty-fifth floor of Trump Tower. My father's office was on the twenty-sixth. One quick elevator trip separated two generations. Don, Ivanka, and I walked into his office—a time capsule that represented his career. Heavyweight championship boxing belts from the Atlantic City casinos littered a beautiful red suede couch. Countless deal trophies and awards, celebrating his most iconic projects, sat on the windowsill overlooking Central Park, Wollman Rink, the Plaza Hotel, the General Motors Building, and so many other projects that made him the icon of New York real estate. Donald Trump's office was a shrine of success. An office I'd spent thousands of hours in, both as a child and as an executive. We sat down. His assistant called Melania, who was in the apartment.

Rarely were we all called to the office at the same time. The tone was different.

I knew what this meeting was about. We all did. The topic had been on the table for more than a year. But still, there was a line to cross.

"I am going to do this. Let's give it a go."

The agreement was brief, mostly unspoken, and enthusiastic yet somber.

Everything we had ever done we had done together as a family. One collective. We were a team. We all worked together, fought together, traveled together. We all represented our family name, fought for the family name, and protected the family name. "Let's give this a go" represented something never before seen in politics. Most political children are hidden, kept out of sight—the cardinal rule of politics: keep family the hell away from campaigns.

But we were different. He was different. We knew what we were getting into . . . sort of.

Just a few days later, he and Melania took that famous trip down the Trump Tower escalator to announce his candidacy for president of the United States. Our whole family was there waiting for him on the stage. One of many things I loved about that moment was America didn't just see a man; they saw a family unit—set in the backdrop of a business empire. A family that would do something that no family had ever done in political history.

Everything changed that day. And almost everyone around us changed, too.

REAL CLIMATE CHANGE

In about fifteen minutes, he went from real estate developer, entrepreneur, and TV star number one to the media's public enemy number one. What had changed?

Donald Trump didn't change, and we, his family, didn't change. He was never considered partisan. In fact, looking back at the panic in the GOP in 2015, people actually questioned if he was conservative enough. Some even called him a "counterfeit Republican."[14] Had he come down the escalator as a Democrat, he would have been treated very differently—except, perhaps, by Hillary.

Companies that had lined up to be featured on *The Apprentice* were suddenly part of an opposition movement. Chief among them was NBC and their many outlets. Donald Trump went from hero to zero in their eyes.

What amazed me was how quickly the political climate changed. As in New York politics, when Donald Trump was needed, they loved him and our family; when he left NBC, they turned on us. In their minds, Donald Trump had changed teams. Was it the fact that his brand wasn't monetizing their network anymore? MSNBC's Joe Scarborough and Mika Brzezinski often came to Mar-a-Lago on weekends. Prior to 2015, they were friends of our family. The same with Oprah (who hosted our family in a 2011 "Trump Family Values" episode, which would be among her very last). The same was true of Erin Burnett on CNN and dozens of others.

As Joan Rivers famously said, "I succeeded by saying what everyone else is thinking." That same authenticity embodied our campaign, but the establishment didn't think it was funny. This was evident in October 2016 at the annual Alfred E. Smith Memorial Foundation Dinner, which raises millions for kids in need in New York City. Traditionally, Democrats and Republicans come together for some laughter and a great cause. (Eight years later, the 2024 Democrat candidate chose to skip the event.)

This particular dinner, which I was honored to attend, was the day after an intense presidential debate with Hillary Clinton. Donald Trump commanded the room—like he had on fourteen seasons in the boardroom—and basically told everyone, "You're fired!"

"Hi Chuck," he said to Senator Schumer, sitting just to his left. "He used to love me when I was a Democrat, you know."

"The politicians. They've had me to their homes, they've introduced me to their children, I've become their best friends in many instances.

They've asked for my endorsement and they always wanted my money. And even called me really a dear, dear friend. But then suddenly, decided when I ran for president as a Republican, that I've always been a no-good, rotten, disgusting scoundrel.

"I know Hillary met my campaign manager, and I got the chance to meet the people who are working so hard to get her elected. There they are—the heads of NBC, CNN, CBS, ABC—there's the *New York Times*, right over there, and the *Washington Post*."

He concluded with this:

I have great memories of coming to this dinner with my father over the years when I was a young man. Great experience for me. This was always a special experience for him and me to be together. One thing we can all agree on is the need to support the great work that comes out of the dinner. Millions of dollars have been raised to support disadvantaged children, and I applaud the many people who have worked to make this wonderful event a critical lifeline for children in need. And that we together broke the all-time record tonight is really something special. . . . We can also agree on the need to stand up to anti-Catholic bias, to defend religious liberty, and to create a culture that celebrates life.[15]

The Art of the Deal: Maximize Your Options
"I never get too attached to one deal or one approach. For starters, I keep a lot of balls in the air, because most deals fall out, no matter how promising they seem at first." —DJT[16]

CHANGING THE CHANNEL

The Apprentice and *The Celebrity Apprentice* were filmed on the fifth and fourteenth floors of Trump Tower. Within a few days of the campaign announcement, those spaces were converted to become our 2016 campaign headquarters.

Personally, I don't believe Donald Trump would have run for president, and won, if it wasn't for *The Apprentice*. The show gave America a chance to get to know him as a mentor, father, and decision-maker. They saw a man who could forgive honest mistakes, but quickly fire someone else for deliberate stupidity. They saw humor and humanity. They saw my father.

Now it was my turn to be the apprentice.

CHAPTER 4

2016

"Our presidential forecast:
92% Hillary Clinton
8% Donald J. Trump"
—THE [FAILED] *NEW YORK TIMES*, OCTOBER 20, 2016[1]

I often find the term *public service* to be a complete joke. Having witnessed every aspect of the American political system as an outsider, it's sad to say that the majority of politicians seem to be in it to serve themselves, not the public. Their only legacy is their ballooning net worth. From Obama and Biden to the Clintons and Nancy Pelosi—and, sadly, many opportunistic RINOs—D.C. has been a place where miraculous transformations in wealth that defy all logic happen.

In my world, people would be in jail for insider trading. What Martha Stewart was convicted of is laughable compared to what certain politicians do *every week*. Whenever an elected official has the courage to write legislation preventing this practice, the problem is brushed aside.

Hearing members of Congress and bureaucrats moan about their years of "dedicated public service" is often insulting. How can they brag to their constituents when so many people they're supposed to serve are working two and three jobs and still worried sick about their children's future?

It used to *cost* people something to serve their country. Now it's become a way to work a few years and fade into the well-financed machinery of the establishment.

Sure, I imagine the white marble walls of the Capitol, the schmoozing lobbyists, the media exposure, and campaign cash can be intoxicating. And the fight for power is corrupting. For most politicians, their career provides the best pay, least work, and most lavish perks of their lives, all on someone else's dime. Who would want to give that up?

The original intent of our representative republic was for working people to get involved in the business of running the country. Today, many lawmakers who have never held a real job or gained genuine real-world experience are the ones writing and voting on legislation that impacts every American's life. They make decisions shaping our economy, communities, and future—often without an understanding of the issues they legislate.

The White House is one of the most beautiful buildings in the world, and what it stands for is iconic. But from the perspective of Donald Trump, Mar-a-Lago and Trump Tower are equally incredible places to call home. The same can be said for Air Force One. It's phenomenal . . . but so is Trump Force One. My point isn't to diminish 1600 Pennsylvania Avenue. It's to show how ridiculous it is to think that my father ran for president because of the "perks." He's been in the limelight for decades and lived a lifestyle few can imagine as a result of hard work and tremendous personal success.

In many ways, stepping into the political arena in 2015 was a step backward for my father.

COULD HE ACTUALLY WIN?

Did I really believe that Donald Trump could beat sixteen established Republicans, and then Hillary—who had led the most influential political family and political machine of the time? That's a difficult question.

From my childhood I had never seen my father fail. His conviction to accomplish whatever he set his mind to is off the charts. And his instincts are second to none. There were a hundred times over the course of my life when the world was swimming downstream and only one person went the opposite direction: Donald Trump.

I believed he could win because I'd seen what he accomplished, and I had a front-row seat to the comeback when most people counted him out. And I believed he *should* win because he was right on the issues.

The number of people at our rallies, and the energy at those events, eclipsed every other candidate, including Hillary, by a landslide. It wasn't even close. Jeb Bush had $100 million worth of super PAC money, but it was gone before South Carolina and he had nothing to show for it. As we would learn, money can't buy enthusiasm.[2]

Donald Trump's approach was different. Despite none of us being "experts" in running a political campaign, he kept climbing in the polls (more on those polls later). That inexperience turned out to be our greatest advantage.

OUR EXPERTS

Campaigns are usually run by experts and consultants, but we knew few people in that world, and, regardless, with sixteen other candidates in the race in 2016, very few consultants were unemployed. The people around the favored faces made tens of millions of dollars, not to mention the elaborate network of commissions and kickbacks paid when various firms hire each other. They gave terrible advice, tied themselves to candidates who couldn't win, and still made a fortune. No matter which candidate wins an election, the consultants never lose.

We worked with people we knew, people in our orbit. I know, a crazy idea. My father was certainly the mastermind, but it was *all hands on deck* in terms of family and the great people we worked with in our businesses. Most people don't realize that the reason our campaign could go from zero to sixty so quickly is because of the deep relationships and trust earned over decades.

Dan Scavino, the former general manager of Trump National Golf Club in Westchester, turned out to have a great instinct for social media and communications. People loved him and he was born for the job. This unconventional, nonpolitical, former GM would become one of the greatest forces in Republican communications. In addition to running our social channels, he remained a great advocate for my father and a friend to our family. Did Dan know anything about political communications? Technically, no. Neither did I.

Brad Parscale, who went on to become campaign manager alongside Kellyanne Conway, was someone I happened to meet on a plane and a person I had hired to do website work for our company. Through the years, I haggled with Brad over small projects as he grew his company and I grew ours. A few weeks after we jumped into the arena, he was running all our digital media, fundraising, and strategy. Like most of our team, what he lacked in experience he made up for in energy, passion, and street smarts.

Corey Lewandowski simply believed. I've always valued the power of positive thinking. Corey was the living proof. He was one of the most politically experienced members of our team and a true catalyst—instilling confidence in his home state of New Hampshire and helping my father jump-start his campaign.

Christl Mahfouz became a friend years before 2016. We both had a love for St. Jude Children's Research Hospital and spent much of our time raising money for this incredible cause. One day she mentioned to me, "Eric, I would love to create your campaign merchandise. It will all be made in the United States, and I can have samples in two days." I remember her presenting what would be the first version of the Make America Great Again hat in the conference room on the twenty-fifth floor of Trump Tower. My father was impressed. Tens of millions of those red hats flew off the shelves—and with them, a movement was born, a movement that would sweep the nation and is still as relevant today as in 2016. All because a friend—a friend who was helping me fight pediatric cancer—came forward. I'm so grateful she did.

Jared Kushner, Ivanka's great husband and businessman, loved operations and became a big influence on the campaign. He, Brad, and I spent enormous amounts of time brainstorming behind the scenes. Jared was a great voice of reason, and would go on to help accomplish so many incredible successes in Washington, D.C., including establishing the Abraham Accords and other major policies that helped foster peace in the Middle East.

Kellyanne Conway, our amazing campaign manager, the first female campaign manager, has a powerful voice. She understood the sentiment of the nation and was an unbeatable defender of our message. Campaign managers aren't typically on the front lines of the media, but Kellyanne wore all those hats, and wore them well.

There are too many others to name here, but I have to acknowledge John Dunkin, our chief pilot. He's not a formal member of the "campaign," but without John there would be no campaign. In the 2016 election cycle he logged 1,042 flight hours, over 382,464 miles, to 202 cities in 45 states.

Political observers know that our team of political apprentices broke the rules and rewrote the playbook. There were no advisors calling the shots. Donald Trump was his own political advisor, his own voice, his own candidate. As everyone should know by now, his social media posts are his thoughts.

While others paid for ads, we received billions of dollars in free "earned" media. This was crucial because Donald Trump self-funded most of the early campaign. We needed to be unconventional and out-work our competitors.

THE LAND OF CORN AND CAUCUSES

In the months leading up to the Iowa caucuses, our family and team canvassed the state. We didn't yet have a commanding lead in the polls, but knew we had to have a strong showing. I found myself on a tour of Pizza Ranch restaurants and other local establishments. "Just hop up on that table and give your talk," I was told. And if that wasn't awkward enough, we would often show up unannounced. I loved every minute of it.

Delivering high-energy speeches and fielding questions while standing on a table or chair was a new experience. (*I could almost hear my mother's voice telling me to get off the table.*) But it was refreshing to see that bullshit had no place in those gatherings, as the other candidates would come to learn. Americans are smart. That's why the vast majority of the GOP candidates sealed their losing fates the very first night of the caucuses.

We were constantly on the move, fueled by Red Bulls and gas station snacks. Some days, I spoke at more than a dozen events. There was no security detail, no organization, no stage or microphones. We had no entourage. It was often just me and junior members of the campaign team, working the mosh pits of supporters and speaking with groups. Day after day, speech after speech, I struggled to keep my voice intact. Handshakes by the thousands. Hugs. Selfies. And more caffeine. It was a movement you had to experience to believe, and that's why the elite media on both coasts missed it.

On February 1, 2016, it was time for our first "election"—our first test in Iowa.

"Eric, we would love you to speak at one of the largest caucus locations."

"Of course," I replied. "But can someone *finally* explain what this caucus is?"

Don't laugh. If you don't live in Iowa you don't know, either. A caucus is a meeting where candidates or their spokespersons make their case at places like schools or restaurants. In these gatherings, after hearing from a candidate or their representative, attendees "vote" on slips of paper and the results are tallied.

It's a process that mandates community involvement. Caucuses bring neighbors together to hear directly from candidates and their team. Speaking on behalf of a man I love was one of the most memorable experiences of my life. I can only imagine how proud my father was to have his family with him—fighting for him every day. That rarely happens in politics.

THE SMILING WARRIOR

That first caucus night took place at the biggest high school I had ever seen, with three massive gymnasiums and a giant cafeteria. Each of the rooms was filled to the brim—and somehow I was slated to speak at all four. I approached one of the organizers and asked, "Would you mind if I spoke first? I'm representing my father's campaign and would love to address the other three rooms."

"You will speak when you're called," he replied. The man was wearing a Ted Cruz shirt. We had virtually no statewide organization. In contrast, Ted seemingly had his people *running* many of the locations. The next two officials I approached, clearly Trump voters, were happy to fit me into the schedule. The final organizer wasn't much better than the first. I didn't want to miss any of the rooms, but it seemed impossible.

I asked Lara, "Honey, can you just sit in one of these rooms for me?"

"Sure."

"And if they call my name, give a speech for me. Okay?"

"Wait, what?"

The timing ended up working out and Lara didn't need to speak that night. But in the months that followed, she became one of the most powerful and respected voices in the campaign. She is eloquent and keeps her composure in the face of unbelievable hate and stupidity. Lara is far from shy. Having been an employee of CBS and a producer on their hit show *Inside Edition*, she was no stranger to the media, but this was new territory for us all. Shortly after Iowa, she started traveling with the campaign and doing TV interviews. One morning, she was interviewed by one of the usual, awful network anchors, and Lara fought back, effortlessly landing punches with a kind, beautiful smile on her face.

Later that day, my father called. "Did you see Lara? I love her, but I never knew she had that in her. She was so incredible. They couldn't touch her. Like water off of a duck's back! Amazing."

As the campaign went on, we needed someone to manage North Carolina, Lara's home state. My father turned to her and said, "Lara, you're from North Carolina. Why don't you take over the state?"

That's when she made the difficult choice to resign from *Inside Edition*. I swear I've cost her more careers than I can count. To raise the stakes even higher, North Carolina was designated a "must-win" state by the Clinton campaign. The race was on!

POLLS, PUNDITS, AND DELEGATES

In 2016, some people were still skeptical of candidate Donald Trump. Maybe they thought it was a publicity stunt. *Was he a real Republican? Is he a Christian? How about the Second Amendment? He's a New Yorker after all.*

Unlike most politicians, he never felt compelled to wear certain issues on his sleeve. He never pandered and he never changed his style. When every other candidate showed up in Iowa in their freshly pressed Carhartts and flannel shirts with the price tags still attached, Donald Trump flew in on his New York helicopter. He walked around the fairgrounds in his signature suit and red tie, while the helicopter flew overhead, giving rides to children from the crowd.

We could feel that a true movement had been born. We came in second place out of twelve candidates. Pretty good for a crew who could barely spell *caucus*.

BACK TO "REALITY"?

Returning home to New York from campaign events was always an emotional roller coaster. On the road, there was no time to watch TV or read much news, but back in New York, we might as well have landed on another planet. According to the media and some polls, "Trump doesn't have a chance." This was from talking heads who never left their studios at Columbus Circle and Times Square.

So let's talk about those polls. The polls are often dishonest because many of the pollsters are dishonest. Take them with a grain of salt and read the fine print. Look for terms like "oversampling"—picking participants to boost a certain demographic—and "weighting," which means recalibrating results to supposedly reflect that group more accurately. In addition to playing with the numbers, a significant percentage of those planning to vote for Donald Trump had no interest in talking to pollsters. That's been true for ten years.

At an ABC roundtable with Kellyanne Conway, I actually made a friendly wager with the president of ABC News, James Goldston, about the election. He told us my father didn't have a chance. I said, "The loser buys a steak dinner at the restaurant of the winner's choice!" Jonathan Karl, George Stephanopoulos, and John Santucci were all at the table. I'm still waiting for that steak and still remind them all of that wager, not that they'll ever forget.

In early 2016, I still maintained some respect for the media. And that's why I didn't understand the disconnect with the polls. The contrast between talking with voters face-to-face versus listening to the media was jarring. *Was I delusional?* Every rally had tens of thousands of people. I had hundreds and hundreds of people show up to every stop I made. But the experts in New York and D.C. said we had no chance. The contrast between the positivity on the ground and the negativity on TV was bizarre. And something else from the early primary season baffled me.

DELEGATES

After Iowa, we won New Hampshire, South Carolina, Nevada, and virtually every other state. I wondered how Ted Cruz was staying in the race even though he wasn't winning many primaries. Our delegate count didn't seem to match the victories, the enthusiasm, or the Republican polls. *Why was it still a horse race?*

I have to hand it to Ted; he'd been in this game a long time. We might win the popular vote, but he understood the system and was wining and dining delegates in every state, an aspect of politics we had simply ignored. A state might have fifty delegates, but some were "bound" and some "unbound"—which meant they could still cast their vote for any candidate at the convention regardless of the popular vote in their state.[3]

As we did with everything else in politics, we quickly figured the system and the tide immediately changed. I remember being asked by Paul Manafort and the campaign team if I could call every delegate in the state of Pennsylvania. I was happy to. I knew the state well from my years at the Hill School—a remarkable boarding school in Pottstown, where Don and I studied and where I later served on the board. I'll never forget those calls.

"Hi, [insert name here]. Eric Trump. I wanted to call and ask for your support in my father's campaign. I know Reading well—in fact I lived down the road for five years. . . ."

These individuals were deeply entrenched in politics. They believed. They fought, often rudderless in the old-school GOP, which had no message or direction. Then came a simple call—a simple act of respect to reach out. From the frontrunner, from the family who had become the first face many saw on TV in the morning and the last they saw before going to bed.

Those calls made us human. A son calling on behalf of his father. No campaign manager, no scripted nonsense. Cell phone to cell phone. Many became friends. I batted close to a thousand. The other GOP candidates didn't stand a chance with our team and our family in the fight. We secured all but a few of the Pennsylvania delegates. Once our team learned how the game was played, we started winning.

The Art of the Deal: Know Your Market
"I like to think I have that instinct. That's why I don't hire a lot of
number-crunchers, and I don't trust fancy marketing surveys. I
do my own surveys and draw my own conclusions." —DJT[4]

WINGING IT

To say we were winging it in the opening months was an understatement.
It left the establishment speechless. But in many ways, running for office was not any different from real estate development. You need a solid
product and a message that connects with people. What we lacked in experience in the political arena we made up for in authenticity, character,
and work ethic.

Winging it with sincerity "trumps" following teleprompters of the
experts. Those so-called strategists of the establishment were almost always individuals who had never won anything in politics themselves, yet
somehow had all the answers. Donald Trump has his own voice. He
speaks the language of America, of patriotism, and of common sense. It
was always a stark contrast between him and other GOP candidates.

I was on *all* the major cable news networks every day, and often
multiple times a day. For months my second office was the greenroom
at Fox News on the Avenue of the Americas (6th Avenue) in N.Y.C. A
big reason my father was on TV so often was the simple fact that he *always* made great television—and drew fantastic ratings. Come to find
out, we did as well.

When the networks weren't interviewing us, they carried the rallies
live—even CNN. Why buy thirty-second ads on the networks for millions
of dollars when you could go on any show, any time, day or night, and get
full segments, or entire rallies, for free. As the campaign went on, the networks realized they were giving us rally-infomercials at no cost. But those
rallies got ratings, and ratings are king. They were unscripted and "politically incorrect." People tuned in by the millions.

Today, it's easy to forget what a huge gamble the 2016 campaign was.
It was not a given that thousands—and tens of thousands—would pack

stadiums across the country. This had never happened before. And it wasn't a given that these rallies would become legendary for their energy. People waited in line for hours, and sometimes days, to get a seat. Lines were often a mile long. We were witnessing a movement—a movement that was bigger than us.

STRANDED IN INDIANA

I traveled solo to campaign events as much as possible. Divide and conquer. If Donald Trump was in Wisconsin, I should be in Ohio, if he was in Pennsylvania, I would be in Michigan. I was able to get into smaller markets that were harder for him to reach—farther away from the big airports that could support Trump Force One and the enormous motorcades to and from his events.

That said, campaigns are lonely and tough—especially for the candidate. Having a friendly face lightened the mood. Having family support changed the energy. Every week I tried to reconnect with my father for a day. It was good for my soul and it was great for his.

One afternoon in July 2016, I flew into Indianapolis, Indiana, for a rally that he was hosting in Westfield. As I came off the plane, I noticed that one of the tires on the back landing gear of the 757 was deflated. People who know me will attest that I've always had an eye for detail. As the wheels began turning in the motorcade of dozens of vehicles, motorcycles, and escorts, I texted, "John. Left Rear Gear. We have a problem."

Governor Mike Pence introduced Donald Trump to the overflowing crowd, and we had a wonderful event. While my father was onstage, with chants of "USA! USA! USA!" ringing out, I learned the plane would be grounded until the next morning. A piece of metal on the runway had punctured the tire during landing.

Backstage, when I told Governor Pence about the delay, he said, "I know a great steakhouse downtown. Karen and I will take you to dinner."

We checked into the Conrad Hotel in downtown Indianapolis. In my father's room there happened to be a framed poster on the wall with the words "I usually have to lay it on pretty thick . . . if I'm going to get anywhere." *Perfect*, I thought. After a long dinner at the Capital Grille with Governor Pence and his wife, Karen, my father and I headed to our rooms.

"What did you think?" I asked.

"I like him. He's the one. Call the kids. It would be nice to have everyone here in the morning." So I made the calls and arranged for them to fly out at dark-thirty for a breakfast meeting at the governor's mansion. If it hadn't been for that piece of metal on the runway, I'm not sure Mike Pence would have become vice president of the United States.

Mike was thoughtful. The first note Lara and I received after the birth of our children came from his office. He didn't draw crowds on the campaign trail, but he didn't need to. Donald Trump was the candidate and had the personality to spare. All Pence needed to do was not make a mistake during the campaign, and he succeeded.

In later years, Pence would become another Michael Cohen, Anthony Scaramucci, et al. Not in terms of *character*—Mike was always a good man—but when it came down to choosing a team. I'm not trying to disparage the former vice president, he has convictions and so do I. But one thing I've learned in politics is that you have to pick a team—you can't be half pregnant.

ELEPHANTS AND RINOS

As more of the sixteen other GOP candidates dropped out, we still had another primary opponent who wouldn't go away, refusing to fully endorse Donald Trump. From day one of the campaign to Election Day—and even after the general election—this adversary was always there, passive-aggressively working against us. Believe it or not, I'm talking about the RNC—the Republican National Committee.

Yes, our party, or at least the establishment and RINOs in the GOP, seemed to resent our success. While they would smile and seem to play along, many didn't understand Donald Trump—nor did they understand his supporters. Even though we were new to the process, it was clear something was off. The organization that was supposed to fight to win seemed half-hearted about our candidate and half-assed in their execution. That hunch became more clear later during the elections of 2018, 2020, and 2022.

MANUFACTURED OUTRAGE AND REAL LOVE

"How dare he say that?!"

It became so predictable. Every month there was freshly manufactured outrage over Donald Trump's words. "Build that wall," "Crooked Hillary," the "Muslim ban," and "America First." Yes, putting our own nation first was a controversial position.

With every fake news story and critically offended talking head, something remarkable happened—Donald Trump's poll numbers went up. The disconnect between the establishment and Americans had never been so clear, and 2016 would forever change the game.

The swamp and the pundits threw everything they could against him. Nothing stuck. People could see through the madness. Voters connected with Donald Trump because they sensed the truth: he genuinely cared about them. He made the powerful uncomfortable. He called out incompetence and hypocrisy whenever he saw it, with a level of unvarnished honesty.

I'll always remember the Nevada caucus on February 23, 2016. People were lined up for a mile. I walked along that line and shook hands with every person who was waiting to go into the polling location. "We love your family. We're here for you. Our family, our church, we are all praying for you!" It was very sincere, and those interactions fueled our resolve.

I called my father as I left the polling location in Las Vegas that night. The sixty-four-story, twenty-four-karat-gold building that I spent so many years building was in the distance, with the Trump name shining over the entire strip. A surreal moment. "Dad, I don't know what you just experienced, but the energy at my polling location was incredible. It felt like we have every single vote."

Minutes later, as I pulled up to Trump International Hotel in Las Vegas, the call came in—we had won the state.[5] That moment marked more than just a victory; it was the first real intersection of my two worlds—the Trump Organization and the unpredictable realm of politics.

AUTHENTIC SUPPORT

There were always more Carhartts and camo than suits at Trump rallies, by a factor of a hundred. What does that say for a candidate who basically lives in a suit?

Since his days working with my grandfather, my father has enjoyed walking construction sites. He'd walk up to an electrician and simply ask, "How are we doing?" And the remarkable thing was, they would always tell him the truth.

My father took feedback from the bosses with a grain of salt. When he wanted to know what was *really* happening, he would talk with the guy wiring up the outlets or installing the plumbing.

That was the same approach we took in the campaign—talk with the people on the ground, the people doing the hard work. The Left's strategy was to get big shots to endorse them, bend over backward for the media, and have them spoon-feed their message to the masses. But let's go back to those construction sites. Why would an electrician or other skilled tradesperson give Donald Trump a straight answer?

First, my father had built a reputation for these kinds of conversations. It was not a show. He cares. He admires hardworking tradesmen—the guys who would walk on I beams in howling winds, sixty stories above the New York streets. No matter their job or title, these were the people building America. I've consistently seen my father cringe at socialites, but light up when talking to foremen at construction sites. That's who he is.

Second, most people genuinely admired Donald Trump. He always stood for success and the American Dream. Our company has never been interested in hiring for Ivy League diplomas, nor do I today. We've always promoted people from within, just as we did with the campaign team. That was the culture at our company before *The Apprentice* and it has never changed.

Brian Baudreau, our general manager at Trump International Hotel and Tower, Las Vegas—a nearly billion-dollar 1,282-room hotel I built on the Las Vegas Strip—was a driver for our company, and family, for years. I've known Brian since I was a kid. His work ethic and excellence outshine any diploma, and he's a close friend to this day. When we originally purchased that piece of land we needed someone to tour architects around the property. Brian had his hand up. Months later, we needed to go through a zoning process. He offered to be in those meetings. He went on to tour bankers, help us secure financing, and so much more. When we needed someone to run the building, Brian's hand was back up. "I know nothing about running a hotel, but I also knew nothing about building a sixty-four-story building, or banks, or architects . . . but we made it all happen." He's been running the hotel ever since.

Our organization is filled with these kinds of stories. Doers, not consultants. It's a different universe than politics. We came from a world of action and results, not bullshit and pageantry.

THE ALTERNATE UNIVERSE

I remember being on Erin Burnett's CNN show on June 22, 2016. Our family had a great relationship with Erin and others at her network, including Donna Brazile. Erin loved my father and our family. Every few months, she would eat at Trump Grill in Trump Tower, but all that changed in 2015. In fact, with Erin, everything changed when the red lights on the cameras went on. After exchanging usual pleasantries before the show, she began the segment with this.

"$42 million for the Clinton campaign, just over $1 million for the Trump campaign. Are you going to close that gap?"

I shot back, "Truly one of the [most] dishonest sound bites. We started raising money on May 28. One million dollars reported for May. Last night we had a fundraiser where we raised $6 million. . . . We don't need the kind of money that Hillary needs. She has 730 people on staff. You know how many we have? We have seventy. Her operation is bloated. It's crazy. We run a lean operation—quite frankly, this country should be run the same way."[6]

Our campaign was almost entirely self-funded to that point, and we were only *one day* into the fundraising. Before the cameras went live, I had seen her question on the teleprompter and told her the question was dishonest, and I explained why. I thought after all the years we had been friends that it would matter. It didn't. They had their script. The Erin we knew was gone. Journalistic integrity went out the window.

I always liked asking the cable hosts when was the last time they visited Iowa, Maine, or Wisconsin. Short of St. Barts, Martha's Vineyard, or the like, most hadn't left New York for years. That question usually kept them off balance for a few seconds. The point is, these people have no idea what life is like outside of N.Y.C. or D.C. The dishonesty, the gotcha questions, and the smoke and mirrors are all designed to create a false narrative for voters, all from the safety of their isolated studios. In reality, they neither knew nor understood America

They wanted to destroy any hope people might place in electing Donald Trump. But the more the establishment tried to vilify Donald Trump, the better he did.

President Obama offered this sage perspective: "The other guy doesn't have the preparation, the temperament or the core values of inclusion and making everybody, you know, have opportunity that would take our country forward."[7] And Chris Christie shared his diagnosis: "I don't think his temperament is suited for that [the presidency] and I don't think his experience is."[8] Ironic, coming from a man embroiled in the Bridgegate scandal—one who would later beg to become vice president.

When the cameras were off, everybody seemed cordial—pundits, reporters, and even primary opponents. When the cameras turned on, they treated my father and my family like Satan. One exception to this was Mike Huckabee. Case in point, the debates of 2016. For some reason, the moderators thought it should be fun to ask the other candidates what they thought of Donald Trump. It's ridiculous, but it showed how much he drove ratings and how far he'd gotten in everyone's head at that point.

All the candidates seized the moment to go negative, except Mike. He took the opportunity to be truthful, and positive, about our family.

After that debate, Mike walked over to me with a smile and confided that his answer had probably ended his campaign, and that he believed Donald Trump was going to be our next president. "I truly believe God is blessing your father's candidacy and that he will be the next president of the United States." Mike Huckabee was the same onstage and off. He is a remarkable human being whom I respect tremendously.

DEFYING CONVENTION

I had stood on tables in Iowa, and now it was time to stand on the stage and address the GOP convention, to hundreds of millions of viewers around the world. This was the Super Bowl of politics. A candidate for the most powerful job in the world, who had never held elected office, was about to be nominated as the Republican pick. And I would have the honor of speaking right before the man selected as Donald J. Trump's running mate. I had put my heart and soul into my speech, knowing that every network would carry it in prime-time. I was prepared. The massive crowd and the swarm of TV cameras and lights didn't bother me. I simply wanted to make my father and my family proud. And I wanted the people of our great country to understand who Donald Trump was, and why he was running for president.

After a hard-fought primary, Ted Cruz had come in second, was the last to drop out, and he addressed the convention directly before my speech. I was backstage waiting for my cue and listening for Ted to endorse my father. This would seal the unification of the Republican Party after a hard-fought primary.

He did not.

I was shocked, and so was the crowd. Booing and jeering rang out in the auditorium. It was deafening.

The country was watching. So was the world. Hundreds of media talking heads were there, most of whom hoped our candidate would fail—and most did everything in their power to see that happen.

"WTF was that, Ted?" I chuckled to myself. Oh well, forget it. I have a speech to deliver. It would be one of the greatest honors of my life.

The opening line of my speech was ready on the teleprompters, but just as I was about to walk to the microphone, I heard the crew panicking. "We lost power. Prompters are down!" Then they told me, "Sir, you have to go. We are still live all across the country."

Murphy's Law . . . today?! In the past year I had gotten good at winging stump speeches, but this was not Pizza Ranch. The teleprompter screen reminded me of a scene from *The Terminator*—the glowing red light—the symbol of his consciousness—faded to black and disappeared. The words—the message I'd put my heart and soul into—were gone.

I started walking. Lines from my speech bounced around my brain in no particular order. Halfway to the podium and the screens were still dead. I paused on the catwalk and pointed to a couple of my buddies from the Connecticut delegation, Jeff Ferraro and Mike Mason, two friends I had placed as delegates, knowing that my father could "shoot someone in the middle of 5th Avenue" and they would still vote for him.

Let's just say that the booing after Ted's speech teed me up pretty well. People were shocked by the lack of his endorsement. The applause I received in contrast was overwhelming. "USA! USA! TRUMP... TRUMP... TRUMP!"

As I made the final steps to the microphone, the teleprompters flashed back on. The first word I spoke was "Wow!" It expressed a combination of months of intense campaigning, joy for my father, the remarkable energy in the room—and relief that those fucking prompters were working. For the first time in my "political career" I wouldn't have to wing it.

The best part? My father was there in the arena.

"My father is running for you.... Vote for the candidate who has never been a politician. Vote for the candidate who has never received a paycheck from our government.... Vote for the candidate who cannot be bought, sold, purchased, bribed, coerced, intimidated, or steered from the path that is right and just and true."

MAGA

Has there ever been a more effective, or enduring, political tagline than "Make America Great Again"? Ten years out and it's still as powerful—maybe more—as the day it was born. The phrase has also been purposely maligned.

At its heart, MAGA is not controversial—it's pure common sense. In 2015, I'm not sure if people really knew what "America First" was, after decades of elected officials putting our nation last. Those two words opened people's eyes to the corruption in government and the fact that our nation was losing our competitive edge and our sense of national identity.

Once you start looking at what's happening in our country—and happening in your community—through the lens of "the safety and prosperity of the United States should be our top priority," the absolute failure of the establishment comes into view.

I can't tell you how many times I've seen my father look up from the newspaper, shake his head, and ask, "What the hell are we doing?" With "Make America Great Again," Donald Trump simply put words to what millions of Americans were thinking.

TIME TO VOTE

In October 2016, experts at the (failed) *New York Times* proclaimed that Hillary had a 92 percent chance of winning.

Every day more polling would come out, and it clarified . . . nothing. We could tell many of the polls were being skewed in Hillary's favor. That bias still shows up today in nearly every poll—a blatant manipulation we'd continue to see in campaigns to come. Clinton was trouncing us with large-dollar donors, but we were winning with smaller donations by a large margin. We were up against the most connected political dynasty in history. Why wouldn't Hillary expect to win?

For her presumptive election night celebration, her team rented the Jacob Javits Convention Center in Manhattan, which my father had helped convince New York City leaders to build, because the ballroom features a "glass ceiling." *Who says Democrats don't have any creative ideas?* They had food, champagne, and a zillion balloons poised to drop from that metaphorical ceiling. It almost makes me sad thinking about all the wasted preparation they put into the celebration that never happened.

We rented a simple ballroom at the Hilton. There was no food, but there was a bar. Honestly, we have always been a little superstitious and didn't want to plan a celebration.

A four-minute drive away at campaign HQ on the fourteenth floor of Trump Tower, Mike and Karen Pence, Steve Bannon, Tiffany, Vanessa, Don, Kai, Ivanka, Jared, Lara, and I were all there, along with Kellyanne and a handful of others from our campaign team.

The states started coming in . . . for Donald Trump.

I remember when Lara's home state of North Carolina officially moved into our column at 11:11 p.m. We were on cloud nine because she had worked so hard for that victory. Frankly, I was just as concerned about winning the Tar Heel State as I was about winning the election. Imagine if we had lost *because* of losing North Carolina? And it was especially memorable for us because November 8—Election Day—was also our second wedding anniversary.

Meanwhile, reliable sources were telling me the Clinton camp was melting down. Then, at 2 a.m., John Podesta crawled out and told the crowd at the Javits Center, "Everybody should head home. You should get some sleep."[9] No sign of Hillary.

We went back up to my father's apartment—the apartment I grew up in as a child—and my father started writing a speech. No, he didn't have a victory speech written beforehand. And despite what NBC falsely reported, no one even considered drafting a concession speech.[10] We were all too busy getting the message out, fighting to the last second in every state and on every possible platform.

We sat at my father's large dining room table on the sixty-sixth floor of Trump Tower, debating ideas and drafting language.

"I want to bring the country together," he told everyone. "I want this speech to be *positive*."

When we arrived at the Hilton to address the crowd and the nation, it was mayhem—in the best possible way. Above the noise I could hear a dear friend who everyone reading this will know (a TV personality who detested Hillary for personal reasons and shall remain nameless) shouting, "Payback's a bitch!" Remember: open bar + no food. At 2:31 a.m., as our family stood backstage waiting for our cue, I saw my father's phone light up.

"You're tough as hell, and you never quit," he told Hillary. "You ran an incredible race."

Then it was time for him to deliver the speech, straight from the heart. Flanked by his family, he began.

Now it is time for America to bind the wounds of division—have to get together. To all Republicans and Democrats and Independents across this nation, I say it is time for us to come together as one united people.

As I've said from the beginning, ours was not a campaign but rather an incredible and great movement, made up of millions of hard-working men and women who love their country and want a better, brighter future for themselves and for their family.

Working together, we will begin the urgent task of rebuilding our nation and renewing the American dream. I've spent my entire life in business, looking at the untapped potential in projects and in people all over the world.

That is now what I want to do for our country.

The forgotten men and women of our country will be forgotten no longer.[11]

That's when our world changed again. Very quickly.

THE TRUMP ORGANIZATION

January 19, 2017

To all my wonderful employees and friends in the Trump Organization :

I am right now leaving for Washington, D.C. for a new and very exciting journey. The journey I have been on with you has been a great one, and one that I will never forget.

I want to thank all of you for your support throughout my campaign. I appreciate it very much, just as I have appreciated your dedicated work throughout the years here at the Trump Organization. All of you have been an important element in my success, and we have truly done this together. Keep up the great work – Make America Great Again!

With my warmest regards,

Donald J. Trump

725 FIFTH AVENUE • NEW YORK, NY 10022 • (212) 832-2000 • FAX (212) 935-0141

PART TWO

UNDER SIEGE

CHAPTER 5

SEPARATION OF COMPANY AND STATE

"Don't smoke, don't drink, don't do drugs, and never trust
anyone."
—DJT TO ELEMENTARY SCHOOL ME

By 2016, I had done virtually all of our golf acquisitions, built much of Trump Chicago, Trump Doral, the Trump Las Vegas hotel, the Old Post Office, Trump Winery, and handled many of our license deals around the world. I knew everyone in the company, many of whom I had hired as we expanded the portfolio. Effectively, I had been running the company since 2015, as my father ramped up his political aspirations. But now the torch had been officially passed.

The new president was now walled off from the business he built, and after almost a decade of working together, it was strange not to walk into his office a dozen times a day. I loved those interactions, those meetings, those laughs.

At a press conference on January 11, 2017, a few days before the inauguration, our attorney Sheri Dillon read an unprecedented statement to the country. While it was not a legal requirement for becoming president, my father had chosen to totally separate from the company that he had spent his life building.

"The president-elect will have no role in deciding whether the Trump Organization engages in a new deal. He will only know of a new deal if he reads it in the paper or sees it on TV. . . . As you can well imagine, that caused an immediate financial loss of millions of dollars, not just for President-elect Trump but also for Don, Ivanka and Eric."[1]

She wasn't kidding. Only years later would we understand the magnitude of the losses, in opportunity costs and the unimaginable legal bills that we'd face when the lawfare began. At the same event, my father mentioned just one of many deals we chose to decline.

"Over the weekend, I was offered $2 billion to do a deal in Dubai with . . . a great developer from the Middle East. . . . I turned it down. I didn't have to turn it down, 'cause, as you know, I have a no-conflict situation because I'm president."[2]

The same month, I became power of attorney for Donald Trump and became an officer of virtually every legal entity in the portfolio, which numbered in the hundreds. No one in recent history had been elected president without holding prior office. Neither had anyone faced the logistical and ethical concerns of transitioning to the White House with a multibillion-dollar international hospitality business and brand that bore their name.

The president *chose* to be disconnected from the business, and I did everything in my power to avoid even the *appearance* of a conflict of interest. For example, how might any changes in the tax code affect our business? What about Middle East policy and international properties?

We brought in the best attorneys and ethics experts. We built a wall between the new president and the company he had built and created. But we chose to go even further.

In our hotels all over the country and around the world, *anyone* can enjoy a meal or book a room by simply going to Expedia or similar booking sites. But what if a customer happens to be a foreign government official? Let's say a Chinese official books a room online at Trump New York. We could be accused of receiving some "gift" from that government and be accused of violating the emoluments clause in the U.S. Constitution—even though we had no idea about the transaction.

I know it's hard to imagine, but there are people who might take us to court for such things.

We decided that every year, in January, the company would write a check to the U.S. Treasury for *any* profits associated with income from foreign government business. That's right, not only did we track clients associated with foreign governments but we also calculated the profit and sent a check to the United States Treasury every single January. None of this was required by law—and, of course, was never touted or even mentioned by the media.

We created our own precedent and regularly sent documentation of these payments to the fake news. They conveniently ignored them. We were accused endlessly of somehow "profiting" off the presidency and sued several times. We prevailed each time, including in a judgment by the Supreme Court of the United States to dismiss the case as moot. But it didn't end the ridiculous slander.

As one example, Eric Swalwell ignorantly asserted, "Unlike other Presidents, Donald Trump has failed to distance himself from his private business interests while serving our nation, and so he and his family are getting richer from Trump companies that receive money and benefits from foreign powers."[3] Ironic coming from a congressman who had a habit of sleeping with Chinese spies named Fang-Fang.

We even decided to avoid any hint of impropriety or controversy and go "pencils down" on many new projects.

We were now the First Family. If profit had been our priority, believe me, Donald Trump wouldn't have spent nearly $100 million self-funding his own campaign against sixteen Republicans and Hillary Clinton. We wouldn't have turned away some of the biggest real estate deals on the planet. We wouldn't have volunteered to end all foreign deals. My father wouldn't have been the first president in United States history to donate his salary, on a quarterly basis, to charity. The presidency came first. Profit was no longer the barometer of success, and I would not allow our companies to be a distraction to President Trump's agenda, as much as the media wanted to paint a distorted picture.

This was uncharted territory in the history of our nation. In my early thirties I would chart a new path for balancing a company and a presidency—something that had never been faced before.

TARIFFS 2019 STYLE

During the presidency, France imposed a "digital tax" on tech companies based in the United States. My father frequently criticized France, and other nations, of ripping us off, over trade imbalances and lack of NATO defense spending. The president wasn't happy about this latest move and made his intentions clear on Twitter on July 26, 2019.

"France just put a digital tax on our great American technology companies. If anybody taxes them, it should be their home Country, the USA. We will announce a substantial reciprocal action on Macron's foolishness shortly. I've always said American wine is better than French wine!"[4]

In conversations with French President Macron, President Trump tossed out the prospect of a 25 percent tariff on French wines. *Maybe even 100 percent.* Not an unusual game of chicken from him, but the Trump Organization happens to own a vineyard in Virginia, the largest on the East Coast. *Was all this a ploy to boost sales of our wine?* Of course not. But these are the sort of complications we dealt with every week and the narrative the media tried to create.

By the way, Macron blinked and canceled the tech tax.[5] Likewise, the tariffs on wine were never imposed.

In 2019, the president proposed hosting the G7 Summit at Trump Doral, in Miami, Florida. The amenities were perfect for such an event, with ten separate lodges, each with about fifty rooms, which could host a different nation's delegates. These events cost host countries tens of millions of dollars. My father offered to host at Doral free of charge to the American taxpayer. Before you could yell, "Fore!" the media lied and accused us of trying to "enrich" the company. A few days later, he removed the proposal—not because he had to, but because no good deed goes unpunished. As a result, the taxpayers picked up the tab.[6]

In 2025 we would see this same America-last "logic" applied when the media wanted to refuse the free use of a $500 million Boeing 747 from a nation we spend billions a year defending. In as long as I can remember, it was one of the first true acts of generosity toward the United States—and it was shunned.

While America started winning again, our company was under siege from the political establishment. This was a new level of attack—the weaponization of government, judges, federal law enforcement agencies, district attorneys, attorney generals, subpoenas, depositions, discovery demands, sham media stories, leaked tax returns, harassment of our employees, and so much more.

My father and mother, Don, Ivanka, and me.

All photos courtesy of the author's personal collection, unless otherwise noted.

LEFT: My siblings and I with our mom, Ivana Trump.

RIGHT: Siblings circa 1989.

With my parents at a party circa 1987.

My entire life has been construction—
it was in our genes from Day #1.

Politics started young. My father introducing Don and I to then First Lady Hillary Clinton.

Summer with our mom.

Front row at the US Open.

A sibling photo with our dad.

My dad and I at my birthday circa 1988.

My beautiful mother in St. Tropez with her beloved dog, Tiger.

My mom was an incredible skier.

Businessmen feared the red nails and teased blonde hair. She was a force in the business world.

The Eric Trump Foundation Surgery and ICU Center at St. Jude Children's Research Hospital will forever be my proudest work.

My friend Colin Toland, a St. Jude patient, and I at the Eric Trump Foundation. Colin never missed an event.

Colin was relentless in his fight against pediatric cancer. Unfortunately, years later, I would give the eulogy at his memorial in Memphis.

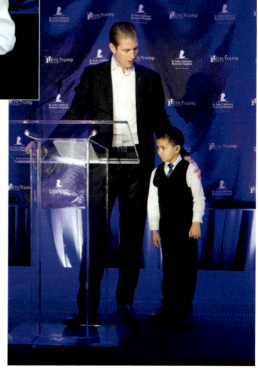

LEFT: Lara and our dog, Charlie, moments after I proposed in 2013.

RIGHT: Lara is a rock star.

Lara and I tied the knot at Mar-a-Lago on November 8, 2014. Years later, we would win the 2024 presidential election under the same chandeliers. COURTESY OF DONNA NEWMAN

My father and I in the boardroom filming *The Celebrity Apprentice.*

Don, Ivanka, and I hard at work.

Overlooking 5th Avenue from the great Trump Tower during Pope Francis's 2015 U.S. visit.

My father and I at the 2015 ribbon-cutting ceremony for Trump Turnberry. COURTESY OF THE TRUMP ORGANIZATION

Celebrating our first political victory in Manchester, New Hampshire, on February 9, 2016.

Iowa caucuses during the 2016 campaign. This would be one of four auditoriums I would speak in that evening.

Family dinner on the trail.

The 2016 rallies were nothing short of electric.

The moment our Digital Media Director, Brad Parscale, said he believed we just won the 2016 election.

The famous call! Hillary Clinton called and officially conceded at 2:31 a.m. on November 9, 2016.

The 2017 Inauguration of President Donald J. Trump. GETTY / MANDEL NGAN / STAFF

A few days after the election, the *New York Post* came out with this cover. I had it framed and proudly displayed in my office.

Our official family photo shortly after my father took office in 2017.

CLOCKWISE: Lara about seven months pregnant with Luke in the White House private residence.

Lara and I backstage with my dad, Melania, and Mike and Karen Pence for my dad's announcement of his 2020 presidential run.

Welcome to the world, Carolina Dorothy Trump.

Celebrating Luke's baptism at the White House—Carolina would follow two years later.

One of the first times Luke realized Mom and Dad were on TV.

In 2018, my father hit the campaign trail again for the midterm elections. Nothing like this had been seen in political history. Every arena filled to the max.

n London for my father's State Visit. Lara vas about seven months pregnant with Carolina.

About to meet Queen Elizabeth in Buckingham Palace.

While in New York for the United Nations General Assembly, we gathered in my father's Trump Tower Penthouse to introduce newborn Carolina to the family.

Some of Carolina's first steps were in the White House.

Behind the scenes on the stairs of Marine One.

Marine One from Joint Base Andrews to the South Lawn of the White House.
COURTESY OF THE
WHITE HOUSE

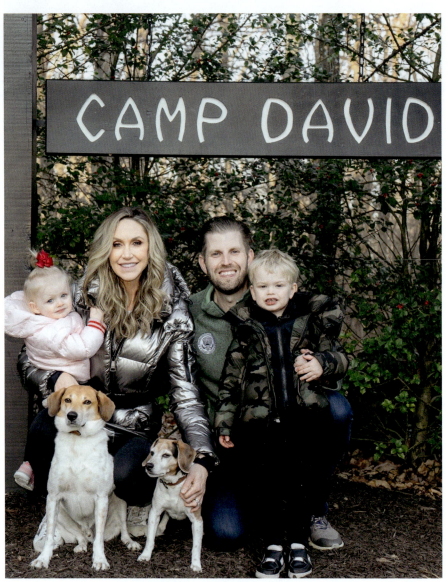

Family weekend at Camp David.

It began with various routine restaurant health inspections. Our properties have always had impeccable standards for cleanliness. But we started to have health inspectors show up with a smirk on their faces. One even told a manager, "I'll be here all day, until I find something wrong." It was infuriating to see great, hardworking employees, who were not involved in the political conversation, getting harassed for no reason other than the political views of their former boss.

Our longtime executive chef in Trump Tower actually got into an argument with an inspector who tried to insist, with a smirk, that a grain of rice was a rat dropping. I'm no rodent expert, but the difference is pretty clear. After eight hours of battle and a proud employee's iPhone recording of the entire charade, our property received a perfect score.

Then the media took a page out of the mob playbook and tried to intimidate our employees and customers. They would learn about upcoming events at one of our properties and call the people who booked the event, including brides and grooms, and hosts of bridal showers, bar mitzvahs, bat mitzvahs, charity functions, and anniversary parties—not to mention business events.

The calls went like this. "Hello, I'm a reporter with [. . .]. We noticed you're planning your wedding at a Trump property, and we wanted to get your comment on the record for an upcoming article."

Can you imagine getting a call like this? You're planning your special day and suddenly receive a veiled threat that your name will be in the paper, just because you like one of our hotels?

Reporters sunk to the same level with our wonderful employees. They would stalk our staff, find their LinkedIns or email addresses, and message them. "I'm a reporter at [. . .]. If you ever hear or see *anything* newsworthy about the Trump family or their business, please contact me." Of course, they would promise to do it on the condition of "anonymity." These reporters sometimes went even further, calling family members of our employees.

We lost business because of these twisted obsessions and harrasment of certain customers, who simply wanted to stay out of the spotlight. But our employees saw through the media game and told us about these disgusting communications.

Despite the constant barrage, some of our biggest deals closed during that period. I filled up many commercial buildings, including some of the largest in the country. My sale of Trump Golf Links at Ferry Point to Bally's Corporation was one of the largest golf deals ever done. In 2022 I sold the Old Post Office (the Trump International Hotel, Washington, D.C.). The sale marked the highest price per key ever achieved in Washington, D.C., the highest price per key in the United States history for a leasehold interest, *and* the largest sale of a historic hotel in over fifteen years.[7]

I was living in two universes. In one, relentless and vicious attacks. In the other, happy customers, and iconic properties—despite the political restraints. Thankfully I had received priceless advice from my father as a kid.

THE GOOD AND THE BAD

For as long as I can remember, every morning started out the same way. Before heading out to school, I would make my way to my father's bedroom and kiss him goodbye. As I was leaving, he would always end by saying, "No Drinking, No Smoking, No Drugs, and remember never trust anyone." Certainly not the words you typically hear a father say to his first grader.

After school, Don would often suggest a trading session with coins from our piggy banks. I happily exchanged one little dime for a few of his shiny pennies. One day, I walked into my father's office with my pile of pennies to show him what a great investment I had just made. He looked at me, explained the concept of value versus quantity, and reminded me, "Eric, what did I tell you? Never trust anyone."

I like to give people the benefit of the doubt, but over the years, I realized that trust cannot be given freely. It must be earned.

The Art of the Deal: Protect the Downside and the Upside
Will Take Care of Itself
"I always go into the deal anticipating the worst. If you plan
for the worst—if you can live with the worst—the good will
always take care of itself." —DJT[8]

THE NEGOTIATOR

I am a firm believer in "ask and you shall receive." And when it comes to negotiating, Donald Trump is the best.

Throughout my life, I've come to learn that most people are fundamentally afraid of hearing the word *no*. Americans live in one of the few societies in the world where everyday purchases aren't routinely negotiated. They can be, but people are simply unwilling to ask.

My father loves negotiating contracts, both big and small, and he's gotten as much value out of the *conversations* as he did from the savings reached in the final agreement. So often we would receive a valuable insight. "Mr. Trump, I know other bidders are proposing that you replace the entire mechanical system. It does not need to be done, sir. That's insane. Here is how I would approach it. You'll save a fortune."

Often, he combined negotiation with the gift of a huge opportunity. "All right, I'm going to give you the job. *Show me what you can do!* Make it perfect. I want your best guys. And no extras." So many long-term relationships were built with those handshakes and many companies were born.

I love hearing from companies we do business with that we negotiate harder than anyone. They often tell me that other clients don't even try, leaving millions on the table and without building a relationship in the process. Open dialogue will tell you a lot about the other party, and you can learn a lot about the challenges and nuances of a job.

Never be afraid to ask. Never be afraid of the word *no*. And negotiate *everything*.

THE BUILDER

There's an old adage: *you are what you think about most.* In order to have a successful career, your work must be your life, and the only way to be truly satisfied with that reality is to love what you do. You'll never be good at something you aren't passionate about.

Donald Trump could have stayed in real estate, but he ran for president. He could have spent his "best years" playing golf, living at Mar-a-Lago, flying to our hotels around the world in his beautiful plane. He could have maintained his private life—full of peace, quiet, friends, family, and gratitude. He could have lived out retirement knowing that he achieved the ultimate American dream, becoming a real estate and television mogul, and then the 45th president of the United States. He could have done all that, and stayed out of the 2024 race. But he didn't.

He wasn't focused on comfort or on lifestyle—he was focused on getting a job done. As a son, his choice makes me proud. I hope my kids, in years to come, understand the same principle is true of me. I often have to leave town for a business trip, miss their bedtime so I can do a TV hit, and I have invested years of my life to be with my father in court and on the campaign trail. It's not easy, as any parent who travels for work knows. "Daddy, why are you leaving?" Those words always break my heart and remind me of similar situations when I was a kid.

But children need to understand, as best they can, that their family is also about building something bigger than themselves. They're learning that we create, operate, and manage properties all over the world, and in addition to that, we're working to save our country. I spare them the details for now, of course, but am always affected by their naïve desire to have a "normal" dad with a nine-to-five career.

"I have to go be with Grandpa. I promise I'll be back in a couple of days." That's usually what I tell them. But it doesn't stop the tears. One day they may read this and understand. And, Dad, now *I* understand.

I appreciate my father even more as an adult. He is a builder. He built skylines, resorts, and businesses. And he built a family.

I'm over forty years old, and my dad still calls me "honey." Yep. Still kisses me on the cheek. I do the same with my kids, and hope I can pass along the same affection that he has for me.

My father is the hardest-working person I've ever known. He never stops. An Energizer bunny in a red tie. He'll sometimes call me at five o'clock in the morning. "Hey, honey, are you awake?"

"I'm awake. . . . I'm talking to you."

He calls me at eleven o'clock at night. "Were you sleeping?"

"I fell asleep a half an hour ago. You got me."

"Eric, I was thinking. The seventh hole at Turnberry, if we made that dogleg a little bit sharper, we could put a trap off to the left-hand side. . . . You push that green back, we could pick up thirty yards, and elevate the tee box. You'd have a better tee shot."

We used to make ridiculous bets over the tiniest details of our properties. "I'll bet you that window is exactly three feet from the corner." Out
came the tape measure, ready to prove the other wrong.

"Well, Dad, I'm three thousand miles away at the moment, but I'll
bet you a dollar it's five feet."

I have a stack of signed dollar bills pinned to the board above my
desk for the bets I've won. The granularity of these conversations is
something that no one would expect from Donald Trump. I definitely inherited his DNA.

LET'S TALK "NEPOTISM"

Nepotism is real and I'll be the first to say that I have been given numerous opportunities as Donald Trump's son. *Opportunities*, not handouts.
Beginning on the earliest construction sites, mentored by tough men, I
showed that I would roll up my sleeves and work tirelessly.

As I earned respect, bigger initiatives were put on my plate. My father always gave his children tasks that felt insurmountable. Trust was
built as each one was conquered. So was confidence. One thousand steps.
That's how the tallest mountains are climbed. That's how family and
business is supposed to work, in my view, anyway.

For the past ten years, as Executive Vice President of the Trump Organization, many thousands around the world have depended on me:
housekeepers and bartenders, security officers and general managers, an
unequaled corporate team and the most meticulous maintenance crews.
I carry the weight of all of them on my shoulders—thousands of lives,
families, children, dreams, aspirations—in the best times and in the
worst. If I didn't deliver, if I couldn't guide the ship, there's a zero percent
chance I would have lasted two months in my role. I would be loved as a
son, but I sure as hell wouldn't be entrusted with the keys.

The other side of nepotism is that I was willing to stand on a stage
very few, in other families, would be willing to tolerate, or even survive. I
am likely the most subpoenaed man in American history—112 so far directed at me and the organization I run—from the far Left in Congress,
radical district attorneys, and attorney generals. I could have crawled
into a cave and avoided the nonsense. Most political "kids" do—or they

suddenly become talented painters. But my love for my father, the pride in my name, our company, his backbone, and my unwavering belief that we are on the right side of history fuels my soul.

Nepotism gave me my start, but the finish was up to me.

THE SAME AND DIFFERENT

In business—and this would include the business of politics—my father and I are similar in so many ways, and I see more similarities the older I get. But we're different, too.

My father enjoys the camera and has used it masterfully his entire life. I, on the other hand, tolerate it. I've learned to use the medium in the business world and as one of his strongest surrogates in the political world, but I'm equally thrilled to turn if off, step away, and go dark.

I'm much happier interacting with a foreman in a hard hat than I am in front of dishonest reporters with an agenda—individuals happy to criticize something they could never build.

When it comes to working with Donald Trump, I often became a mediator of sorts for people who might be intimidated by a man who has achieved so much. After all, he built a business empire, became a top-rated television star by saying, "You're fired," and is president of the United States. I can't tell you how many people talk big in the foyer and just melt in a meeting with Donald Trump. I've seen it in business and in politics, and the shrinkage is fascinating to watch. When I can, I enjoy helping people articulate their case, and find a way to deliver something great, for the business or their career.

VISION AND ACTION

My "yoga" is a sharp chainsaw in the woods, by myself. That's my stress release—along with the shooting sports, fishing, skiing, and building.

In high school, I spent most of my free time in the wood shop. One of my projects was a twenty-two-foot rowing scull. (These are the long skinny rowing boats with sliding seats that you see gracing Olympic races.) I won the arts award every year, not because I could draw, but because I could build. I love the art of complex joinery, mortise and tenons, hand-cut dovetails, and sharp chisels. I have equal love for complex metalworking, to .001 of an inch. I'll cut threads on a manual lathe or run a Bridgeport as well as anyone—it allows me to combine two of my hobbies, building and precision-shooting sports, with my OCD personality.

I shot competitively and participated in virtually every discipline in the shooting sports my entire life. Moreover, practically every rifle in my collection I built from the ground up, blueprinting actions, chambering barrels, cutting throats, and setting headspace, muzzle threads, crowns, bedding, and so much more. The process, the discipline, and the satisfaction are all connected.

Building is in my blood—as is my insane attention to detail. I love and appreciate craftsmanship, and I love people who are capable of creating something beautiful with their hands. We live in a world where many people can't hang a picture on a wall correctly. I'm thrilled to see billions in federal funding diverted from the likes of Harvard and into trade schools—teaching kids meaningful skills instead of some nonsense major and their typical leftist brainwashing.

UNIMAGINABLE?

As I write this, I'm struck by the reality that all the varied experiences in my childhood and college years prepared me for what was to come, both in business and in politics.

Who would have imagined that? My parents probably did.

CHAPTER 6

WELCOME TO WASHINGTON

"Let me tell you, you take on the intelligence community,
they have six ways from Sunday at getting back at you. So
even for a practical, supposedly hard-nosed businessman,
he's being really dumb to do this."
—SENATE *MINORITY* LEADER CHUCK SCHUMER,
REGARDING PRESIDENT-ELECT DONALD J. TRUMP
CRITICIZING THE "INTELLIGENCE COMMUNITY," JANUARY 3, 2017
(SEVENTEEN DAYS BEFORE INAUGURATION)[1]

Thanks for the warning, Chuck.

In January of 2017, Donald J. Trump, the new president-elect, questioned the conclusions of the FBI and CIA regarding "Russian interference" in the election. And right on cue, Chuck was very quick to offer his opinion—just as quick as he had been to ask our family for donations for decades. It wasn't friendly advice, and I doubt he even realized how telling his statement was.

"They have six ways from Sunday at getting back at you."

So let me get this straight. As Americans, we are not allowed to question unelected bureaucrats and government employees—*and neither is the president*? And if we do, we better watch our backs?

I believed in the integrity of our intelligence agencies, and never thought their immense power would be used against law-abiding Americans, including those who won a democratic election and now lived in the White House. Regardless of Schumer's intentions, he was correct.

At noon on Friday, January 20, 2017, Donald J. Trump was sworn in as the 45th president of the United States. Nineteen minutes later, the *Washington Post* ran an article with this headline: "The Campaign to Impeach President Trump Has Begun."[2]

OUT OF THE WOODWORK

Back in 2015, when my father told us he was running for president, he said that we would "quickly learn who our true friends are." He was right. Many would run for the hills—often the very ones you believed were the strongest, the most loyal, the best of friends. But some of the people you would least expect to stand by your side were the most resilient. Those who seemed toughest often proved to be weakest, and vice versa.

On election night 2016, from the moment Hillary conceded, I received more text messages and phone calls than ever before in my life. It seemed as if every person I had ever known wanted to tell me how happy they were, that they were "in our corner," and had been working to rally voters. After almost two years of campaigning, I was exhausted. Many of these messages were beautiful, others were fake and truly full of shit. The volume was overwhelming.

"Eric. Congratulations!!! Sorry I've been quiet, I know how busy you have been and didn't want to disturb you. I've been a supporter the entire time." Translation: *Holy crap. Trump beat Hillary! Is it too late to join the team? Feels like a convenient time to reengage.* Everyone had doubted him—and our family. But when we won, they all came crawling out of the woodwork. In the days of social media, you know where people stand politically. Unfortunately, I had seen too many shameful social media posts—joining the mob—from people I thought were friends, many of them the same ones who suddenly found my phone number. If you didn't get a response, now you know why.

But the worst experience involved one of my closest friends and his brother. The three of us grew up together, traveled together, spent most holidays together. We were inseparable. The day after the inauguration, I was scrolling through my social media and saw a post that shocked me. His wife had posted a photo of herself and their daughters at the "Women's March" in D.C., protesting the new president. They wore those crude pink beanies and held up a vile sign . . . about my father.

No f-ing way. I immediately called him. "Buddy. I just saw your wife's post. That can't be real?!"

"Eric, um, I'm not going to tell my wife how to think." I hardly recognized the voice on the other side of the phone.

"I am not telling anyone how to think," I said. "We're practically family. Your brother and I are best friends. I was in your wedding party."

Silence. And to this day, the silence remains from both of them.

Maybe I was naïve. I had seen many people betray my father and our family, but this one cut deep. Thousands of hours of memories together. Parents who treated me as their own, and who I adore to this day. I just would have never imagined these two brothers.

Over the years, I became well acquainted with hostility and lies, but this manufactured hysteria in 2016 went beyond anything we had seen before. People who knew better—those who could finish your sentences—chose to get swept up in the polarizing venom and nonsense. Then there were those who tried to play both sides. One woman, whom we had helped when she fell on hard times years earlier, suddenly reemerged after the inauguration, with a letter.

"Dearest Donald," she wrote. "While I did not vote for you, and voted for Hillary Clinton, I would like to be the ambassador to Iraq, because my parents were born there. . . ."

In classic Donald J. Trump form, he circled that opening sentence, wrote, "Not a smart way to ask," initialed it, and sent it back to her with a simple *D*—a brevity that usually signaled he was either pissed or didn't have the time for the matter.

My family and I had certainly been around the block before Donald J. Trump was sworn in, but I must admit, by January 2017, we had stepped into a whole new arena. You never know who has backbone until they step into battle. Then you quickly see who can take the arrows—and who can't. The toughest personalities often turn out to be the weakest, while the humble and unassuming prove to be the strongest.

History will judge Jeff Sessions on his decision, as U.S. attorney general, to recuse himself under the pressure of the so-called "Russian collusion" investigation. Regardless, he would have never made it through what was to come. Who knows if the entire *Russia, Russia, Russia* scam could have been stopped in its tracks by someone with the balls to simply call out the lies and bring the truth to light. Years later, Tulsi would do what he and others didn't have the courage to do—shine a bright light onto the Obama administration's hoax.

In 2015, Macy's CEO, Terry Lundgren, someone my father had called a dear friend, pulled Trump Ties and other items from his stores across the country. Ironic, and sad, considering the Donald J. Trump Collection had been Macy's top-selling items for years.[3] This "cutting ties" didn't stop with politicians and timid businesspeople. Several relatives, whom I won't call family, turned their back as well. This included individuals who shared our last name—people who had eagerly accepted invitations to White House events and significant financial support, only to cash in later with poorly written books about how terrible we were.

None of this surprised my father, but I won't say it didn't hit hard. He's always been better at forgiveness than I am. I detest disloyalty. I know plenty of people spew hate online—keyboard warriors hiding in their basement shadows. But during the campaign, and even now, I probably encountered fewer than ten people who were truly rude or made a scene in person. And nearly all who've tried to insult me face-to-face have been males—typically beta males.

One exception occurred in a Chicago restaurant, where I had a business dinner. I walked in, and a young woman who I thought was the hostess approached. Instead of a greeting, she recoiled and spit in my face.

That was a first.

The Secret Service immediately arrested her, and Chicago police asked if I wanted to press charges. I didn't, but was happy to take my time at the restaurant and let her wait in the back of the police car, handcuffed, for a couple hours. To be fair, she *looked* a lot like Rachel Maddow, which should come as no surprise.

I have always been baffled that having a different political opinion could justify something so vile.

Another interesting moment happened on the way to my birthday dinner at RiverMarket in Tarrytown. Don and I picked up the traditional Trump family birthday cake—Fudgie the Whale from Carvel. As we headed to the door on our way out, some lunatic started yelling, "Mueller is coming, motherf-ers! Mueller is coming!" This "boy's" date looked mortified. Don and I just laughed. Looking back, the only thing Mueller found was dirt on Hillary Clinton. The irony.

It might surprise you, but despite the media noise and online bots, negative encounters are shockingly rare—and that's after shaking tens of thousands of hands and meeting countless people. For every hater or betrayer we faced, we gained hundreds of loyal friends. The love and support I have received is nothing short of contagious.

THE MOMENT IT HITS YOU

The day before the inauguration, we checked into Blair House, the traditional residence where the First Family–elect spends the night before the transition. Considered the "guesthouse of the president," Blair House sits just outside the gates of the White House and has long served as the official residence for visiting dignitaries, foreign heads of state, and important delegations. You could feel the weight of the history.

Shortly after, we departed for Arlington National Cemetery. Two impressions of that visit will forever stand in my memory: the profound quietness that filled the grounds and the awe-inspiring views stretching beyond the endless rows of white marble headstones—each one perfectly aligned.

As my father placed a wreath on the Tomb of the Unknown Soldier, I looked on the seemingly countless resting places of our nation's fallen heroes. You have to see it in person to grasp the solemn significance of the hallowed grounds that represent the best of America.

The views of D.C. from Arlington were breathtaking: the Capitol, the White House, and other historic landmarks stretched across the horizon. The only sounds heard in that moment were the clanking footsteps of the Army Guard on the white Georgia marble and the relentless shutters of cameras from the gaggles of press and paparazzi. I never imagined D.C. could be so quiet.

The enormity and immense significance of it all struck me in that moment: the battle of the campaign, the new role as First Family of the United States, and most of all, the magnitude of my father's role as Commander in Chief—the most powerful man on earth. In any strong family, when a heavy burden falls on a father or mother, the entire family inevitably shares the weight. Typically, the number one rule in politics is to keep the family out of it. But we were determined to win—and win together—just as we had in business, television, and everything else.

Though I had been running much of the company for years, all I could focus on was the deep love and admiration I felt for our great nation. At thirty-three, I suddenly realized I stood with one foot firmly rooted in business—and the other, albeit indirectly, in government. One world I knew inside and out; the other was completely foreign. That day, I truly felt the weight of that divide.

INAUGURATION DAY

On the morning of the inauguration, we attended the historic St. John's Church across from the White House—a place that would later be set ablaze by BLM rioters in 2020. Every president since James Madison had been there, including Abraham Lincoln, Franklin D. Roosevelt, John F. Kennedy, George W. Bush, Barack Obama, Donald Trump, and Joe Biden—Franklin D. Roosevelt (in 1933) began the tradition of holding a private prayer service at St. John's on Inauguration Day morning. Yet another unforgettable moment.

At the Capitol, the weather was chilly as we awaited the ceremony. Former presidents and their spouses were there with us—Barack and Michelle Obama, George W. Bush, Jimmy Carter, and of course, Bill and Hillary Clinton. After her "unexpected" loss, I can only imagine how uncomfortable it must have been for Hillary to sit just feet away from our family on that podium beneath our nation's Capitol. As Chief Justice John Roberts swore in my father as the 45th president of the United States, using his personal family Bible given to him by his mother when he graduated from Sunday school, the moment was sealed. I was tremendously proud of my father *before* that day, but that moment with the hundreds of thousands of onlookers lining the National Mall was surreal.

As guests made their way into the Capitol, I exchanged greetings with several former presidents and first ladies. President Obama was very gracious. "Congratulations. I saw you on TV a lot." Michelle followed, looked at me, and said something along the lines of, "You guys worked hard for this. Now don't mess it up." At that point, my tolerance for BS was nonexistent. I chuckled and kept walking.

We departed the Capitol shortly after, traveling toward the White

House in an enormous caravan of Secret Service agents and, for the first time, military assets. I will always remember seeing the Oval Office for the first time. I had never been in the building before—strange, given all the years I dedicated to rebuilding the Trump Old Post Office, just blocks away. It's hard to put into words what it means to be in the most powerful office in the world. Elegant yet comfortable. The power was tangible, but so was the weight of responsibility. I reflected on the amount of stress and heartache that played out in that very room over the years—the Cuban Missile Crisis in 1962 under President John F. Kennedy, the Vietnam War escalation under President Lyndon B. Johnson, the Watergate scandal in the 1970s under President Richard Nixon, the 9/11 attacks and aftermath in 2001 under President George W. Bush, just to name a few.

Our next stop in my father's new home was the residence, where he, Melania, and Barron were already moved in. As the new First Family, we were invited to spend a few nights in the White House. Lara and I stayed in the Lincoln Bedroom—an honor, a history lesson, and, admittedly, a bit . . . unusual. The actual Gettysburg Address is displayed in the room, which President Lincoln used as a personal office and the White House cabinet room. On the nightstand was a small oval-shaped painting of Lincoln and his son William "Willie" Lincoln, who died on February 20, 1862, at age eleven in the White House. The sense of history is palpable.

On the floor above the main residence are extra bedrooms, a gym, a media room, and access to the roof. When we visited over the next four years, Don and I would occasionally go up there with cigars—the white marble of the Washington Monument standing prominently on the National Mall. We never took that view for granted.

On his first full day as president, we went to the National Cathedral, where a beautiful blind child, Marlana VanHoose, sang "How Great Thou Art," and her voice filled the room. An extremely powerful moment that brought tears to the eyes of most in that beautiful soaring Gothic masterpiece—a room lined with stained glass windows, the most incredible vaulted ceiling, and countless stone columns that echo with grandeur. During the service, I was reminded of these lines from my father's inaugural address from the day before.[4]

Today's ceremony, however, has very special meaning. Because today we are not merely transferring power from one Administration to another, or from one party to another—but we are transferring power from Washington, D.C., and giving it back to you, the American People.

Washington flourished—but the people did not share in its wealth.

Politicians prospered—but the jobs left, and the factories closed.

The establishment protected itself, but not the citizens of our country.

That all changes—starting right here, and right now, because this moment is your moment: it belongs to you.[5]

THE BIGGEST ENTERPRISE IN THE WORLD

Weeks into the presidency, I was still trying to grasp the idea of my father as Commander in Chief. My phone rang with no caller ID. While I would never do so today, I decided to answer.

"Hello."

"This is the commander of Air Force One. Please hold for the president of the United States. . . ."

"Hi, honey," my father laughed, hearing the introduction. "Can you *freaking* believe this?!"

Sure, my father had airplanes and helicopters, but few understand Air Force One and the entire apparatus that surrounds it. It is on a different level. Walk out of the West Wing of the White House and two helicopters await, with more circling overhead. Hop on Air Force One and you are accompanied by an armed fleet of the most sophisticated aircraft, along with the most advanced security and communications on the planet—a plane designed not just for comfort, but for the possibility of nuclear war.

Trump Chicago was almost a billion-dollar building when we opened its doors. Trump Las Vegas cost roughly $640 million at the time of completion. I don't care how big of a business you run, nothing compares to the size and power of the United States government. The Pentagon's budget makes the revenue of Walmart, Amazon, and Apple look like small potatoes. If the Pentagon were a country, its military budget alone would rank as the eighteenth- or nineteenth-largest economy in the world.

A big development deal for us might be a billion dollars—no small

endeavor. But now it was time to step into the biggest of big leagues—
what would become Donald Trump's greatest calling and unmistakable
domain. Suddenly, as commander in chief, my father was negotiating
some of the largest government contracts in world history—from the
border wall to state-of-the-art fighter jets and more.[6]

As just one example of hundreds, the price tag from Lockheed Martin
on an F-35 was outrageous—over a trillion dollars. My father was familiar
with the competing F/A-18 Hornet—originally developed by McDonnell
Douglas but now produced by Boeing—which costs roughly $75 million
per plane. He had the team send photos of the newer "Super Hornet" and
scheduled a meeting with Lockheed Martin.

There in the Oval Office with the executives and generals, he held up
a photo of the F/A-18. In true Donald Trump fashion he stated matter-
of-factly, "Your contract is out of control. And the Super Hornet is a
better-looking plane. I can buy ten of these for every one of yours." Sure
enough, Lockheed Martin reduced the price of the project by billions.[7]

And let's not forget how Donald Trump negotiated for Air Force
One—which is actually two planes. Boeing wanted five and a half billion dollars to develop and build the new 747 for the president. But
there's never been a president who already owned his own 757. Sure, a
brand-new 747 is an expensive plane—400 to 500 million bucks—but
not five and a half billion.

President Trump: "Why is this a five and a half *billion* dollar contract?"

Generals: "Sir, we want a slightly larger APU [Auxiliary Power Unit] in
the back of the plane. So, the back of the plane has to get redesigned. We
want to be able to take off in four hundred less feet . . . So now the wings
need to be redesigned and the engines need to be more powerful. But if the
engines are more powerful, the wings need to become stronger. So now . . ."

You get the idea. Not only that, but the timeline included three years
of testing. Typical government nonsense.

President Trump: "No, we're not doing this." My father would later
renegotiate the contract with Boeing executives, including then-CEO
Dennis Muilenburg, and threatened to cancel the contract unless costs
were brought down significantly. He saved taxpayers a billion dollars
with only a few minutes of negotiation.[8] [9]

How many presidents before him negotiated like this on behalf of
taxpayers? None. And I can tell you—my father relished every minute of

it. For us Trumps, negotiation is in our DNA. My father thrives on the challenge, just like Don and I did back in our teenage days, hustling on construction sites and fighting tooth and nail for that extra dollar an hour. Those early battles were where we truly learned the art of the deal.

It's one thing to negotiate a million dollars off a real estate purchase, but in January 2017, he got to play in a really big sandbox. Donald Trump was the Department of Government Efficiency before he ever created DOGE!

DECENTRALIZE

A major way my father applied his business experience to the office was by empowering those around him to get results. In his first month in office, Lara and I were having dinner at the White House and he told us this story.

"It's crazy, this general in the Pentagon keeps calling me in the middle of the night and asking, 'Mr. President, there's a bad guy, who we've been trying to locate for many years . . . and we need your approval.'

"On the first call I said, 'Tell me about it.' The second time I told him, 'I trust your judgment.' But the third time he called, I asked him, 'Where did you go to school?' The general went to a prestigious military academy. 'I trust your judgment.'"

"'Sir, this is the protocol President Obama put in place.'"

The military changed overnight. The handcuffs were removed.

I personally heard time and time again from great soldiers and others in the military that this approach made a world of difference. "Eric, please tell your father thank you. He empowered us. He stood behind us. He gave us the tools to get the job done. It was a hundred and eighty degrees from the previous administration. All the bullshit disappeared instantly." Instead of being micromanaged, and threatened with court-martials, our warriors were free to do their job. And they did—better than anyone in the world.

TOP SECRET?

Just a few months after the inauguration, in May of 2017, I received a call through my Secret Service detail. We were told that there was a credible threat to the company, and the FBI wanted to personally brief me on it—at their N.Y.C. headquarters, just blocks away from Trump 40 Wall Street, a seventy-one-story commercial building I oversee virtually every day. Within the hour, my detail drove me to the FBI offices, taking every precaution to keep my visit out of the media. I was processed through various checkpoints, signed countless documents, and forfeited my phone before entering a secure SCIF (sensitive compartmented information facility).

In the briefing room, I endured about thirty minutes of them telling me . . . absolutely nothing. Vague cybersecurity and cyberattack threats were mentioned, along with generalized regions of the world. Any IT department with basic skills can see malware and cyberattacks daily. Nothing they were telling me was new or the least bit shocking. Despite this, I was repeatedly reminded that the details, or lack thereof, of this briefing were "extremely confidential" and to remain secret.

I left underwhelmed, but appreciative. Maybe where there is smoke there is fire. I trusted the agency.

As we were driving out of the garage, my cell phone rang. It was a reporter from ABC News, someone I've had a friendly journalistic relationship with for years. I answered on speakerphone.

"Eric, I heard you were just down at FBI headquarters."

There's no greater fan of law enforcement than me, and their repeated requests for confidentiality rang in my ears. I replied, "I have no idea what you're talking about."

"Don't bullshit me, Eric. I know exactly where you were and what you were doing there."

"I have no idea what you're talking about," I repeated. "Where did you hear this?"

"From the FBI press office in Washington, D.C. They just called to tell us you were in their office and they were briefing you on a threat to your company."

I don't know who was more pissed—me or my Secret Service detail leader, Scott, in the front seat. I had never seen him so angry, clenching his fists in rage. Any remaining trace of naïvete left me that moment. This was the swamp in action.

Before I had even *left the building*, it seemed clear that bureaucrats in the FBI, in both New York and D.C., were spreading a misleading story to the legacy media. Back at my office, I fielded a few press inquiries, and confirmed, "We absolutely were not hacked."

A few days later, headlines like this emerged: "FBI Probing Attempted Hack of Trump Organization, Officials Say: Trump's Sons Were Summoned to an Emergency Meeting with FBI, CIA Officials."

The FBI bosses wanted to be perceived as team players—like they were watching out for us, doing their job. But it became increasingly clear that the senior leadership in the agency at the time cared more about the public relations game than keeping Americans safe and bringing criminals to justice. The twisted agenda went even deeper. If they could be *perceived* as actually protecting my father and our family, the fake scandals might be seen as more credible by American citizens. Don't believe me?

The ABC News report about the events played right into the hoax.[10] Their "expert contributor" and former FBI official was quoted as saying, "If the FBI saw that kind of hack, they'd have to track that. There's no telling what a hacker could get that's connected to the president, corporate records, financial records, even things that were going on during the transition." And he added this cryptic comment: "There could be stuff in there that they do not want to become part of a separate criminal investigation."

The "Russian collusion" mantra was still gaining momentum, and the same ABC article made sure to mention a trip Don made to Moscow *nine years* earlier, announcing that our company had received trademark approval in Russia.

Another setup, designed to keep the words *Trump* and *Russia* in the headlines, stir up suspicion, and make it clear that there was a target on the president.

As for all those documents I signed at the FBI, whoever orchestrated this sham briefing knows where they can put them.

Years later the same senior officials again asked to "brief" me on a new "threat." I declined that invitation. I told my Secret Service detail that if there was a serious matter—if there was a physical threat to my safety—they could simply fill me in, but I wouldn't allow them to use me as their media pawn. The men and women of the Secret Service are some of the greatest people in the world. As are 99.9 percent of FBI agents, a few of whom are incredibly close personal friends—heroes who believe in fighting crime and haven't succumbed to political games and pageantry.

THE STEELE "DOSSIER" AND RUSSIAN "COLLUSION"

One benefit of *winning* the election was that we could *begin* to uncover the various ways the government had been weaponized against the president. After *years* of telling America that he had been spied on, and years before the FBI admitted it, President Trump sat down for a *60 Minutes* interview with Lesley Stahl in October of 2020.

> President Donald Trump: "The biggest scandal was when they spied on my campaign. They spied on my campaign, Lesley."
> Lesley Stahl: "Well, there's no, real evidence of that."
> President Donald Trump: "Of course there is. It's all over . . ."
> Lesley Stahl: "No. [. . .] Can I, can I say something? You know, this is *60 Minutes*. And we can't put on things we can't verify."
> President Donald Trump: "No, you won't put it on because it's bad for Biden."[11]

We knew—and the intelligence community knew. It would take a few more years to dispel any doubt that the FISA warrants the Department of Justice used to spy on members of our team were not valid and contained "material misstatements" and "factual misstatements and omissions." Translation: political weaponization.[12]

Robert Mueller spent years, and millions, looking for something to pin on the president and found nothing. You and I lived through years of "Russia" insanity, so I'll be brief on these pages. Anyone who's been paying attention should know these facts by now.

The entire collusion accusation was fabricated.

Yet I was the one who got the calls from the *Washington Post* and the *New York Times*. "Eric, I hear you have a secret server in the basement of Trump Tower that's connected to the Kremlin—and the FBI has opened an investigation into the Trump Organization."

Welcome to D.C. That's one way the game is played. The second Trump White House set the record straight, once and for all, explaining that Fusion GPS was hired to manufacture a false "dossier" designed to steal an election—then used as a pretense to question an election. All claims about "Russian collusion" have been proven to be intentional lies.[13]

The Democrats and Hillary created it—with the help of some Republicans, along with Obama and his corrupt administration. One of the lies was deliberately spread by Clinton herself, in October 2016 statements, where she accused Donald Trump of having a "secret server"—confirming the axiom that Democrats always accuse others of exactly what they are doing.[14]

Adam Schiff lied to Americans about it.[15]

At least twenty-six associates of Donald Trump were spied on, according to reports.[16]

The media put it on repeat. "Russia hacked the election."

Social media spread it, while censoring and suppressing the truth.

Many in our government played along, and involved foreign governments to spy on Donald Trump.

Investigations cost Americans hundreds of millions of dollars.

They pitted the two largest nuclear superpowers against each other—made communication awkward and uneasy, based on lies and deceit. All because some bitter, power-hungry, career politician wanted a few more votes in 2016. All because someone needed an excuse as to why a small group of people, who couldn't spell "politics," created the greatest political movement in American history and beat them overwhelmingly at their own game, despite being at a five-to-one monetary disadvantage.

The lies cost America at least three years of focus, productivity, and taxpayer dollars—and destroyed lives.

The only people who won were the lawyers—on both sides of the fray.

What an evil distraction. And it almost succeeded in its ultimate goal given the unwavering loyalty the establishment media has to the Democratic Party.

But there's another aspect that has not received the attention it deserves. The vile fantasies in the Steele dossier, cooked up by some James Bond wannabes, were also put forth to hurt my family *personally*. They were going after my father and all his important relationships—including his marriage.

I have lost count of how many times the media—and even our own government—have tried to divide and conquer our family. But no matter what, we never broke.

BORN IN A CROSSFIRE HURRICANE

Here are a few excerpts from the investigation by John Durham, published in 2023.[17]

"Indeed, based on the evidence gathered in the *multiple exhaustive and costly* federal investigations of these matters, including the instant investigation, neither U.S. law enforcement nor the Intelligence Community appears to have possessed *any actual evidence* of collusion in their holdings at the commencement of the Crossfire Hurricane investigation."

"Based on the review of Crossfire Hurricane and related intelligence activities, we conclude that the (Justice) Department and the FBI *failed to uphold their important mission of strict fidelity to the law* in connection with certain events and activities described in this report."

". . . at least on the part of certain personnel intimately involved in the matter" there was "a *predisposition* to open an investigation into Trump."[18]

Durham's report shredded the intelligence agencies for opening an investigation founded on "raw, unanalyzed and uncorroborated intelligence," and confirmed that investigators relied on "confirmation bias," ignoring clear evidence that disproved their claims.

When speaking about the reforms the FBI put in place—and which Christopher Wray publicly apologized for—Durham noted, "Had those reforms been in place in 2016, the missteps identified in the report could have been prevented."[19]

Bottom line: "An objective and honest assessment of these strands of information should have caused the FBI to question not only the predication for Crossfire Hurricane, but also to reflect on whether the FBI was being manipulated for political or other purposes," his report noted. "Unfortunately, it did not."[20] [21] [22]

In April and July of 2025, hundreds of pages regarding Crossfire Hurricane were released, and the findings again confirmed it was all a hoax—and so much worse. A simple trip to the basement of Trump Tower could have quickly ended three years of hell.

HAD HE PLAYED ALONG

Does anyone think that Donald J. Trump would have faced never-ending legal and political persecution if he had simply focused on real estate and sent in the legal-maximum donations to candidates around the country? From presidential and congressional candidates, to local district attorneys, to city council representatives, he could have written hundreds of checks like this for the next ten years, and the total would be a small fraction of what he's spent on legal fees.

Maybe it sounds simplistic, but when my father challenged—and rightly ridiculed—the status quo, when he flicked the hornet's nest over and over, he became public-sector enemy number one. In the Republican debates in August of 2015, he delivered this truth.

> Hillary Clinton, I said be at my wedding, and she came to my wedding. She had no choice because I gave to [her] foundation. . . .
> I will tell you that our system is broken. I gave to many people before this—before two months ago I was a businessman. I give to everybody. When they call, I give. And you know what, when I need something from them two years later, three years later, I call them. They are there for me. That's a broken system.[23]

Donald Trump speaks the truth and fights for the truth.

In a world drowning in lies, that's why so many Americans trust him. During his first term, he and our family endured lie after lie—and we still do today. "Russia," the Mueller investigation, two baseless impeachments, the Kavanaugh Supreme Court drama, Charlottesville, and more—all built on complete fiction. But none of it ever changed him.

CHANGING OF THE GUARD

I remember the week that my father moved his office out of Trump Tower. From one iconic structure to the next; from a skyscraper on 5th Avenue to the West Wing at 1600 Pennsylvania. That short period felt very strange—his larger-than-life presence left a huge void in the building and the business he built over many decades. The twenty-sixth floor—the floor that I grew up on—the office that had become so synonymous with his success would never quite be the same.

Before the first election, his office had an energy that was off the charts. One day we might have rock stars or celebrities stopping by, applying to be on *The Celebrity Apprentice*, the next day we would host a head of state, as he was running for president. You simply couldn't script who would come through those doors—it was a circus, in the best possible way. And out of that very same space, we were building the best projects on earth—focused on every piece of steel, every crystal chandelier, every slab of marble, and every office lease.

The week was bittersweet. I was very excited to take the reins—to focus on an incredible company and our thousands of employees—yet looking back we were all naïve about what was to come. I wanted to build on our already incredible brand, continue my father's legacy, focus full-time on our operations, standards, and capital investments, but unbeknownst to me, in those first four years I would spend more time keeping the company alive amid relentless attacks, political prosecution, and the weaponization of every facet of life imaginable than on day-to-day operations.

For the first time in my life, I fully understood the difference between being a boss and being a leader. As the one ultimately responsible, there was no safety net, nor any room for indecision.

Leadership meant standing firm when chaos hit. It meant being present, not just at meetings, but emotionally present for the people who depended on me. During those early years, I found myself acting as a counselor as much as an executive—helping team members navigate fear, uncertainty, and pressures we had never faced before.

My father's leadership style had always been rooted in big-picture thinking while still being incredibly micro in terms of the smallest details. He trusted his team to bring ideas to the table fully formed, but would always surprise a team with the most granular question or observation.

My approach was similar—incredibly hands-on but deeply involved from the outset in the smallest details. That level of engagement was necessary in the beginning, especially during a time when trust and focus were under constant assault.

But as time passed, I've come to appreciate and adopt more of his style. You cannot scale vision without stepping back. After nearly a decade of leading this business, I've learned when to let go, how to empower others, and when to zoom in—or out—depending on what the moment demands.

Donald Trump has a rare ability to distill complexity into clarity. He can take the most nuanced and complicated issue and reduce it to one unforgettable line. It's a superpower—one that arguably won him the presidency—and a critical leadership trait in a world of information overload.

Watching him work in the Oval Office was like watching someone balance two worlds at once. His attention to detail was second to none, yet he could appear in front of the press and convey the visions in a few simple words. He could go from negotiating a contract with Boeing, giving sports stats on any baseball player, golfer, or boxer, and in the next moment pivot to a global policy issue or a national security briefing, all without missing a beat.

When he asks questions, it's not just to get answers. Usually, he already knows them. People with a fast mouth but little substance do not last. It is never the talkers who win in his orbit, it is the doers.

He always jokes that I was the "sleeper," quietly exceeding expectations—not by boasting or demanding attention, but by steadily getting things done. Much of my approach came from his mindset—probing, challenging, forward-looking—and it deeply influenced the way I lead today.

He led by example, even amid chaos. He never let it consume him. He stayed accessible, engaged, and always focused on results.

Donald Trump knows how to get things done. He always has. And that's a legacy I strive to carry forward every day.

The Art of the Deal: Deliver the Goods
"You can't con people, at least not for long. You can create excitement, you can do wonderful promotion and get all kinds of
press, and you can throw in a little hyperbole. But if you don't
deliver the goods, people will eventually catch on." —DJT[24]

THE FIGHTER

The very trait Donald Trump is most often criticized for is ironically the
one that makes him exceptionally great. He is a fighter. He does not hesitate
and he does not quit.

It is what made him a successful candidate and what makes him a
transformational president—by every measure. Without the fight, there
are no victories. Without the fight, he might as well have packed it in on
day one, because he would have been finished.

The siege dragged on through the next election, and I was stunned
by just how low they were willing to go.

CHAPTER 7

NO GOOD DEED

"My wonderful son, Eric, will no longer be allowed to raise money for children with cancer because of a possible conflict of interest with my presidency. He loves these kids, has raised millions of dollars for them, and now must stop.
Wrong answer!"

—PRESIDENT-ELECT DONALD J. TRUMP, DECEMBER 2016[1]

Before the campaigns, before the vicious lawfare, our family was always involved in supporting charities. Who could be against that? You would be surprised. Actually, by now, you probably wouldn't be.

In Christian tradition, St. Jude is known as the "patron saint of hope and impossible causes." What a fitting name for a research hospital that helps terminally ill children who need a miracle.

You know about St. Jude Children's Research Hospital. You have seen the commercials and the images. Many people look the other way, and I can understand why. Who wants to stop and consider what these innocent children and their families face? Beautiful children simply drew the short straw in a world that can be so ugly and unfair. It truly is too much to process.

Roughly 15,000 children are diagnosed with pediatric cancer each year in the United States.[2] The littlest and most precious members of our society have been left behind by Big Pharma. *Why devote resources to thousands of cancer permutations in such a small subset of our population when we can create Ozempic, Viagra, and opioids that are easy to produce, generate billions in profit, are addictive, and finance their lobbyists?* The

National Cancer Institute only allocates about 4 percent of its budget to pediatric cancer research. These innocent and precious children are worth more than 4 percent.

A REALIZATION

I still don't know why the moment happened. I had just graduated college and should have been focused on the next happy hour and the beginning of my career. That's what twenty-one-year-old men are supposed to do, right? Driving home on the Jersey Turnpike one day, all I could think about was how fortunate I was.

I had just graduated from Georgetown University in Washington, D.C. My future looked promising. But I was also struck by another blessing: I had resources—I had the ability to help others who couldn't help themselves.

I saw so many charities do it wrong. Rubber-chicken dinners, where invited guests neither comprehend nor care about the cause at hand. Then you have the lavish celebrity charity events, where people are there to rub shoulders with the "right" people, get their picture taken, and appear on "Page Six." Some charities employ dozens of staff so the founders and board do not need to lift a finger. Their events pay hundreds of thousands for entertainment, and only a small percentage of the money raised actually goes to the cause they supposedly embrace.

I wanted to do the opposite.

I have seen six-month-old babies in the intensive care unit hooked up to countless machines being kept alive thanks to the miraculous work of doctors, nurses, and researchers at St. Jude. I have watched six-year-olds with a grim prognosis laugh and play—celebrating the gift of life we so often take for granted. In any other country or at any other time in history, they would have no chance of seeing another day.

I was young and green, with no experience in the nonprofit fundraising world. Somehow, I *knew* I could help.

MY INFOMERCIAL

Like its namesake, St. Jude brings hope to those with little hope. They have a meaningful guiding message: "We are not only here to *treat* your child, we are here to *cure* your child."

Not all hospitals are created equal, nor do many have the resources, equipment, or expertise to fight pediatric cancer. Moreover, traditional hospitals are businesses, and those businesses are ranked on "survival rates." This metric affects grants and funding, salaries and bonuses, recruitment and retention. It's why terminally ill patients are turned away from the most "prominent" medical institutions every day. Patients who are looking for hope are faced with impossible-looking odds—odds that would destroy the very metrics used to rank those institutions on prestigious lists.

Added to this cruel irony is the fact that St. Jude largely cannot collect insurance money for many treatments, because their innovative treatments are often considered "experimental," even though their track record, and survival rates, are unmatched. Beyond that, they do not charge a dime for their services. Thanks to generous donors, patients will *never* receive a bill at St. Jude, and they will never be denied the best possible treatment.

For example, retinoblastoma is a rare cancer of the eye that has been researched extensively at St. Jude; it affects a relatively small group of kids, so Big Pharma doesn't see it as a viable business model for investment. There's no ROI for developing a drug for cancers that affect a few hundred children per year. St. Jude not only does the research to find the cure, they also have to produce their own pharmaceuticals to treat those children.

I hope you're beginning to see what a special place this is. St. Jude is one of a kind, but it costs billions to keep their operations going.[3]

Their human genome project (the Pediatric Cancer Genome Project) includes storing cells from tens of thousands of patients going back to the 1960s. The goal is to break down the genome of every cancer patient and find clues to causes and cures. St. Jude has one of the largest supercomputers dedicated to this mission, and they freely share their data and findings with other hospitals around the world.[4]

In simple, human terms, every child who enters those doors will receive the most up-to-date care available. And here's where I ask you to take out your checkbook.

Just kidding. But not really.

HOW DIFFICULT CAN IT BE?

What I determined to fundraise for St. Jude in our first year was a drop in the bucket compared to what we raise now. But it was a start. Instead of calling people to ask for donations, I first called friends and told them about the kids I met at St. Jude, and the team of doctors, nurses, and scientists. Everyone I spoke with felt the passion. A team was born.

We created events, made phone calls, stuffed envelopes, collected auction items, and tried to raise every penny we could. What we didn't know about fundraising we made up for in enthusiasm and the unique benefit of owning and operating the finest golf properties on earth. We could utilize those golf facilities free of charge, or at cost, subsidize our expenses and labor, recruit our members, and call in favors from our vendors. It was a winning combination that resulted in an *extremely* low expense ratio, allowing more funds to go directly to the children of St. Jude.

The Art of the Deal: Get the Word Out
"You can have the most wonderful product in the world,
but if people don't know about it, it's not going to
be worth much." —DJT[5]

Our first Eric Trump Foundation event in 2006—when I was twenty-two—was an unbelievable success. We received our first $10,000 check and raised a total of $230,000. St. Jude was amazed that a group of kids could hold their largest golf fundraiser of the year with no employees and on a shoestring budget. The following year, we doubled that amount and continued this upward trend for many years.

During my ten-year "tenure" as president of the foundation, our total expense ratio encompassing every dollar spent was about 9.2 percent, with a large amount of that being third-party credit card processing fees. Almost no other charity in the country had such a low expense ratio—we were truly unbelievable at what we did.

I would call every vendor and simply ask. "I give you a tremendous amount of business. Can you help provide steaks and lobster for our upcoming gala for the children of St. Jude?" "We love your AV company. I know you have done twenty weddings with us this year alone. Bret Michaels is headlining our charity event for St. Jude—you probably saw him on *The Celebrity Apprentice*. Would you do the stage, lights, and sound?" To pitch companies like TaylorMade I would say, "You are such a significant partner at our golf courses. We need gifts for our charity tournament players who are supporting the kids. Could you donate a putter for everyone at the event?" To increase the effectiveness of our fundraising, we'd simply ask companies we worked with to donate products and services.

The answer was always yes, mostly because of the miraculous work of St. Jude.

Another way we cut expenses to the bone was the fact that the foundation didn't have a single employee for the first nine years. Volunteers unpacked boxes, set up rooms, decorated tables, and made calls. Board members, including myself, flew coach to every event—more money to the kids, no private planes, and no Clinton Foundation nonsense.

We quickly grew into one of St. Jude's largest noncorporate fundraising partners, with one of the lowest expense ratios of any charity in the world.

INTENSIVE CARE

As our partnership with St. Jude grew, I committed $20 million to building St. Jude's Intensive Care Unit (ICU) and Surgery Center. I can't tell you how daunting of a goal that was for a twenty-something-year-old, and I still remember the anxiety of signing that enormous pledge.

Long story short, in much less than ten years we fulfilled our commitment and far surpassed our goal. The facility would become known as the Eric Trump Foundation Surgery & ICU Center, the most state-of-the-art ICU dedicated to children anywhere in the world.

As the foundation grew, it also grew within the heart and soul of the company. Our employees began wearing the beautiful St. Jude pins. Not because it was required, but because they believed.

Each property did a different fundraiser, and it all happened organically. Chicago would decorate one of our incredible high-speed elevators, turning it into "the Gingerbread Express" with toy trains, a faux fireplace, stockings, and all the trimmings. *Make a donation and ride the Gingerbread Express.* Housekeepers would hold employee bake sales. No effort was too big or too small. The various properties even competed to see who could raise the most money for St. Jude, with the winning property receiving a large Stanley Cup–style trophy and bragging rights for the next year.

Across our portfolio, we were raising hundreds of thousands of dollars annually through these special promotions alone. Each year, we brought some of our employees to St. Jude to tour the hospital. These visits were both life-changing and deeply inspiring experiences for everyone involved.

BLINDSIDED

My phone started ringing early one day in 2017. Friends called to tell me that New York's attorney general, Eric Schneiderman, was holding a press conference that morning about me. "I don't understand," I replied. "What does it have to do with me?" So I turned on the TV and watched in absolute disbelief.

"We're going to investigate the Eric Trump Foundation."[6]

Hours afterward, I received the subpoena. It was my first (of 112 and counting). Today I'm numb to the nonsense, but that one hit me like a rock. We ran an amazing charity. We raised millions. We had the lowest possible expense ratio—no one even came close. I sat on St. Jude's advisory board. The hospital named us Charity of the Year. We became the "poster child" of how to do fundraising right. Nothing made sense . . . until it did.

* * *

A few months earlier, in 2016, the Clinton Foundation was getting hammered in the media. (*Hammered* is a relative term, of course, when it comes to scrutinizing Democrats.) They accepted millions of dollars from those connected to foreign governments while Hillary served as secretary of state. The FBI and the Department of Justice were publicly discussing corruption within her foundation. There were ethical red flags about overlaps between Clinton campaign donors and foundation donors. Several of the largest foundation donations were connected to companies lobbying the federal government. Their expense ratios were insulting, including more than $50 million spent on travel since 2003.[7]

I wondered how many times my team and I visited St. Jude versus how many times Bill and Hillary went to Haiti. Does anyone think they gave a shit about Haiti? Call me a cynic, but looking at the rotten fruit of their foundation's work there, it seems clear to me that the Clinton Foundation was primarily an influence-peddling apparatus. After she lost the election in 2016, funding plummeted. Strange coincidence, right?[8]

The publicity was terrible and the Left needed a distraction—a counternarrative. Enter the Eric Trump Foundation.

One of my best friends from college, Paige, who had been an integral part of the foundation since the beginning, was there at our office when the subpoena arrived. I handed the papers to her and said, "Welcome to politics, Paige."

Over the next several months, Paige led the grueling task of collecting all the requested documents going back several years. They had asked for *everything*—every check received and every check written, every invitation to every event, every expense, every tax return, and every financial record. They knew it was all bullshit. It took almost three full months to gather all the requested information, but that wasn't the worst part . . .

I was being accused of *embezzling* money from sick children and somehow profiting from the foundation.[9]

The only perceivable purpose of the investigation: they wanted headlines. And they got headlines. Oh, and all this happened in 2017, just months after Donald J. Trump was sworn in as president.

We had seen the same pattern before: the press runs a story that "raises questions," they hand it to an attorney general in a deep blue state, and give Leftists an excuse to open an investigation, which leads to endless damaging headlines. The "scandal" snowballs—all coordinated and all by design.

It was probably the first time in my life I was deeply "hurt." In fact, I don't think I'll ever use that word again. I put a note on my desk that still sits there today: "No good deed goes unpunished."

As a charity, we helped fund the cure for retinoblastoma, saving thousands of children, their vision, and their lives. We built one of the largest intensive care units in the world dedicated to children with terminal cancer.

Then I woke up to the ABC News headline: "Eric Trump Funneled Cancer Charity Money to His Businesses, Associates: Report."[10]

Honest question. If a nonprofit has single-digit expenses, what is left to "funnel"? Maybe the only people more angry and confused than me were the incredible CEO, staff, and patients at St. Jude. We weren't just fundraising partners, we were friends.

Other than answering some simple questions over the next few months, we didn't hear back from the AG's office. As for New York Attorney General Eric Schneiderman, he resigned in disgrace in 2018 after allegations that he assaulted multiple women.[11] The irony: the highest law enforcement authority in the state of New York used his power to take action against a wonderful children's charity, but was then forced to resign because he was allegedly hitting and choking women.

By the way, have you ever heard of "the Biden Cancer Initiative"? I didn't think so. Founded in 2017, the foundation reportedly gave out *no* grants its first two years, and spent millions in salaries. These revelations came to light in 2020, and I don't remember any lawsuits or scandals during that election year.[12]

Eighteen months later, when a reporter asked the current attorney general, Letitia James, if the investigation into our foundation was still active, her office suddenly remembered the case and "reopened" it. The entire investigation was bullshit, but the damage had already been done.

The foundation was squeaky-clean, but I did not want to create any more noise for my father, who had only been in the White House a few months, and honestly, my spirit was shot. I called Paige and said, "Let's put the foundation on hold. As long as I'm involved, they will attack every dollar raised. Any check, big or small, from any donor, will be labeled as unethical—and then they will target our friends and donors."

Paige was not having any of it, so I made her an offer she couldn't refuse.

"Will you lead the foundation?"

As someone who was a true believer and had donated to St. Jude even before we first met, she accepted the challenge, agreeing that my name would be removed from the organization during my father's time in office. Of course, I would stay involved as an ambassador, as I am to this day. Paige and the board, some of whom are my best friends, rebranded to Curetivity—combining the words *Cure* and *Activity*, because you have to take action to find a cure.

The Art of the Comeback: Be Passionate
**"This is a key ingredient to success and coming back.
If you don't have passion about who you are, about
what you are trying to be, about where you are
going, you might as well close this book right
now and give up." —DJT[13]**

MY FRIEND COLIN

I have gotten to know many wonderful patients and their families through our work with St. Jude. Over the years, I celebrated milestones with them such as birthdays and "no more chemo" parties. . . . I have also given eulogies at their funerals.

We met Colin at St. Jude when he was two years old and first diagnosed. He and his family lived in Ithaca, New York, and quickly became a huge part of our Eric Trump Foundation/Curetivity family. Colin and his family attended many of our events, sharing his journey with all of us. After many ups and downs, Colin's cancer returned and he left us at the age of ten. Lara, Paige, and I—along with other members of the board—flew to Memphis for the memorial.

I have spoken on some of the world's largest stages, but a funeral, for a beautiful ten-year-old boy who had spent his whole life fighting . . . this was the most difficult of all.

I shared what an inspiration Colin was, and continues to be, and his mission of not letting challenges get in the way of pursuing dreams. Colin was very passionate about becoming a police officer. And he *did*. Before he passed, he was inducted as an honorary sergeant of the Ithaca Police Department. Colin was an amazing kid.

To date, we have raised over $50 million for St. Jude. We fully funded the Eric Trump Foundation Surgery & ICU Center. Now we are funding the Curetivity Floor, located in St. Jude's "Inspiration4 Advanced Research Center," where they conduct groundbreaking research on pediatric neurological disease.

One of our proudest moments came during a State of the Union address, when ten-year-old Grace Eline—a brain cancer survivor who had completed treatment at St. Jude Children's Research Hospital—was introduced as a guest of First Lady Melania Trump. She received a rare, minutes-long standing ovation from both sides of the aisle. Politics should *never* have a place in the fight against pediatric cancer. Seeing that young girl receive an ovation, seeing the greatest pediatric hospital in the world recognized for their outstanding work, and seeing the support for a cause that I've dedicated so much of my life to, validated the mission I love so much.

To this day, I occasionally hear "Eric stole money from children." It's infuriating. If Donald Trump were a Democrat, and if my name was Malia or Sasha, I would have been given the Nobel Peace Prize for what I created. The viciousness of politics is hard to comprehend. This was just the tip of the spear.

I still have that note on my desk about "no good deeds." It sits next to Colin's photo. Not to discourage me from helping those in need, but to remind me of the duality of life.

If you wonder how I can keep the political, legal, and business attacks in perspective, I'll tell you a secret. I think about those kids at St. Jude. When I open the doors to that ICU and see a tiny baby fighting for life—surrounded by tubes, hooked to beeping machines, enduring unthinkably toxic cancer drugs—I remember. Compared to those children, we have absolutely nothing to stress or complain about.

Nothing.

And, as Colin taught me, and can teach us all, nothing is hopeless or impossible if we never quit.

CHAPTER 8

DEFEAT BY A
THOUSAND CUTS

"You never want a serious crisis to go to waste."
—RAHM EMANUEL, FORMER CHIEF OF STAFF TO PRESIDENT
BARACK OBAMA, FORMER CHICAGO MAYOR[1]

"Eric, this is Chicago Mayor Lori Lightfoot. I just want to let you know nothing's going to happen to your building."

Late-night phone calls are not rare for me, with a huge portfolio of projects around the world, but this was the first time I had received a call from the mayor. It was late May of 2020. Election season was heating up, as were the Black Lives Matter protests, and COVID concerns and confusion were turning the entire world upside down. Huge BLM riots erupted nationwide, including in D.C., where monuments were defaced and stores looted. Days later, rioters even set fire to St. John's Episcopal Church. After repeatedly and publicly condemning the violence, my father—joined by my sister Ivanka and others—walked to that very church, where he defiantly stood, Bible in hand.[2]

The night Mayor Lightfoot called, the city—and our nation—was burning. Several large mobs were in Chicago and they were getting closer to downtown, where Trump International Hotel and Tower Chicago is located. It was out of control. Protesters numbered in the thousands and were throwing bottles, shooting fireworks at officers, carrying bats, and breaking windows. Law enforcement officers were being hurt.

Lightfoot held a press conference saying that the protests had "evolved into criminal conduct."[3] That night, as the mobs moved closer, our team kept asking city officials why they weren't lifting the bridges on the Chicago River to keep the mayhem from spreading.

"Ms. Mayor, I really appreciate the call," I replied. "This is not political for me. I care about Chicago. We have over 300 hotel units, 430 residences, hundreds of owners and guests—and hundreds of employees relying on our building for their livelihood. Our team is currently treating many of your wounded officers from all across the city in the retail space in our hotel. I'm not sure if you've heard this from Chicago PD, but everyone is asking that you lift the bridges . . . now."

She assured me the bridges would be raised, then shared something fascinating about the riots. The mayor made it clear that the mobs were orchestrated and controlled from the outside. She told me that undercover agents knew that the crowds were being "led" by outside instigators. It was a coordinated siege, steered through the city and around police, by Leftist organizers in high-rise buildings and on rooftops. And as we would later learn, thanks to DOGE, many of these protests were actually fueled by funds from the federal government via the United States Agency for International Development (USAID). How ironic that they seek to develop other nations while destroying our own.

Minutes after our call, I watched the scene unfold live on television as the bridges were lifted.

Was Lori Lightfoot losing sleep because she cared about our building? I doubt it. Politically, she was far from an ally. But if anything happened to a Trump building during a Trump presidency and just a few months from an election, the optics would have seemed incompetent if not vindictive. As horrible as her policies were for the city and the people of Chicago, she seemed to comprehend this. In addition, the Chicago police have always been big fans of Donald Trump—he was the one person who relentlessly defended their livelihood in a city known for race-baiting and quickly turning on their own.

In Chicago and in blue states around the country, these violent protests were being orchestrated by people outside of the mobs. Why were people funding hysteria? Why were pallets of bricks being left on the sides of the streets? *And where were the congressional hearings about these riots?*

Was the death of George Floyd the cause for all the uproar—or an excuse to change the narrative in an election year?

I am not a conspiracy theorist, but it was clear that those opposing President Trump's reelection would seize every possible opportunity to affect the outcome. Leverage multiple layers of mayhem? Absolutely. Manufacture outrage? Easy. The Main Street Media became the de facto communication arm of the DNC. It is no different than the lawfare we have experienced. This insanity does not just form out of thin air.

"FIERY BUT MOSTLY PEACEFUL PROTEST"[4]

Were the protests and the COVID virus created to impact the 2020 election? Were they *leveraged* by the establishment? I'll let Rahm answer that one.

Rahm Emanuel, former chief of staff to President Barack Obama and Chicago's mayor preceding Lori Lightfoot, famously said years earlier, "You never want a serious crisis to go to waste. And what I mean by that, it's an opportunity to do things that you think you could not do before."[5]

In August 2020, a report in the *Washington Post* ran an article with the headline "How the Coronavirus Pandemic Helped the Floyd Protests Become the Biggest in U.S. History." The story asserted that "people who lost money or jobs because of the pandemic response were more likely to protest with Black Lives Matter."[6] [7]

According to the *New York Times*, between 15 million and 26 million people participated in protests by late June 2020.[8] Remember, this was still during "lockdowns" that closed businesses and schools. Weddings had been canceled, funerals forbidden, and any gatherings—including in people's homes—were not allowed in many states.

But BLM protests weren't merely tolerated—they were encouraged. Even the ones CNN absurdly labeled "mostly peaceful" as cars and buildings burned in the background. At the peak of the lockdowns, countless left-leaning health officials openly urged people to join the crowds. The irony was staggering.[9]

This is Washington Politics 101.

LOCKING DOWN AND STIRRING UP

It is important to understand that the COVID pandemic wasn't a single chapter in history. Politically, I see it as three distinct chapters. First, there was the panic and pain. People were dying and facts were scarce. It was a truly dark time. Second, there was the season during the Trump presidency when the administration worked to bring calm. The third and darkest, after the 2020 election, was a season of exploitation by the swamp, led by the Biden administration. They sure didn't let the crisis go to waste.

The radical Left turned the pandemic into profit centers and seized the opportunity to expand government control in many aspects of our everyday life. Work from home? Absolutely. Hand out billions in untraceable money? No problem. Expand surveillance powers using apps to collect personal data and "contact tracing"? Why not?

The consequences were predictable: rampant fraud in relief programs; massive corporate windfalls, especially for Big Pharma, where stock prices soared to staggering highs; censorship of dissent; government pressure on tech platforms to silence COVID "misinformation" and Biden family "disinformation"; and runaway inflation. But why?

Look at the actions of the Biden administration and their allies in several states and localities.

Closures were handled on a state-by-state basis, and New York's response was a mix of Marxism and mayhem. Most appalling, the policies put in place by the state contributed to thousands of deaths. Then they lied about it, according to a 2022 report, which concluded: "The public was misled by those at the highest level of state government through distortion and suppression of the facts when New Yorkers deserved the truth."[10] The state also "misled" (i.e., "lied to") us about the over nine thousand hospital patients they sent to nursing homes at the height of the pandemic, putting tens of thousands of residents at risk and causing needless deaths, according to reports.[11]

Was anyone ever held accountable? You know the answer.

As a reminder of how insane the narrative was at the time, Governor Andrew Cuomo, hoping to use the crisis to jump-start a 2024 presidential run, published a book in October of 2020 about his "leadership lessons."[12] When Cuomo fell, the vultures circled—including Letitia James and Kathy Hochul.

From an economic and business perspective, the power-grabbing policies didn't even make sense. Why were liquor stores and marijuana shops open, but hardware stores, gyms, and churches forced to close? The people implementing these rules were often the very people trying to subvert them.

Michigan Governor Gretchen Whitmer declared that people could not visit their vacation homes, even if those homes were in the state. For some reason, she also ruled that motorboats could not be used. In the retail sector, she forced the closing of areas "dedicated to carpeting, flooring, furniture, garden centers, plant nurseries, or paint." During the pandemic, she and her husband took several trips—including one to my home state of Florida.[13]

Police and firefighters were told they would be fired if they didn't get the vaccine. Airline pilots were refusing and resigning in massive numbers. Entire military platoons were faced with the prospect of complying or being "dishonorably discharged." A member of my former Secret Service detail, who will remain unnamed, was told he must either be vaccinated or be fired. He was just six months from being able to retire with the full pension he spent his career earning. "Eric," he told me, "I'm about to lose everything I have ever worked for! I can't believe what this new administration is doing."

These corrupt politicians are always looking to increase their power, with zero regard for how it affects people. So much for "my body, my choice."

SHUT IT DOWN?

In 2020, while the world was closing down, our phones were ringing off the hook. Office and retail tenants were calling me and they were panicked. "Eric, we are out of business. I need help!" We worked, around the clock, with every single one of them. "John, let's cut your rent in half and draw down your security deposit. Your firm is amazing, we've been together for years, and I know you'll be there when the world comes back around."

So many other companies took the f-you approach: *you have a lease, you need to pay*. But we worked with our clients and found creative, win-win agreements. We were flexible and maintained a long-term view.

We kept our buildings full and kept our tenants happy. I give the credit to our team, who spent thousands of hours on the phone negotiating—and often simply listening. They are remarkable people, and they know who they are, and how much I appreciate them.

That was my commercial leasing challenge. But I also had some of the largest hotels, golf resorts, retail outlets, estates, private clubs, and restaurants to run. "Eric, you have twenty-four hours to shut down the hotel. No one will be allowed in the building. Your lights are going to go dark. Shut down your restaurants, spa, and all other functions. You are hereby closed." That's what I was told by countless government officials in March of 2020. The City of Chicago gave us twelve hours to shut down Trump International Hotel and Tower.

How do you "turn off" a building with 2.6 million square feet of space? It was unprecedented. Do I get rid of fire command, mandated by law, which monitors all life safety systems, and compromises the safety of hundreds of people who make the building their home? Turn off the HVAC systems, lock down the elevators, and send those technicians home? Should tenants be locked in their units with no power or lights? How about the hundreds of employees who earn their livelihoods in those very jobs?

Air travel was crippled. Vacations and corporate conferences were canceled. On a state and local level, to say these mandates were not well thought-out would be an understatement. In a matter of weeks, our entire industry was shut down.

Imagine having to call the brides of every wedding booked for the foreseeable future to tell them their wedding needed to be canceled—the biggest day of their lives, upended. Despite the narrative from mayors and governors, it was not as easy as turning the lights off and locking the doors. We had obligations to guests, residents, patrons, and employees.

On top of that, we had to continue to make our loan payments and pay our utilities and overhead. Like so many businesses, our expenses never changed despite the lack of revenue. The mayor of New York City forbade businesses from going into the office—a difficult problem when the very checks needed to pay New York real estate tax were issued from the location we were forbidden from visiting. I largely ignored that rule, and along with a small executive team, I went to Trump Tower to keep everything rolling.

We were constantly trying to figure out how to pay housekeepers when there were no guests, and how not to lay off our cooks when there were no patrons walking the streets. The grass keeps growing during a pandemic—who would mow it? And would the powers that be designate them as "essential"? For over a year, I did not take a salary. If our housekeepers and cooks were out of work, so was I.

When the Paycheck Protection Program (PPP) was enacted in March 2020 to help businesses cover rent and payroll, our companies and our family were explicitly excluded from receiving any benefits. No other hospitality company was carved out—not Four Seasons, not Hilton, or Marriott, just Trump. Why? Because Donald Trump was president. Despite this, major news outlets accused our company of receiving PPP because various unrelated office tenants had applied for PPP benefits.[14]

Through it all, the Trump Organization stood strong. We did not waver. We adapted faster and smarter than any other company. Not a single corporate employee lost their job and there were no pay cuts. I am proud to say that as I write this, the Trump Organization has never been stronger.

ESCAPE FROM NEW YORK

In October 2020, we were on a plane ride home from a weeklong campaign trip in Minnesota and Wisconsin, while the president stayed in D.C. We boarded a plane from Wausau to New York when I received a message from my father's assistant reporting that he had tested positive for COVID. "How is he?" I replied.

"He's on his way to Walter Reed."

I was in disbelief. The screening to get into the White House in the midst of the pandemic was nothing short of scenes in a sci-fi movie. Doctors, mandatory testing, and endless paperwork. Social distancing was the norm, and beyond that my father has always been a bit of a germaphobe. *If the president of the United States could get COVID in those circumstances, anyone, anywhere could.*

My father had always been indestructible, but this was a bad case. Yes, we were *very* concerned. People were dying. The "experts" were giving wildly conflicting advice that seemed to change daily. We wanted to visit, but simply could not. That fact alone was excruciating.

The news of his hospitalization dominated the headlines. Supporters gathered around the hospital with well-wishing signs. Their love was tremendous.

Ironically, Walter Reed Hospital was named after a United States Army physician who discovered how yellow fever—the pandemic of that era—was transmitted

At one point during his stay, my father insisted on leaving the presidential wing, "Ward 71," so he could have the limo drive him around the hospital. He wanted to wave and personally thank everyone who had taken the time to show their support. The media predictably erupted in outrage. In a small way, this moment foreshadowed what he would later display on the stage in Butler—a powerful show of strength to the American people amid crisis and personal hardship.

All over the world, the headlines announced "The President Has Been Placed on Regeneron," an experimental treatment of monoclonal antibodies to neutralize viruses. I couldn't ignore the irony that a former friend of the family who disappeared from our lives due to political differences happened to be the CEO of the company that manufactured the drug we were now entrusting to save my father's life. The irony. It has certainly been an interesting life.

PANDEMIC PANICANS

That night, I began getting strange, late-night texts from an official at our son's school in New York. The messages were barely coherent but carried one clear demand: "Since your father has COVID, do not drop your kid off at school. We must protect our classrooms from infection."

"My father lives in D.C.," I replied. "That's 240 miles from here. Lara and I will be bringing him to school. I don't have my medical license, but I am certain COVID can't be transferred via a cell phone."

This was the last straw of insanity for Lara and me. We had another life-changing decision to make. Should we stay in New York, a state that meant so much to us, or get the hell out and move to Florida? Our company had a large footprint in Florida, our kids could be free of classroom indoctrination, and we would save a fortune in taxes—taxes that were funding the very people who made our lives hell. At our dining room table, Lara and I made a list of pros and cons. The only con on our list: sentimental value.

"Honey," I said, "we can create that anywhere."

Today we are grateful to call Florida home. It was the best move we ever made, but it was also sad in many ways. We love New York. I was born and grew up there. The Trump name dots skyscrapers across the city and I still run those properties today. We didn't want to leave, but why live somewhere you're not welcome? Hundreds of thousands of other New Yorkers felt the same way and have left the city in one of the largest exoduses from any state in the history of the nation. So sad for a state whose motto, "Excelsior," means "ever upward."[15]

After six months of logistics, moving, unpacking, and getting the kids settled in, Lara said, "Honey, we're finally here. Let's celebrate." We stepped outside to try our patio furniture for the first time, and I popped open a beer. Before the carbonation left the can, my phone rang. It was one of our property managers in upstate New York.

"Eric, our cart barn is on fire."

"How bad is it, Brian? Can we put it out?"

"The building is gone."

Celebration delayed. Another fire to put out and structure to rebuild. A pretty good analogy of how we, and so many other Americans, endured those years, punch after punch.

LOCKING DOWN THE MEDIA

The *New York Post* broke the news about Hunter Biden's "Laptop from Hell" in October 2020, just weeks before the election. Panic hit the Biden camp, and the Democrat war machine went straight into action.

The first tactic was to ignore the story. As National Public Radio's managing editor put it, "We don't want to waste our time on stories that are not really stories, and we don't want to waste the listeners' and readers' time on stories that are just pure distractions."[16] When ignoring Hunter's laptop was not working, the government and media went into the censorship business. And make no mistake, it was, and is, a business.[17]

Almost two years after the 2020 election, Mark Zuckerberg finally confessed to Joe Rogan about the lie our government was peddling regarding Hunter's laptop. "The background here is that the FBI came to us—some folks on our team—and was like, 'Hey, just so you know, you should be on high alert. We thought there was a lot of Russian propaganda.'"

Right. The same guy who later removed Donald J. Trump from his platform was concerned about propaganda in the campaign?!

Then Zuck continued. "When we take down something that we're not supposed to, that's the worst."[18]

Yeah, the worst. And the $400 million he put into tilting the 2020 election in Democrats' favor.[19]

Other platforms followed in lockstep. Less than one month before Election Day, Twitter blocked users from sharing posts related to Hunter's laptop, including information that removed any doubt about the Biden family's corruption. They later banned Donald Trump, the 45th president of the United States, from the platform altogether, while terrorist organizations including the Taliban, Boko Haram, Al-Qaeda, Hamas, Hezbollah, and the Ayatollah in Iran remained free to tweet to the masses.

If locking down almost all media and social media was not enough, it was time for the "experts" to weigh in. Fifty-one former intelligence officials signed a letter saying that the whole laptop story was "Russian disinformation." Former Director of National Intelligence James Clapper, former Secretary of Defense Leon Panetta, former CIA Director John Brennan, and their cosigners rode those talking points right through Election Day.[20] Former intelligence indeed.

And in June of 2024, we learned from the House Judiciary Committee that these officials coordinated with current CIA officials and top members of the Biden campaign: "The 51 former intelligence officials' Hunter Biden statement was a blatant political operation from the start. It originated with a call from top Biden campaign official—and former Secretary of State—Antony Blinken to former Deputy Central Intelligence Agency (CIA) Director Michael Morell." The committee further noted that "high ranking CIA officials, up to and including then–CIA Director Gina Haspel, were made aware of the Hunter Biden statement prior to its approval and publication."[21]

Bottom line: partisans in the CIA actively used their influence to change the outcome of a debate, the news, social media, and an election.

Would hearing a story about a laptop have made a difference in how people voted? According to a congressional hearing on "protecting speech from government," a survey found that "70 percent of Biden voters would not have voted for the Biden-Harris ticket if they had known about the Biden laptop, but many Americans did not know about it because of the coordinated cover-up by Big Tech, the swamp, and mainstream news. Now, mainstream media outlets have verified the laptop, but the damage has been done."[22]

According to NBC News, "From 2013 through 2018 Hunter Biden and his company brought in about $11 million via his roles as an attorney and a board member with a Ukrainian firm accused of bribery and his work with a Chinese businessman now accused of fraud."[23] Joe Biden was vice president during most of this time and "exchanged emails with his son Hunter's business associate 54 times while he was serving as vice president."[24]

No one questioned the emoluments clause then. This was before the world saw Hunter's elicit photo album or read his emails about "the big guy." Would I or my siblings have been given the benefit of the doubt in similar circumstances? Of course not. These are the same people who targeted me for raising funds to save *terminally ill children* at St. Jude!

American voters should have known about Hunter's laptop—and a whole lot more—before the 2020 election. Including the truth about Sleepy Joe.

On October 18, 2020, less than three weeks before election day, CNN's Jake Tapper interviewed Lara on the topic of Biden's capabilities and supposed "stutter." The Democratic emperor had no cognition, and everyone knew it.

Tapper: "How do you think it makes little kids with stutters feel when they see you make a comment like that?"

Lara: "First and foremost, I had no idea that Joe Biden ever suffered from a stutter. I think what we see onstage with Joe Biden, Jake, is very clearly a cognitive decline."

After Tapper accused her of not being qualified to diagnose anyone, she answered, "I'm not diagnosing. I'm saying that we see the Joe Biden of today is not the Joe Biden of five years ago, of ten years ago. [. . .] We can clearly see that Joe Biden is struggling. . . . And it's very concerning to a lot of people that this could be the leader of the free world."[25]

Remember, this was in 2020—before Biden was president!

As usual, Lara was right. And as usual, CNN later deleted that video from their site. America knew Biden wasn't fit for office. But the political machine was in overdrive and churning out ballots. It's worth noting that Tapper called Lara to apologize in 2025, right before his book came out, ironically named *Original Sin: President Biden's Decline, Its Cover-up, and His Disastrous Choice to Run Again*. If you wonder why so many Americans detest the media, this is example 9,754.

SOCIALLY DISTANCED VOTING

In an August 2020 statement in the White House Rose Garden, President Donald J. Trump once again predicted the future.

"I thought I'd start by talking about some mail-in voting that just was revealed. . . . Half a million incorrect absentee ballot applications were sent all across the state of Virginia, including to many dead people. This was an unprecedented mailing flub that's heightened concerns about the integrity of expanding mail-in voting and mail-in voting efforts. It's a disaster—all over Virginia, half a million votes. . . . We don't want to have a rigged election, I know that."[26]

The lockdowns set the stage for unprecedented changes in how Americans voted. "Never let a crisis go to waste." Remember, national elections are run by individual states—not the federal government. Mail-in ballots and other shadowy tactics amounted to a death by a thousand cuts. Even now, as I write this, more and more unmistakable evidence emerges revealing the extent of the "irregularities" that marred the 2020 process.

To name just a few:

In 2024 the Georgia election board reprimanded Fulton County— Fani Willis's district—for how it handled the 2020 election, and ordered the 2024 election to be monitored. Among other issues, thousands of ballots were double-scanned and seventeen thousand ballots went "missing." Biden "won" by fewer than twelve thousand votes.[27]

Nationwide, as NPR reported in 2020, "just 44,000 votes in Georgia, Arizona and Wisconsin separated Biden and Trump from a tie in the Electoral College."[28] New revelations come out about Georgia's electoral dysfunction every week.

Journalist Mollie Hemingway summed it up well in her 2024 statement to Congress: "Instead of having total security and a verifiable chain of custody for ballots being issued, cast, and counted, we flood addresses across the country with tens of millions of unsupervised mail-in ballots months ahead of elections, frequently to locations from which voters, if they're even alive, have long since moved."[29]

During the Biden autopen administration, various government agencies gave voter registration forms to noncitizens.[30] U.S. Attorney General Merrick Garland called proposed voter ID laws and election reforms "discriminatory, burdensome, and unnecessary."[31]

The issue of election integrity is really not complicated. One side always tries to create more gray areas and excuses, and the other side is working to create more accountability and transparency. I'll let you guess which side is blue, and which is red.

IT'S PROBABLY A DUCK

From my standpoint, having been on the front lines of three campaigns, the energy going into November 2020 was even greater than in 2016, and the numbers proved it. In addition, our campaign organization was light-years ahead of the previous election.

America had low inflation, low gas prices, low taxes, low interest rates, and record low unemployment for every demographic. Biden drew hundreds to his campaign events, while my father's crowds were in the tens of thousands. Supporters would camp out for days before just to get a seat. Even for me, someone not on the political ticket, I cannot count how many rallies I did every week in every swing state that drew thousands just to hear me speak.

I saw every demographic: bikers for Trump, farmers for Trump, factory workers, union members, outdoorsmen, police and firefighters, Blacks for Trump, Asians for Trump, Hispanics for Trump—I even visited Assyrians for Trump. I spoke in churches, town halls, VFW posts, factories, refinery platforms, farms, and backyards—often into a bullhorn, standing on a John Deere tractor or a picnic table. It was surreal.

I'll never forget an event in Pennsylvania. Directly across the street from me, Joe Biden, the candidate himself, had just a few dozen people show up for his event. His yellow, social-distancing circles remained largely empty. My venue was standing room only and I wasn't the person on the ballot.

I would leave those rallies with my pockets filled with challenge coins, given to me by law enforcement, military, and Purple Heart recipients. I still display several hundred of them on a special shelf in my home. I'm not an unbiased observer, and these measurements are subjective, but it sure seems like the enthusiasm gap was huge in 2020, especially against a man who rarely left his Delaware basement. I tend to think that Biden's statement a few days before the election was Freudian.

"We have put together, I think, the most extensive and inclusive voter fraud organization in the history of American politics."
    —CANDIDATE JOE BIDEN, OCTOBER 24, 2020[32]

I want facts, investigations, and the truth. So do all honest Americans. If something looks like a duck, quacks like a duck, and swims like a duck, it's probably a duck. There was something very "off" about 2020. Actually, thousands of things were off. Here are some unique dynamics of that election.

Elected officials and countless bureaucrats using the pandemic to close schools, businesses, and gatherings in violation of the Constitution—while ignoring lockdowns themselves?

Okay.

Intelligence agencies coordinating with the media and social media companies (before and after the election) to censor free speech?

They're protecting the public from disinformation!

Riots?

Fine. They are "mostly peaceful."

Requiring citizens to show up at polling places to cast their vote?

Unsafe! We need mail-in ballots and drop-off boxes or millions will die!

Lawfare against the president, against my family, against me as the head of the Trump Organization, and against our wonderful team and clients?

As long as it saves "democracy."

Surprise election tallies at 2 a.m.?

Well, those ballots are hard to count, especially under supervision.

Do not tell me there were zero problems with the 2020 election because that would be stupid, naïve, and dishonest—or all three. Some addresses received multiple ballots in the mail, often sent to the same name, or to former residents. Post-election, questions about irregularities were dismissed as crazy, suppressed by the media, and denounced with legal actions as "election denial."

As for legal recourse, as you've seen in the past few years, a case brought forward by Republicans often stands zero chance before a Democratic judge. Moreover, too many conservative judges don't have the backbone to create waves, and frankly, in 2020 the RNC was caught unprepared to present evidence and win cases in the aftermath. That is a mistake we corrected in 2024, thanks to a beautiful woman named Lara (who is staring at me as I write this sentence).

The message from politicians, media, and the swamp was "Get over it and move on, losers."

We did have to move on, and it was gut-wrenching. Our family and team went from zero doubt of winning to zero doubt that something was wrong. How did we lose an election to an incoherent candidate with no message?

DO NUMBERS LIE?

On November 3, 2020, Joe Biden was declared the winner. Let's look at some interesting voter numbers from the previous four presidential elections.

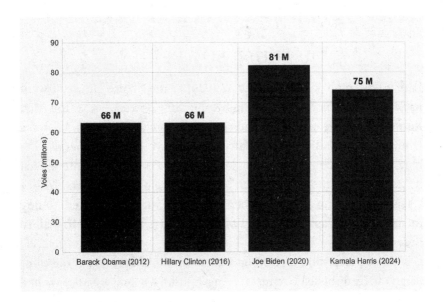

Barack Obama in 2012: 66 million

Hillary Clinton in 2016: 66 million

Donald J. Trump in 2016: 63 million (defeated Hillary Clinton)

Joe Biden in 2020: 81 million (Over 15 million more votes than Barack Obama reported in 2012?)

Donald J. Trump in 2020: 74 million (Eleven million more than in 2016. More enthusiasm equals more votes.)[33]

Kamala in 2024: 75 million (6 million fewer than Biden in 2020)[34] [35] [36]

Seeing these totals makes me shake my head. President Donald J. Trump earned 11 million more votes in 2020 than he did in 2016. This set a new record—by a mile—for a candidate seeking reelection.[37] That part makes perfect sense. But somehow, Joe Biden amassed 15 million more votes than Hillary did four years earlier—and 15 million more than Barack Obama's reelection total—despite campaigning from his basement with no crowds or enthusiasm. This was despite President Trump's incredible track record and a movement widely seen as virtually unstoppable. It simply doesn't add up.

DISTRUST BUT VERIFY

Late in the night of November 3, 2020, at the White House, I went back and forth between the Blue Room and downstairs to the Map Room, where the campaign had set up its watch operations. We were winning and trending consistently in every swing state. Generally, the blue states and counties are the last to report votes. Convenient, isn't it? Especially if they could "find" the right number of ballots. Notice I say "ballots," not "votes." Then the 2 a.m. updates started rolling in, and we watched in disbelief as the numbers began to shift—all in Biden's favor.[38]

No one slept that night. The next morning, six o'clock, at the campaign office: disbelief. Confusion. Anger. Just a few hours earlier we had been winning. In a flash, trends reversed. A basement candidate was pulling away from an incumbent—with statistically impossible spikes in last-minute ballots. The Clintons were a powerful dynasty, and we had crushed her four years earlier. But Joe and Kamala?

It seemed like we had won all the battles, but lost the war.

In the back of my mind, I was trying to process a new reality: *Would this be our legacy?* Or—equally daunting—*Would we have to do it all again?*

We had left it all on the field, which we always do as a family. Unlike 2016, we could read the room. Every quantifiable metric—and every gut metric—had pointed toward a resounding win.

Our internal polling was completely at odds with the "official" results. The difference in energy between Biden and Trump was night and day.

Lara and I held a campaign meeting at the headquarters in Virginia.

It was difficult. We saw so many sleep-deprived team members drained of emotion and excitement. They knew we were robbed.

Four years earlier we had snuck up on Hillary. Her ego and hubris did not allow her to believe that she could lose to the "reality TV star," especially with the media in her corner. I know the Biden team took note, and they did everything possible—and "impossible"— to win.

We decided to go to Philadelphia to get to the bottom of what was really happening with the reported results. Representing the campaign, I showed up at the convention center where ballots were being counted—only to be denied entry.

"You're not coming in here," growled the severely overweight, street-hardened doorman.

In all my years running the Trump Organization, I've dealt with tough characters in New York—but this encounter felt straight out of the mob. I calmly explained I was there not as the president's son, but as a campaign representative and poll watcher.

"You are not coming in this room." The message was clear. Unless we brought our own mob and broke down the door, no Republican was getting inside the convention center that day. It wasn't only me—Republican poll watchers were being denied access across the city. As I argued, I heard a whisper from my Secret Service detail leader. "A mob heard you're here and they're running in this direction. It's time to go."

What kind of third-world shit was this?

That's just one story from the day after the election, and I have heard hundreds like it. But redemption is coming, in the form of facts about the 2020 election—including documentation of Chinese interference in voter rolls.[39]

The Art of the Comeback: Be Paranoid
"I have noticed over the years that people who are guarded or, to put it more coldly, slightly paranoid, end up being the most successful. Let some paranoia reign! You've got to realize that you have something other people want. Don't let them take it away." —DJT[40]

THE QUIET RETURNS

The transfer of presidential power occurred at around noon on January 20, 2021. Our family prepared to fly back to Florida together that morning. We arrived at Andrews Air Force Base before our father, and watched Marine One fly him in. A large crowd of supporters, friends, and staffers were there to see him off.

Lara and I stood on the tarmac that morning, believing this was the last time we would see Marine One land, and our final time to board Air Force One. A six-year story, a tireless battle, was coming to an end.

Melania shared a few heartfelt words.

"Being your first lady was my greatest honor. Thank you for your love and your support, you will be [in] my thoughts and prayers. God bless you all. God bless your families, and God bless this beautiful nation."

Then my father spoke, and I still do not know how he managed to hold himself together in that moment. Many of his friends in the crowd could not hold back their tears as they watched, emotions pouring freely down their faces.

And I can only say this: we have worked hard. We've left it all as the athletes would say, "We've left it all on the field." . . .

We're not going to be looking at each other and saying, "You know, if we only worked a little bit harder." You can't work harder. And we had a lot of obstacles and we went through the obstacles. And we just got 75 million votes and that's a record in the history of sitting presidents. . . .

The first thing we have to do is pay our respects and our love to the incredible people and families who suffered so gravely from the China virus. It's a horrible thing that was put onto the world. We all know where it came from, but it's a horrible, horrible thing. So be very careful. Be very, very careful. But we want to pay great love, great love to all of the people that have suffered including families who have suffered so gravely.

So with that, I just want to say, you are amazing people. This is a great, great country. It is my greatest honor and privilege to have been your president. I will always fight for you. I will be watching, I will be listening.[41]

As we flew home, the mood was somber. What truly weighed on us was knowing our work had to stop—at least for now. My father, his administration, and our family had fought so hard and accomplished so much against unthinkable odds, yet so much remained undone. No one wanted to quit.

On Air Force One, several clocks display times across the globe. I looked up and watched them tick down, each second bringing us closer to the moment a new president would be sworn in. It felt like a bomb tech looking over a timer, knowing the inevitable end was coming.

Few words were needed. It was the look in the eye.

We had witnessed the lies of politics, the chaos of the election, and the manufactured storm of January 6. We had to face, at least for the moment, how powerful the current was in the Potomac.

As we flew south, one of the wonderful military staff—whom our family had come to know well aboard Air Force One—pulled me aside. With a quiet smile, he unbuttoned a few buttons on his perfectly pressed white dress shirt beneath his crisp dark jacket, revealing a Make America Great Again T-shirt.

I invited him into my father's office. "Dad, our friend has something to show you." After years of serving multiple administrations aboard the world's most famous aircraft, I doubt he ever imagined unbuttoning his shirt in front of a president. We could feel the love in that moment—it made us all smile.

The same is true of so many in the United States Secret Service, who became far more than protectors—they became close personal friends. Lara and I love and care about them deeply. After four years, thousands of travel miles, and countless shared moments, many became extensions of our family. Coincidentally, several of those individuals would be on that famous stage in Butler, Pennsylvania, years later. They are patriots and professionals. And on January 20, 2021, they shared our heartache as we shared theirs.

After landing in Florida, a motorcade took us to Mar-a-Lago. We weren't prepared for what we saw. From the airport exit and almost all the way to Mar-a-Lago, the streets were lined with cheering supporters. Children on fathers' shoulders, retirees waving big American flags, veterans saluting.

The Secret Service isn't known for driving slow—you can probably guess why—but that day, we crawled east along Southern Boulevard (renamed President Donald J. Trump Boulevard in July 2025), the road connecting Palm Beach Airport to Mar-a-Lago. Every street was blocked off by the flashing lights of beautiful police Harley-Davidsons. I had never seen anything like it and sure do not remember any outgoing president receiving such a beautiful homecoming. These were true patriots—not the paid "protesters" the Left depends on. My father has always been far more than a mere politician, and there's no doubt that what we were seeing out the window was the greatest political movement in American history.

Many of the people who were part of the first administration were notably absent and quiet that day. But it was never about them—it was about the citizens.

Minutes after pulling into Mar-a-Lago the presidency officially ended. Air Force One would fly back home to Andrews Air Force Base, and in departing Palm Beach International Airport, flew directly overhead what had become affectionately known as the Winter White House.

Would the movement end here? It was a real question.

I thought back to Inauguration Day four years earlier and the solemn stillness at Arlington National Cemetery. We had entered the arena with quietness and now we had exited in quietness as the noise from those four giant turbofans faded into the distance.

Growing up, my father often talked about the ups and downs of the nineties. "Kids, there were days when the phone stopped ringing."

That day, I fully understood what he meant.

CHAPTER 9

SHOW ME THE CRIME

"Show me the man and I'll show you the crime."
—LAVRENTIY BERIA, SECRET POLICE CHIEF FOR
THE USSR'S JOSEPH STALIN[1]

The weaponization of the United States' justice system is real. These are words I never thought I would write.

In hindsight, the siege had begun even before Donald J. Trump first ran for president. When he came down that iconic escalator in 2015, our family knew we were entering uncharted territory. We knew the fight would be challenging, but no one could have prepared us for what was ahead. The siege we would encounter in the years that followed would not only change history, they would alter the very perception of our nation's judicial system.

I often wonder: How does the son of a president—a man who's never touched drugs, never been in trouble—end up facing 112 subpoenas? A man who, by age thirty-four, had raised over $30 million for terminally ill children at St. Jude Children's Research Hospital; who was never on any Ukrainian energy board and had not sold overpriced finger paintings to foreign political influencers. What could he have possibly done to become the target of relentless investigations and slanderous media attacks?

Scour my laptop—you will find pictures of two beautiful children and an amazing wife—a far cry from the son of a president to follow.

And how is it that my father—who spent over four decades in the public eye, never once received a speeding ticket, triumphed in the 2016 campaign, and became president of the United States—was suddenly charged with almost every crime imaginable, and many unimaginable, in the aftermath?

The answer is shockingly simple. He dared to run for president, again.

The legal siege is reminiscent of Stalin's reign of terror in the former USSR. Once they had their target, all they needed was a fictional crime or two—or in Donald Trump's case, ninety-one.

PROSECUTORS GONE WILD

Irrational hatred for all things Donald Trump seems to run the bloodline of New York State attorney generals. I never thought I'd live in a time when prosecutors would raise campaign funds on the promise of taking down a political opponent. Enter Letitia James, who campaigned for New York State attorney general in 2018 on a heavily reinforced platform of "getting" Donald Trump. She did not even try to mask her hatred.

"I will never be afraid to challenge this illegitimate president."[2]

"Oh, we're going to definitely sue him. We're going to be a real pain in the ass. He's going to know my name personally. . . .

"I look forward to going into the office of attorney general every day, suing him, defending your rights and then going home."

On the evening of her victory, she declared her intentions with reckless speculation: "I will be shining a bright light into every dark corner of his real estate dealings, and every dealing. . . ."[3]

At the time I thought her words were mere bravado. But within days of her entering office there came the flurry of subpoenas—directed at me, my family, my father, and our company—and they were maliciously broad. "Send every document and email you have with the word 'value,' 'statement,' 'International,'" and so on. Most of our hotel and golf properties wear the term Trump "International" and that word would be in almost every email signature of every email in the company.

There was no crime, no evidence of a crime, and no incoming tips about a crime—no victims, no loan defaults, no losses. So Letitia James went fishing.

Our team and our family was forced to turn over *tens of millions* of pages of private correspondence, costing us tens of millions of dollars, so

Letitia James and her office could somehow try to build a case. It was unrelenting. It was their strategy.

MEANWHILE IN MANHATTAN

In a coordinated effort with the New York AG's office, the Manhattan district attorney decided to continue on the path of "get Trump." In 2018, Manhattan DA Cy Vance opened a case against sitting president Donald J. Trump, which included so-called "hush money" payments, looking into "overvaluing assets," and pursuing the public release of my father's tax returns along with millions of pages of documents from our accounting firm. He also persecuted our company's chief financial officer, Allen Weisselberg. (Remember his name.)

Democrats in Congress were doing the same, sending us subpoena after subpoena. Cy Vance—and later, Alvin Bragg—would follow suit. In Vance's case, they didn't even bother to do the work. Without any basis, he copy and pasted a congressional subpoena tied to Donald Trump's tax returns—clear proof this fishing expedition was solely about launching an investigation at any cost.[4][5]

Normally, one would assume the number one job of a district attorney is to keep dangerous criminals off their streets. With women being thrown onto the tracks of the New York subway, fentanyl infiltrating all "street drugs," children being shot in Times Square, homeless people taking over subway cars, citizens being robbed and murdered in broad daylight, police officers getting shot and killed, you would think the DA's office would have their hands full keeping citizens safe.[6][7]

But Cy Vance and Tish James suffered from Trump Derangement Syndrome, and wrongly assumed that all their constituents shared the same illness.[8] Both the state and local prosecutor's offices had found their *man*. Now they just had to find a *crime*—or create one.

When the well-trained prosecutors at the Manhattan DA's office couldn't find a credible theory of a crime, it became clear that Mark Pomerantz and two associates from the Paul, Weiss law firm mysteriously appeared to help manufacture one. Eventually, a few prosecutors with integrity walked away from the DA's office, refusing to be part of the charade—and the never-ending witch hunt.

THE 2019 CASE

In 2019, on behalf of the State of New York, Letitia James began the now-famous investigation to explore whether my father's "annual financial statements inflated the values of Trump's assets to obtain favorable terms for loans and insurance coverage, while also deflating the value of other assets to reduce real estate taxes."[9]

The investigation was led by a former Obama DOJ operative, Matthew Colangelo.

It wasn't long before I was called in for one of many depositions. When I arrived for my second deposition, a seasoned investigator pulled me aside: "Mr. Trump, I've been an investigator for over twenty years. Everyone knows this is bullshit, and a disgrace to this office and my profession. I'm sorry."

OUR COMPLAINT

Given what seemed to be obvious, documented displays of Letitia James's political bias and unlawful harassment, we filed an ethics complaint on December 20, 2021.

Unlike James, we had the evidence—the videos, her tweets, campaign statements, fundraising solicitations, and her outrageous subpoenas. These clearly showed her conflicts of interest, and we demanded her removal.

We still haven't heard back on our complaint.

Guess who selects the ethics officers in the state? Governor Kathy Hochul—supporter of Letitia James. In one video I highlighted on social media, you can see Hochul clapping and cheering as Letitia said this about my father: "All that he stands for is a violation of our value and who we are as a people and society."[10]

You're starting to see what a corrupt mess New York is, and we have barely scratched the surface.

"When the debate is lost, slander becomes the tool of the loser." That's a statement often attributed to Socrates. Regardless of the source, it is true today.

THE ACCUSATION

James's case boiled down to accusing Donald Trump—along with Don, Ivanka, and me—of overvaluing our business assets to gain some advantage on loans. (Can someone investigate Hunter Biden for overvaluing his "art"?) The underlying claim was that we defrauded banks out of millions of dollars and somehow harmed the citizens of New York. It was utterly insane and had us all scratching our head.

When an average consumer applies for a mortgage or home equity loan, they fill out a mortgage application. On that application, they list their bank account balances, assets, and liabilities. Then the bank does their own analysis—including their own detailed appraisals. These big banks have teams of people who scrutinize every valuation, every borrower, every document, and every property before lending a dollar to a borrower.

We are talking about the largest and most sophisticated lenders in the world, like Deutsche Bank, with loan applications that are hundreds of pages. We had phenomenal relationships with our banking partners, and still do. Not once did we breach a covenant, miss a payment, reach a default. In fact, I paid off every mortgage on time or early, made our banks hundreds of millions in interest, all while investing hundreds of millions of dollars into the properties—further decreasing the risk for the lenders by greatly increasing the value of their collateral.

Banks referred to us as a "platinum borrower" and were always courting our business. They described Donald Trump as the "big whale." When called to testify, bank employees confirmed this with nothing but praise for our company.

But all these facts still point to the core question: Why in the world would an attorney general make it her life's ambition to find something wrong with a win-win banking relationship, between two sophisticated parties, that spanned decades? It was obvious—a presidential election was approaching.

Two years of employee harassment, endless subpoenas, millions of private emails searched, and tens of millions of dollars spent on attorney fees. Fined without a crime? Guilty until proven innocent? I thought it was supposed to be the other way around. It was all an effort to find one "bad" email, one mistake, amid dozens of projects, hundreds of transactions, thousands of employees, and millions of documents.

The attorney general weaponized a patchwork of consumer protection laws—meant to protect vulnerable New Yorkers from being overcharged for things like phone bills—to falsely accuse the Trump Organization of ripping off global banks. These same banks, which thrived on our business and made millions, were suddenly cast as victims in a baseless smear.

Nothing could be further from the truth.

THE JUDGE

Every case needs a judge. And every sham case needs . . . a sham judge. For the attorney general the first step was to steer the case away from the "commercial" division courts and into a friendlier venue—the civil division, which would normally handle small disputes.

But, Eric, isn't this a commercial case?

Correct, and that's the next layer of insanity.

The commercial division was set up within the court system to hear more complex cases, because New York is home to some of the biggest financial institutions and insurance companies in the world. As such, the judges in this division tend to be more sophisticated and experienced in business matters. There's also a widely practiced threshold of steering matters involving more than $500,000 to the commercial division. Our case *allegedly* involved hundreds of millions.

The case met all the criteria to go to the commercial division, so we immediately wrote a letter to the administrative judge and asked that it be reassigned. The judge refused, citing that the case was still in the "discovery" phase (read: fishing expedition) and had not yet moved to enforcement.

Two years later, in 2022, when the case moved to enforcement, we again asked the administrative judge—a different judge—to put the case in the commercial division. We cited the clear precedent that cases involving a dispute of more than half a million dollars go there. This judge also declined. For context, when Donald Trump and Mary Trump were in court regarding the slanderous lies in her book, that case was tried—

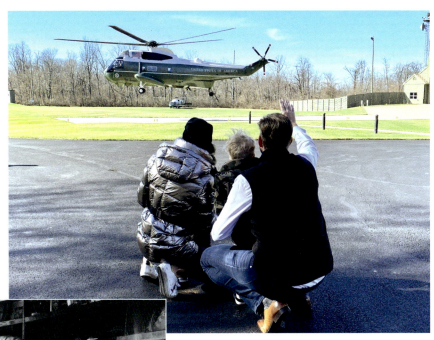

Lara, Luke, Carolina, and I waving goodbye to my dad as he takes off on Marine One.

All in a day's work.

Two worlds collide in 2019: Tiger Woods received the Medal of Freedom from President Donald J. Trump in the Oval Office. COURTESY OF THE WHITE HOUSE

Don and I visiting Dad during his first term and walking the portico from the Oval Office. COURTESY OF THE WHITE HOUSE

We took the kids to the 2020 White House Christmas Party and Luke enjoyed running down the portico.

Back on the campaign trail.

Luke and I with the Coast Guard protecting the famous seawall at Mar-a-Lago.

During the campaigns, I would often park myself behind a desk doing interview after interview across the country, for hours on end.

A very fun rally stop—Bikers for Trump.

Oftentimes we counterprogrammed our rallies. Joe Biden was across the street. My crowd was five times the size.

The Trump Organization has the greatest employees in the entire world.

We share a love for the game.

Enjoying quality time together at Trump International Golf Club Palm Beach. This is the same course where the second assassination attempt occurred.

Eric Trump: There's No GOP Anymore — It's Trump Party Now

toddstarnes.com/politics/eric-trump-theres-no-gop-anymore-its-trump-party-now/

Newsmax   August 18, 2022

The inflexible days of the Grand Old Party have come to an end, said Eric Trump, executive vice president of the Trump Organization and son of former President Donald Trump.

"There's no Republican Party. It's actually the Trump Party now," Eric Trump told Newsmax Monday night, while appearing on "Eric Bolling The Balance."

Eric Trump was speaking matter-of-factly when discussing his father's record-endorsement record — which in vast count resides in the neighborhood of 176-6, or a 96.7% success rate.

"That's incredible! No one's ever had a record like that," said Eric Trump, while telling anecdotal stories of former President Trump having breakthrough interactions with Latino and Black voters through the years, with each group believing in the principles of America First.

"My father has literally brought in a whole new party from the RINO [Republican in name only] class of the Republican Party," said Eric Trump.

The Trump family takes great pride in knocking off establishment-type RINO-type candidates.

The family's also happy to end political dynasties in electoral races — regardless of party affiliation — whether it's the Bush family of Texas, the Clintons of Arkansas/New York or the Cheneys of Wyoming.

On Tuesday night, Harriet Hageman, a virtual unknown in national political circles, crushed Rep. Liz Cheney, R-Wyo., in Wyoming's House GOP primary, accounting for more than 113,000 votes and upending the incumbent Cheney by 34 percentage points. **Continue reading at Newsmax.**

Eric — a wonderful son told me — even such a nice review though it's 100% true! You're great — Love Dad

My father has always loved sending notes—both in business and in life.

My father and I at Trump Scotland in 2023. COURTESY OF THE TRUMP ORGANIZATION

A winter visit to Trump Aberdeen to check in on the new course I was building. COURTESY OF THE TRUMP ORGANIZATION

CLOCKWISE: Travel day with Grandpa.

Moments after my father was indicted in the sham DOJ documents case, Carolina asked Grandpa if he was going to a "trampoline park to celebrate his birthday."

Post–Christmas dinner naps.

I pulled off the impossible for Lara's fortieth birthday— a 400-person surprise party.

I had the honor of marrying two incredible people and lifelong Trump Organization employees, Mike and Gia Vergara.

Luke settling into the new Florida lifestyle.

Luke takes the campaign stage with Grandpa in North Carolina.

On the water for one of the iconic Trump boat parades. Thousands of boats showed up in support of my father and our fight to Make America Great Again.

Speaking to a sold-out crowd at Madison Square Garden— surreal given the thousands of hours I have spent in that arena throughout my life. It was our homecoming—just on steroids.

Unusual to be in bathing suits and T-shirts on the campaign trail.

A very early call time for me to join *Fox & Friends* during the 2024 Republican National Convention.

A picture I took of my father reviewing his acceptance speech, moments after winning the 2024 election.

Taking the stage for the 2024 Republican National Convention.

Letting my father know he just won Pennsylvania on election night 2024.

Lara, Luke, and Carolina running through the Blair House right before the 2025 inauguration.

Sibling photo after my dad was inaugurated at the Capitol.

LEFT: The day after my father was sworn into office in January 2025, we took the kids back into the Oval Office.

RIGHT: All aboard Air Force One! On our way to Daytona, Florida.

Riding in "the Beast" on the steep banking at the Daytona 500, as Thunderbirds roared overhead and the NASCAR field trailed behind.

Grandpa was the Grand Marshal for the 2025 Daytona 500 and Carolina got to join in on the fun. COURTESY OF THE WHITE HOUSE

My father officially signed the legislation to rename the Gulf of America during a flight on Air Force One to the Super Bowl. Our flight was the first to ever fly over the Gulf of America.

Lara and I at the Capitol before the 2025 Joint Address to Congress.

Celebrating the debut of Lara's show, *My View with Lara Trump*, with an intimate party at Mar-a-Lago.

Triggering the Left with a hat that reads Trump 2028—it's too easy.

At home with my family in Florida.
COURTESY OF ERICA ROURKE

Carolina and I getting ready for her daddy-daughter dance.
COURTESY OF ERICA ROURKE

It was the honor of a lifetime to help create a Medal of Sacrifice, an idea that was born after the tragic loss of three officers from the Palm Beach County Sheriff's Office.
COURTESY OF THE WHITE HOUSE

Luke and Carolina in the Lincoln Bedroom.

LEFT: Carolina reading the real Gettysburg Address in the Lincoln bedroom.

RIGHT: Luke sitting in the White House residence, overlooking the South Lawn, the National Mall, and the Washington Monument.

Luke and Carolina take the stage for the Army's 250th anniversary parade. COURTESY OF COURTNEY REED

Our nightly prayers, hugs, and wrestling routine.

and won—in the *commercial* division, and in a case of substantially lower monetary value.

We were shocked. But not as shocked as we would be by the judge they assigned the case to, Judge Engoron. One attorney, a political opponent, who shall remain nameless, referred to him as "the dumbest guy in the courthouse."

Well, you could appeal the judicial assignment, right? Wrong. That wasn't allowed. Behind the scenes, Letitia and her team started celebrating—before the trial even began.

Here's the truth. Our company borrowed money from large financial institutions, including Deutsche Bank. We repaid every penny, on time, with interest. And the banks that lent us the money made millions in profit.

Real estate valuation is subjective, and the bank made their own valuations before approving our loans. The attorney general's case was based on a warped view of "consumer protection" laws, held together with duct tape and malice.

As with all this corrupt lawfare, the people who *are* hurt are our fellow citizens, who live with increasing crime and violence, while their elected officials spend their tax money and years "seeking justice" on a political opponent.

THE TIMELINE

In case you're not tracking, this lawfare started in 2019, or well before, if you look at the efforts of previous officials in New York State, Manhattan, and Congress. When the trial finally started in 2022, our team was given only six months for our discovery. The prosecution had millions of documents and *years* of depositions.

Given various executive protections afforded by the Constitution, including the Supremacy Clause (Article VI, Clause 2), they couldn't frame my father in Washington, D.C. So I became target number one. I was a Trump. I was the company. I was the extension of everything he had ever built—which they wanted to see crumble. I had no constitutional protections, and they tried to set the traps.

Perjury was the Left's go-to play in their playbook. Ask a thousand questions on obscure subjects, under oath, of course, and hope someone remembers incorrectly or answers imprecisely. I would not fall for the setup. Questions were designed to elicit inconsistent answers, exploiting memory lapses or confusion in the moment. A false statement did not need to be related to a crime—any lapse would be used against you, as they had done repeatedly with people like Michael Flynn, Paul Manafort, Roger Stone, Jeff Sessions, Allen Weisselberg, and others. Moreover, with DA investigations and the Southern District of New York involved, anything I said could be used against me in any way—including in new criminal charges they were actively working to create.

I had to show up for the depositions, but I did not have to take the bait. First, the prosecution refused to tell me the topics—nothing. And just in case you thought I was paranoid, they had already seeded the media, with *Newsweek* running the headline: "Eric Trump Could Open Himself Up to Criminal Charge, Ex-Prosecutor Warns."[11]

THE DEPOSITION

In October of 2020, I sat down in the conference room on the twenty-sixth floor at Trump Tower—a room where I had inked my first major real estate deal, Cap Cana in the Dominican Republic—a floor that had been so pivotal to our company, *The Apprentice*, and Donald Trump's career.

My father's office was down the hall—walls with magazine cover after magazine cover depicting my father, our properties, and the so many successes that came out of those very rooms. The same place I grew up building Lego towers, where my first office cubicle was, and where my father had taught me the art of the deal. Ironically, the same floor where he told my siblings and me, "They're going to come after us in ways we can't even imagine."

The deposition began.

> "Mr. Trump—What's your understanding of The Trump Organization?"
>
> [My attorney]: "Mr. Trump will respond to the question with an assertion of rights from here on forward. Mr. Trump, if you'd like to assert your . . ."

And I began reading my written statement:

The Attorney General of the State of New York has abandoned fairness, justice and impartiality when it comes to my family and our businesses.

Before Letitia James even took office, she stated publicly that she had *already* concluded that The Trump Organization had engaged in wrongdoing, and that she was going to use the power of her office to investigate our company, target my family and go after my father, The President of the United States. She said that if elected, she would use her office to look into "every aspect . . . of my father's real estate dealings," she swore that she would "definitely sue him," she claimed that he was an "illegitimate President," she boasted on video that she would be, and I quote, "a real pain in the ass" and she declared "just wait until I'm in the attorney general's office . . . I've got my eyes on Trump Tower." In perhaps her most egregious statement while campaigning, she said that "we will join with law enforcement and other attorney generals across this nation in removing this President from office." . . . "It's important that everyone understand that the days of Donald Trump are coming to an end." Letitia James made those statements without a shred of evidence, all while using them to fundraise and solicit financial support for her campaign.

After the Attorney General was elected, she followed through on these promises, publicly stating that she would be using "every area of the law to investigate President Trump, his business transactions and that of his family." She almost immediately launched what is now an 18-month-long fishing expedition, wasting tens of thousands of hours and millions of taxpayer dollars. She blatantly took an active adversarial political position, leading the endorsement of "Democratic Attorney Generals for Joe Biden" and conveniently chose the first day of the Republican National Convention, moments before my family was set to take the stage, as an appropriate time to file suit against our company. The Attorney General has continued to make public statements and pronouncements that reflect clear bias, and this conduct, for an elected official who is supposed to act without prejudice or favor, is unlawful, unethical, and grossly improper.

As we sit here today, less than a month away from a United States Presidential Election and with my father in Walter Reed Hospital, it has never been more clear that Letitia James has weaponized her office to target my father and influence the upcoming election. The Attorney General's knowing politization of her duties and responsibilities as an elected official violate every known rule of ethics, impartiality and justice. She has a politically motivated vendetta against my father and our family, and her actions flagrantly violate my due process rights as well as the oath she swore to uphold.

After seeing Letitia James' videos and statements, Attorney General of Louisiana Jeff Landry stated: "this is what an abuse of prosecutorial discretion looks like." "No prosecutor should run on a platform of threatening an innocent American citizen, his family and his private businesses with investigations and lawsuits—all for political gain."

The United States Supreme Court has stated that in court cases like these, parties are "prohibited from engaging in arbitrary fishing expeditions," "initiating investigations out of malice or an intent to harass," or "using their power to try and interfere with a President's official duties." Furthermore, the Supreme Court has made it very clear that any "effort to manipulate a President's policy decisions or to retaliate against a President for official acts through issuance of a subpoena" is unconstitutional.

Years ago, the Supreme Court ruled that "one of the Fifth Amendment's basic functions . . . is to protect innocent" individuals. Given the circumstances, it is clear that the is *not* proceeding impartially and is *not* proceeding without bias or favor. She is carrying out a deliberate, biased political agenda that she promised as a candidate in order to hurt my family and to help the opposing political party. This is a fundamental violation of due process. It is a fundamental violation of my rights as a citizen.

Accordingly, under the direction of my counsel and for *all* of the above reasons, I respectfully decline to answer the questions under the rights and privileges afforded to every citizen under the United States Constitution and all parts thereof and amendments thereto, including but not limited to, the Separation of Powers Doctrine, the First Amendment, the Fourth Amendment, the Fifth Amendment, the Sixth Amendment, and the Fourteenth Amendment as incorporated through the Fifth Amendment Due Process Clause.

This will be my answer to any further questions.

For all these reasons—along with another sham investigation brewing simultaneously and knowing they were desperate to set a perjury trap—I pleaded the Fifth and was immediately presumed guilty by the media.[12]

For every insane question they asked, I began reading the same statement. After the third question it was agreed that "same answer" could be used and my statement would be included in the record.

The lawyers' reaction? Fury. Their big opportunity had slipped away. Dozens of gotcha questions orchestrated for weeks . . . useless. Another ally to Donald Trump, his own flesh and bones, would not be added to their takedown list.

But that wouldn't stop the hundreds of headlines that followed. *Huff-Post*: "Eric Trump Pleaded the Fifth More Than 500 Times in Deposition." MSNBC: "Eric Trump Takes 5th in New York Probe into Trump Org. Finances."[13]

Years later, my father would explain it best: "I once asked, 'If you're innocent, why are you taking the Fifth Amendment?' Now I know the answer to that question. When your family, your company, and all the people in your orbit have become the targets of an unfounded, politically motivated Witch Hunt supported by lawyers, prosecutors, and the Fake News Media, you have no choice."[14]

And now it was time for the public circus to begin.

THE TRIAL

As with the charity I founded, it would be the attorney general back behind that podium, in front of that same seal of the State of New York—a well-orchestrated press conference scheduled to hit prime-time television. As always we were the last to know the details. Not surprisingly, the *New York Times* and *Washington Post* were usually the first. This was her moment. This is where Letitia James would make a name for herself.

As the trial crawled forward, Letitia decided to run for governor of New York. It's clear to me that she was instrumental in "offing" Governor Andrew Cuomo in a coordinated effort to gain even more power. And true to form she once again campaigned on "getting Donald Trump."[15] Her "Tish for Governor" campaign lasted about thirteen seconds, with virtually zero support in the polls and a horrible fundraising number. She pulled out of the race, but the verbal and legal attacks continued.

When she wasn't in the front row of the courtroom with her shoes kicked off, she was meeting with federal officials in Washington. For someone representing the citizens of New York State, Letitia James sure made a lot of trips to D.C. In both July and August of 2023, she reportedly attended events with the then vice president. According to White House visitor logs, James visited there on three occasions during the trial.[16] [17] Not surprisingly, like everything else, it was all being orchestrated with Washington, D.C.

THE VERDICT: FRIDAY, FEBRUARY 16, 2024

I was in my office in Florida when the judgment came down against us. Over $464 million, including over $100 million in interest. The verdict was larger than the gross national product of some *countries*. Even more baffling, to everyone involved—including the judge—was the "formula" used to reach those numbers. The judge did not even seem to understand the difference between proceeds and profits—and named our Ferry Point golf course, even though it was never involved with any loan and was unnamed in the case.

The judge, it seemed, also ignored the statute of limitations. He then said I was not credible when I testified that I had nothing to do with my father's personal statement of financial condition. A $4 million fine was leveled on me and on Don and we were barred from serving as a director of *any* New York corporation.[18] Three times in the trial it was made clear that we had no involvement with the particulars of the loan applications—and multiple witnesses, from our accounting team, to our outside CPA, to Michael Cohen, all testified that I was not involved, as court records in the case clearly showed. Not that there was any wrongdoing to begin with. It was insane.

"Allen Weisselberg corroborated Eric Trump's testimony by testifying that he did not rely on Eric Trump for any of the information contained in the SFCs."

"Eric Trump's testimony was corroborated by all the witnesses, including witnesses called by the Attorney General who were predisposed to give testimony beneficial to the Attorney General (i.e., David McArdle, Donald Bender, Michael Cohen, and Claudia Mouradian)."

"Eric Trump was not a party to any of the subject transactions and had no obligation to submit SFCs."

Behind the bench, Engoron was a different person than the one I spoke to in the judge's chamber. He was a puppet. It seemed like somebody had gotten to him. This was not justice, it was a political hit. I called my father. "The judge had clearly made up his mind from the start," I said.

My father's response was low-key, as usual—a mix of disbelief and determination. Donald Trump spent weeks in various courthouses from New York to Georgia to Florida. He had his mug shot taken. I do not know how he did it, but he took it all in stride and kept going.

My mind was racing. *How can we appeal? What will happen in the meantime? How will this affect our employees and customers?*

I went home late that day. Numb. "Honey, it was an expensive day."

That night I tweeted: "In an attempt to destroy my father and kick him out of New York, a Judge ruled that Mar-a-Lago, in Palm Beach Florida, is only worth approximately '$18 Million dollars' . . . Mar-a-Lago is . . . arguably the most valuable residential property in the country. It is all so corrupt and coordinated."

As one of dozens of examples of lawfare and judicial malpractice— and the striking irony of a case centered on real estate valuations—the prosecution argued for an appraisal of Mar-a-Lago that was just a fraction of its true market value.

In contrast to the almost half-a-billion-dollar bond we were ordered to come up with, Bernie Madoff posted a $10 million bond for orchestrating the largest Ponzi scheme in recent history, defrauding forty thousand investors of billions in savings. Sam Bankman-Fried—a $250 million bond for defrauding thousands of crypto investors out of billions of dollars, and financing donations to Democrats and anti-Trump Republicans so they would look the other way. In the wake of the two Boeing 737 MAX tragedies, where over 346 people lost their lives, Boeing was fined $243 million for "Conspiracy to Defraud the United States by Misleading the Federal Aviation Administration."[19] Donald Trump was fined double that amount for never missing a payment, never defaulting on a loan, and paying back all debts ahead of time, to the most sophisticated financial institutions—the very people who would testify that we were exemplary "borrows." This was the most Soviet-style financial injustice ever perpetrated in American history.

Later that evening my father sent me a message. "I don't know how, but we will WIN."

THE FALLOUT

I'm sure there were celebrations in some circles (including judge's chambers), but reasonable people, and even those who weren't fans of our family, could see through the sham. The business community's confidence was rightfully shaken, with countless high-profile entrepreneurs sounding off and encouraging investors to reconsider any dealings in New York. *Shark Tank*'s Kevin O'Leary said repeatedly, "It was already on the top of the list of being a loser state. I would never invest in New York now. And I'm not the only person saying that."[20] Grant Cardone stated that he had planned to invest $500 million in the city,[21] but redirected the funds to Florida, citing the ruling and Judge Engoron's actions as reasons for his decision.[22]

As more repercussions followed, New York Governor Hochul tried to do some damage control, but stepped in her own hypocrisy.

"The law-abiding and rule-following New Yorkers who are business people have nothing to worry about, because they're very different than Donald Trump."[23]

That says it all—as long as you're not Donald Trump, there's nothing to worry about.

Donald Trump posted this on Truth Social:

> Through hard work, talent, and luck, I currently have almost five hundred million dollars in cash, a substantial amount of which I intended to use in my campaign for president.
>
> I have no doubt that those leading this lawfare used financial disclosure rules to help calculate that amount.
>
> The often overturned political hack judge on the rigged and corrupt A.G. case, where I have done nothing wrong, knew this, wanted to take it away from me, and that's where and why he came up with the shocking number which, coupled with his crazy interest demand, is approximately $454,000,000.[24]

The *New York Times* weighed in with a revealing post: "Donald Trump owes $454 million by Monday or risks losing some properties. But experts say pinning a value to the buildings would be a guessing game."[25]

Are you kidding me?! After accusing us of overstating the worth of our properties, *now* valuing assets is a guessing game?

THE BOND

I began the search for our bond to cover the outrageous verdict. It proved to be an impossible task. To add insult to injury, I remember hearing directly from two industry CEOs that Letitia James's office was sending them a clear message. *Don't touch that Trump bond. You are a New York–regulated financial institution. We are watching.*

If we did not get the bond, it was game over. Think about having to sell assets to pay for an insane judgment, only to have the judgment reduced or removed on appeal. James was both the arsonist and the fire chief—exactly as she wanted. She also wanted the skyline of Manhattan changed forever—the beautiful Trump signs removed for the ages.

Even though Engoron thought Mar-a-Lago was only worth $18 million, pundits on CNN and elsewhere suddenly salivated that my father could sell it "quickly for hundreds of millions" to pay the judgment. I don't know whether to call that hypocrisy or stupidity, or both.

Our first step was to ask for a "stay" on enforcement so we could get our ducks in a row. Engoron denied our request. What company could post a half-a-billion-dollar bond on the Friday night of a judgment? We had one hope: a successful appeal.

Meanwhile, James was posting daily interest and penalty amounts on social media, and threatening to seize our properties. "$464,576,230.62" posted on February 23, 2024, then "+$114,553.04" posted one day later. And on and on.[26]

Add to this the constant barrage from other cases in New York, Georgia, and Florida, those aimed not at financial devastation but rather imprisonment. We were truly under siege. None of these cases were about justice, they were all about destroying a man, a family, a company—and a movement.

My father made this comment to the media:

We'll be appealing. But, more important than that, this is Russia, this is China, this is the same game, [it] all comes out of the DOJ. It all comes out of Biden. It's [a] witch-hunt against his political opponent, the likes of which our country has never seen before, you see it in third world countries, banana republics, but you don't see it here.

So I just want to say this: You build a great company. There was no fraud. The banks all got their money, 100 percent. They love Trump. They testified that Trump is great, great customer, one of our best customers. They testified beautifully, and the judge knows that. He is just a corrupt person and we knew that from the beginning. We knew it right from the beginning because he wouldn't give it to the commercial division.

Letitia James, that's another case altogether. She is a horribly corrupt attorney general and it's all having to do with election interference.[27]

MY EMAIL TO EMPLOYEES

February 16, 2024, at 4:18 PM

Team,

Today's ruling comes as a shock to no one. From the moment my father announced his Presidency, they have done everything possible to take down my family and attack our great company. The Attorney General of New York ran on this campaign promise—that she would "get Donald Trump," "sue him every single day" and use her office and the legal system to pursue her political vengeance. You have all seen the videos—I have never seen such corruption in my life.

As you all know, we have never missed a loan payment, breached a loan covenant, or been in default with any lender in this case. We have made our banks hundreds of millions of dollars all while having built and operated the most iconic properties anywhere in the world. It's a disgrace to New York and to a skyline shaped by one man's vision—it's also a disgrace to the thousands of incredible associates that are part of this amazing corporate family.

I know you all know this, but my family, and this company is incredibly resilient because of you.

We have the greatest, most dedicated and honest employees. Employees who have become our extended family. Moreover, we are the strongest we have ever been financially. We will not waiver and we will continue to run this organization with heart, grit, pride, and the very professionalism we have always demonstrated.

Our best days are ahead and I appreciate you all,

Eric

THE APPEAL

The appellate division, in a previous case, had already declared that anything pre-2016 was barred by the statute of limitations. Much of the "damage" James, and Engoron, referenced came well before 2016.

The appellate court took our case and lowered the amount of the bond to $175 million, and the stay order halted enforcement of the ruling that barred Don and me from doing business in New York. A huge victory for the rule of law. But the appellate win was bittersweet, after sham charges and legal warfare were hitting us week after week for over four years. There were hundreds of millions in legal expenses and opportunities missed.

And imagine the price the people of New York paid, and are still paying. All that time and energy could have been put into making the state and city safer and more prosperous.

The Art of the Deal: Fight Back
"In most cases I'm very easy to get along with. I'm very good to people who are good to me. But when people treat me badly or unfairly or try to take advantage of me, my general attitude, all my life, has been to fight back very hard." —DJT[28]

"HUNT THEM DOWN"

People know the whole investigation was a sham. Even Andrew Cuomo admitted it in June of 2024. "The Attorney General's case in New York, frankly, should have never been brought and if his name was not Donald Trump, and if he wasn't running for president, I'm the former AG in New York, I'm telling you that case would have never been brought, and that's what is offensive to people."[29]

Shortly after the original verdict, Letitia James spoke to a gathering of FDNY firefighters, and was loudly booed, along with chants of "Trump, Trump, Trump." That wasn't acceptable to James and her friends. The FDNY commissioner, Laura Kavanagh, opened an official investigation through its Bureau of Investigation and Trials to find out who had dared to express their voice. Yes, really. And it gets worse, if that's even possible. FDNY Chief of Department John Hodgens sent an email to our brave firefighters that read in part: "I recommend they come forward. I have been told by the commissioner it will be better for them if they come forward and we don't have to hunt them down."

Hunt them down? This is where the attention of our elected officials was focused?

Our cities are hurting, violent crime is rampant, and your taxes are going toward hunting political opponents and FDNY firefighters who expressed disagreement.[30] [31]

I can't say it enough—this lawfare isn't just about Donald Trump. The same people who despise him despise you. The ones who have relentlessly persecuted him won't stop until they come after you, too. This is a battle for all of us, and unless we raise our voices and cast our votes to stop them, no one will be safe from their relentless assault.

CHAPTER 10

IT'S ALL CONNECTED

"This is bigger than Trump.
This is bigger than me.
This is bigger than my presidency."
—DONALD J. TRUMP, MAY 31, 2024

"**G**uilty."

May 30, 2024. I was seated behind my father in a New York courtroom. We listened, motionless, as the jury read their verdicts.

"Guilty," they announced—a total of thirty-four times. At this point, having been under siege for so long, I was not surprised. But the outcome was still surreal. *How could this have really happened in the United States of America?*

Outside the courtroom, my father addressed reporters:

"This was a rigged, disgraceful trial. The *real* verdict is going to be November 5th by the people."[1]

THE SWAMP: WEAPONIZED

I used to think the proverbial "swamp" was passive-aggressive bureaucrats and perpetually elected officials. A pain in the ass, but basically harmless. That view was naïve. They're out for blood. And America was catching on.

The swamp spied on their political adversaries, created fictional "dossiers," interfered with elections, conspired with law enforcement to manufacture bogus claims against a former president, and ran a shadow government to prop up a president with dementia—then, in the summer of 2024, pushed out that president to install a cardboard candidate. We were way beyond secretive motives and cloaked attacks.

They openly tried to destroy cabinet appointees in President Donald Trump's first term (and in 2025) and slander Supreme Court nominees. Even members of the judiciary are neck-deep in the swamp—Colorado and Maine both tried to remove my father from the ballots in 2024 without legal standing, an attempt to subvert the will of the American people.

I have written a lot in this book about the FBI, DOJ, and law enforcement, so I want to be very clear about something important. While I consider these agencies to be deep in the swamp, I adore law enforcement and the frontline agents, many of whom are dear personal friends. The hundreds of challenge coins I've been given reaffirm the mutual respect. It's not the gun carriers—the people risking their lives to protect our country and our communities—who I'm talking about. It's the bureaucrats and political appointees in their fancy offices who wage legal lawfare out of their personal agendas and career aspirations. Those leaders often met some DEI criteria, but are not the best and brightest, as we would see with the U.S. Secret Service leadership under Kimberly Cheatle. Have them take the basic fitness or firearms qualification tests of the very agencies they command, and they would likely fail. I view these people as unelected politicians, not law enforcement.

My heroes are the men and women who put themselves in harm's way every day. And to our friends in the Secret Service, you know who you are, and you know how much Lara, Luke, Carolina, and I love you. Thank you.

THE MATRIX OF LAWFARE

Alvin Bragg and Juan Merchan

THREATEN AND INTIMIDATE

Allen Weisselberg worked for the Trump Organization as CFO for almost five decades. He is a wonderful man who dedicated his career to the

Trump Organization. The Left sent him through a meat grinder, simply because they saw Allen as a way to get to Donald Trump. Mark Pomerantz and associates openly threatened him; if he did not spill dirt they would charge him and go after his family.[2]

As a by-product of hundreds of subpoenas, depositions, and days in court, Cy Vance, Alvin Bragg, and Letitia James finally found one needle in the golden haystack.[3] [4] Allen had, among other small items, not included his company car and apartment on his personal tax returns, and they smelled blood, believing they could leverage Allen to get Trump. Surely the CFO of the Trump Organization would spill some dirt on his former boss if they applied enough pressure. There was no dirt. They treated him like a violent criminal, confinscated his cell phone in the middle of the street, and later handcuffed and perp walked him through the courthouse and in front of the global media. They found him guilty in 2023, and sent him to the Rikers Island jail. At age seventy-six. *Jail* for a company car? While thieves and murderers were being set free by Alvin Bragg's office?[5]

They threatened him, and when that tactic produced no results, they threatened to go after his son. Allen stood firm: *I will not lie. We run a great company and have done nothing wrong.* In a certain deposition, Allen once misstated the square footage of Donald Trump's apartment. Remember the perjury trap I mentioned? Another gotcha moment. Effectively the backroom conversations went like this: "We think you perjured yourself about *when* you realized the square footage of the apartment was wrong, and so we're going to send you back to Rikers. If you cooperate we will leave you alone." Allen was just a pawn in their game. They destroyed some of the best years of a great man's life, all in their crazed quest to "get" Donald Trump and his family. Under threat of spending the rest of his life in jail at the hands of a questionable judge, Allen finally "admitted guilt" in mistaking a number and was sentenced to five months at Rikers—conveniently timed so he couldn't testify in my father's criminal trial and counter Michael Cohen's muddy testimony.

Who was the judge in Allen's 2022 case? Juan Merchan. Remember that name.[6]

Alvin Bragg campaigned for district attorney of New York County (effectively Manhattan) on a platform of not pursuing "nonviolent" criminals so that his office could focus on cracking down on violent crimes. Once elected in 2022, his "day one" mandate of "making incarceration a matter of last resort" sent the city even further into chaos. Bragg pledged to invest more in "alternatives to incarceration"—whatever that means. Anyone with even a shred of common sense could have predicted the chaos and crime wave before it exploded.[7]

His office immediately made good on his promise to not prosecute criminals—downgrading 52 percent of felony cases in his jurisdiction to misdemeanors. And his office won barely half of the felony convictions they pursued. I could go on about how many violent criminals he is responsible for releasing back into New York neighborhoods, but you have probably seen the headlines.[8]

Shortly after Alvin Bragg took office, Mark Pomerantz resigned as special assistant district attorney and sent a scathing public letter to Bragg. They do this publicly—for personal PR and to pile on political pressure. Unsurprisingly, just as we've seen over and over, the letter was splashed across the front page of the New York Times. In it he wrote, "I believe that your decision not to prosecute Donald Trump now, and on the existing record, is misguided and completely contrary to the public interest."[9] [10] Pomerantz was fixated on my father, and the so-called hush money, which was in fact a standard nondisclosure agreement (NDA).

The criticism clearly got under Alvin Bragg's skin. Within months, Bragg had brought in Matthew Colangelo from the Biden administration's Department of Justice in Washington, D.C., to work on charges against Donald Trump. Colangelo was—you guessed it—a former Democratic National Committee consultant.[11]

Why the hell would the number three guy at the DOJ leave that job to work with Alvin Bragg with the sole mission to prosecute Donald Trump?[12] Was it the free doughnuts? Or an obsession with taking down a presidential candidate, whom they detested?

THE NEW YORK POWER CENTER

Before working for Cyrus Vance and Alvin Bragg's DA's office, Mark Pomerantz worked with one of the premier law firms in New York, Paul, Weiss. Bloomberg news called the firm the "Biden-Era N.Y. Power Center." After

Pomerantz resigned from the Manhattan DA's office, he returned to the law firm. He also wrote a book titled *People vs. Donald Trump*.[13] [14]

And what other swamp creatures are connected to the firm? Chuck Schumer's brother, Robert Schumer, is a partner at the firm. Robert also has served on his brother's "Judicial Selection Committee," which is known to help Chuck fill U.S. attorney roles and judgeships.[15] [16] [17]

There are so many tangled connections here, it's sometimes hard to fathom. But then again, so is the case Bragg's team cobbled together.

THEIR CASE

Bragg, Colangelo, and team patched together a case that, three years earlier in 2019, the Southern District of New York declined to pursue. One of the main reasons was the "unreliable" testimony of Michael Cohen. The Federal Election Commission also dismissed the matter in 2021 and ruled to not move forward. This was indeed a "zombie" case that they simply wouldn't let die.[18] [19] [20]

The case centered on just $130,000—yet the government spent tens of millions of taxpayer dollars building what many saw as a sham case. They spent millions more shutting down the FDR Drive, one of the busiest highways in the world, and fencing off half of lower Manhattan for months during the trial. All of it over $130,000. It defied logic.

The transaction was 100 percent legal—a simple nondisclosure agreement, which are commonplace to every business. To make matters worse, the exact crime that Bragg was pursuing was never disclosed, until after we made our final case—after our defense rested.

Thirty-four counts—intentionally expanded into a confusing array of "crimes," when there was, in fact, no wrongdoing. And even if a similar case had any merit, the statute of limitations in such cases is two years.[21]

As we did on the day of the raid on Mar-a-Lago, my father got out ahead of the story, and stole Bragg's podium moment in the spotlight.

"I will be arrested on Tuesday," my father posted on Truth Social on March 18, 2023. My phone rang immediately from all the networks, and back on TV I went.

Elon Musk posted, "If this happens, Trump will be re-elected in a landslide victory." Even the rational individuals on the Left recognized that public backlash against blatant lawfare would only boost my father's support.

On April 3, 2023, the day Donald Trump was arraigned, I sent this message to our legal team.

> Team,
> The streets were lined for miles with supporters as I pulled into the airport. Please never forget that this fight is larger than all of us. . . . This small group represents a man, the beliefs and the sentiment of half of this nation. We will likely never be part of something more important. . . .
> —Eric

APRIL 4, 2023

Here are a few of my notes on that day.

Arraignment day. Charged with thirty-four felony counts. Called DJT: "It's all rigged. The entire system is rigged."

Went to the office and then up to apartment. The streets were a zoo. Thousands of people and hundreds of press outlets. When I went upstairs, he was working on his speech in the living room, dictating to Jason, Susie, Dan, and Natalie. He was about to go downtown.

He came down to 25 to have a meeting with the lawyers, Joe, Susan, Todd, Habba, Dave, Kise, and me. I took him down to the car. He walked out the doors, fist pump in the air, and waved to the people on the street.

His strength, his backbone. He was a rock. Private and public.

He sent a post from the car. "Heading to Lower Manhattan, the Courthouse. Seems so SURREAL—WOW, they are going to ARREST ME. Can't believe this is happening in America. MAGA!"

I also posted, "Alvin Bragg has shut down the entire city, called up 38,000 NYPD police officers, closed down the FDR Drive and is spending an estimated $200 million of city funds, all for a $130,000 NDA. I never thought I would see this level of corruption in the United States."

I met him on the plane, headed back to Palm Beach. Every channel had nonstop coverage as we watched from the air on the flight home. Everyone saying that the case was a sham. Five years of investigation and they didn't even spell out a crime.

We landed. Jumped in the Beast with Sean, his Secret Service detail leader. As we drove the streets between PBI and MAL, there were lines with thousands of people. American flags. Trump flags. The Palm Beach County Sheriff's Office motorcycles closing off the intersections as we rolled through. My father waving out the window. "Gentlemen, let's go slow. These people are here out of love."

The last time I was in that car seat was the day he left the White House on January 20, 2021. It was the same reception. It was beautiful. Thousands and thousands of people who loved our country. People who wanted to Make America Great Again.

That night at 8:15 he addressed the nation. The message was perfect.

I went on Hannity and drove home with Lara. It was a hell of a 36 hours.

THE SUITABLE JUDGE

Enter Judge Juan Merchan. "Randomly" selected for my father's case, as he had also been for Steve Bannon's case, and the persecution of our CFO, Allen Weisselberg.[22] What are the odds? Simply put, they defy statistics. It was clear to me and our legal team that this judge was handpicked, for anything Donald Trump. Merchan donated to an anti-Trump campaign fund, in clear violation of a New York rule for judges—he was indeed their perfect choice.[23]

His daughter is Loren Merchan, who made a nice career in political consulting for people like Kamala Harris and Adam Schiff. Her Democrat clients reportedly raised $90 million based on leveraging the lawfare against Donald Trump, and Adam Schiff fundraising emails contained disgusting lines like "Donald Trump indicted by Manhattan grand jury. This is an important moment for our democracy, but our work isn't over."[24]

My issue is with Judge Merchan, not his daughter, and the fact that he ignored the established ethic of not having a conflict of interest in any case he accepts. As Representative Elise Stefanik put it in her judicial complaint, "Acting Judge Merchan is in clear violation of section 100.3(E)(1)(d)(iii) of the Rules of Judicial Conduct for the New York State Unified Court System as his family has enriched itself through anti-Trump fundraising mentioning this case directly. His family's wealth is directly tied to attacking President Trump."[25]

Later that summer after exhausting all our legal options, my father posted on Truth Social, "Can you believe this? The New York Courts refuse to act. This is happening right before the voting begins on September 6th. Suppression and manipulation of the vote. Voter interference."

Despite repeatedly insisting that Merchan recuse himself, the only thing Donald Trump received was more gag orders.

THE GAGS

The trial was going just fine (sarcasm) until Judge Merchan decided that the defendant exercising his free speech rights might interfere with the scales of justice. But how could Donald Trump *not* talk about a daughter—a person who was reportedly fundraising off of the very case her father controlled?

Merchan placed a "gag order" on Donald Trump and his entire legal team, and started assessing thousands of dollars in fines for alleged violations. Subsequent gag orders also included limitations on talking about the judge's daughter. They were terrified of the world knowing the truth.

The leading Republican candidate for president was told he could not exercise his First Amendment right of free speech—not only on the campaign trail, but speaking out in his own defense on the sham case. The good news: I could. I savagely defended my father every day. I was banned from speaking in the courthouse, so I improvised—I walked outside and faced the press gaggles on the courthouse steps.

While the prosecution and their circus of witnesses were being interviewed all over the media (and while disgruntled ex-employee Michael Cohen was doing every interview possible and selling anti-Trump merch on TikTok) the court selectively silenced only my father. In one instance, the judge politely suggested to the prosecution that Cohen consider toning it down. The former president on the other hand, in the middle of a campaign, was gagged and fined through this deliberate lawfare anytime he was asked a question by the media, or sent a post on Truth Social. It was blatantly unfair and unconstitutional.[26]

When we tried to call our expert witnesses in our defense, Judge Merchan denied our requests.

Who were these experts? Allen Weisselberg, our CFO and a former member of the Federal Election Commission,[27] who believed the case was insane and without merit. So much for a just and speedy trial.

As my father said at the time, "The expert witness that we have, the best there is in election law, Brad Smith, he's considered the Rolls-Royce, or we'll bring it back to an American car, Cadillac, but the best there is. He can't testify. He's not being allowed to testify." The Left tried to spin this with legalese about the "scope of questioning," but the fact remains that a preeminent election expert and our CFO were not allowed to speak in Donald Trump's defense.

In the finale of this clown show, Judge Merchan issued the most convoluted set of instructions to the jury in the history of juries. I'll admit, I still cannot make sense of it, so I'll defer to Professor Jonathan Turley.

"Merchan just delivered the coup de grace instruction. He said that there is no need to agree on what occurred. They can disagree on what the crime was among the three choices. Thus, this means that they could split 4-4-4, and he will still treat them as unanimous." Essentially, Professor Turley was saying that the jurors didn't need to agree on how a crime was committed, only that a crime was committed. The prosecutors offered three different theories, and each juror could believe a different one of the three. It would still count as a unanimous guilty verdict.[28]

"Before the jury entered, the judge told the parties not to go into the law, 'that will be my job,'" Turley said of Merchan's instructions. "The judge has allowed this jury to believe that there were federal election violations by Trump and his campaign. At the same time, he has allowed the jury to disagree on what crime was being committed and still treat the verdict as unanimous."[29]

This might be funny if it wasn't the state of political lawfare in the United States today. But the reality was in fact surreal. Thirty-four felony counts over a $130,000 NDA signed by a lawyer.

THE VERDICT

On May 28, 2024, I stated in a press conference outside the courthouse, "While New Yorkers watch murders in the streets, women getting thrown in front of trains, and kids getting shot in Times Square, the entire DA's office is lining that courtroom. They're laughing, they're giggling. This is their moment. This is legal lawfare."[30]

On May 30, 2024, shortly before the "guilty" verdict was being read thirty-four times, three madmen were randomly hacking and terrifying people with a machete at a McDonald's in Times Square—a horrific-yet-timely example of the failures of Bragg's policies. So much for freeing up resources to go after violent criminals. "How many people in New York died because the entire NYPD wasn't doing their job because they were dealing with Alvin Bragg's political charade?!"[31]

As Elon Musk posted the next day, "If a former President can be criminally convicted over such a trivial matter—motivated by politics, rather than justice—then anyone is at risk of a similar fate."[32]

Even after the verdict was delivered, Colangelo argued that the gag order should stay in place. That was a convenient position for him, since it meant that his unusual work history would remain off-limits for my father to bring to light. Thankfully I wasn't mentioned by name in the gag order, so I spoke out relentlessly about the injustice. This was the fight of our lives and I was going to do everything I possibly could to make sure the American people knew the truth about what was happening within our justice system.[33]

Georgia's Fani (Willis)

Believe it or not, the case in Fulton County, Georgia, was not about Attorney General Fani Willis or her love life. Behind her scandalous soap opera, involving hiring attorney Nathan Wade, was a charge of "election interference." She accused my father, and others, under their Racketeer Influenced and Corrupt Organizations (RICO) act, of trying to obstruct the state's certification of the 2020 election. Historically, RICO is used to go after the Mafia and gangs, allowing prosecutors to seek longer sentences. For example, John Gotti was convicted under RICO. In this "case" the supposed crime was questioning a sketchy, pandemic-weakened election—one that made little sense from any quantifiable perspective, and that had most of America scratching their heads.

Shortly before indicting Donald Trump in 2023, she and her romantic-partner-colleague, Nathan Wade, attended multiple events at the Biden White House with the vice president (and at the VP's residence).[34] [35]

Did Donald Trump need a mug shot? Of course not. He's the most recognized person on the planet, but they thought this would add to the "embarrassment." In fact, it just pissed off the country and boosted his appeal, especially in minority communities. Our campaign raised $7.1 million in the three days after the photo was taken. Honestly, not a bad portrait—showing his defiance and strength.

"Honey, is this the first time in history that being indicted is good for someone's polls?!" my father sarcastically asked. We both knew the answer.

The more scrutiny that was applied to Willis's case, the more it became a sideshow—highlighting incompetence and the fact that the entire case was a political witch hunt.[36]

The July 1, 2024, ruling from the U.S. Supreme Court on presidential immunity gutted this case once and for all.[37] Another gigantic waste of time, money, and energy. They tried to use all these cases to make our lives hell—including my life and the organization I run. As just one of the hundreds of examples, New Jersey tried to revoke all of our properties' liquor licenses using "Donald Trump's conviction" as the reason to hurt us—even though his name wasn't on the licenses and despite the fact that he was not involved in the businesses in any way. But never let a crisis go to waste.

At least my father got a great photo out of the deal. Millions of dollars were poured into the campaign as a result of that mug shot, and the entire country, once again, saw the siege.

Documents at Mar-a-Lago

On June 13, 2023, Donald J. Trump made a required court appearance in Miami, Florida, where he was charged in the Southern District of Florida on *37 felony counts* related to the supposed "mishandling of classified government documents stored at his Mar-a-Lago estate," courtesy of special counsel Jack Smith and U.S. Attorney General Merrick Garland. The support from crowds outside the courthouse was unbelievable.

That morning I wrote myself the following:

We met at Doral. My father's strength and confidence was amazing. Solid as a rock. Wrote the Truth about the "sad day for the nation." At the same time we all fully understood the political power of the moment. I walked him to the car. Lara brought the kids down to give him a kiss goodbye.

Love you pops. Go get 'em.

He went down to the courthouse surrounded by massive support. Susie Wiles: "Sir, you own Florida."

When he returned from court, I greeted him at the top of the stairs of the plane with Lara, Luke, and Carolina. Carolina, who was three years old, ran up to him, shouted "Happy Birthday!" and gave him a big hug. "Grandpa, are you going to a trampoline park for your birthday tomorrow?" The following day, June 14, marked his 77th birthday.

The cruelty of the world met innocence.

"My girl," my father said. "Isn't she the most beautiful. Man, you two make the most beautiful children."

A huge smile washed over his face, and we all felt the tension disappear. This is what life is all about. None of the other crazy games matter.

We departed Miami en route to Bedminster watching the very plane taxi on the large TV screen in the center cabin from news helicopters overhead. And his poll numbers went up another 3%. This after 37 felony counts.

McDonald's was served on the flight.

We watched Cavuto discussing if Trump might be a flight risk. "Isn't he the worst?" my father asked rhetorically. "How about Biden's documents in Chinatown?"

We landed in Newark and got into the Beast. "Let's drive right to the podium." Sean Curran once again in the front right seat.

Dana White called. "Sir, I'm in the tough guy business and you're the toughest of them all."

He turned to me. "This is very unfair to you, honey."

We both smiled.

THE CASE AND COORDINATION

Former president Donald J. Trump was falsely accused of taking "classified documents" when he left the White House and keeping them at Mar-a-Lago. You will remember from the introduction to this book that the FBI's raid supposedly came at the direction of the National Archives and Records Administration (NARA). As our legal team rightly pointed out, that's as ridiculous as sending in the local SWAT team to retrieve an overdue library book.

Among the "classified documents" were boxes of the president's and first lady's personal items, including passports, photo albums, newspaper clippings, medical files protected under HIPAA regulations, and items marked for "attorney-client privilege." All of it, and more, was taken.[38]

But in my father's case, there wasn't even an overdue book.

It was all coordinated, and Attorney General Merrick Garland "personally approved" the raid.[39] [40]

Despite President Biden saying, "I didn't have any advance notice. None. Zero. Not one single bit." Give me a break.[41]

You may know already that Joe Biden, Hillary Clinton, and Mike Pence have all also admitted to having classified documents, and weirdly, their homes were never raided. Let's not forget the photo of Joe Biden's garage showcasing the collection of boxes he had stored away next to his Corvette—in a house formerly rented by his degenerate son. Or Hillary's "private" server in Chappaqua, New York, which miraculously deleted 33,000 emails. God only knows who had access to those documents.[42]

Shortly before leaving office in 2021, President Trump declassified documents known as "Crossfire Hurricane." These are reported to contain info that Bill and Hillary Clinton, Barack Obama, Joe Biden, and other members of the swamp—including those in the DOJ—do not want the public to see. Unsurprisingly, the DOJ worked to block the release of those files.

But there is no question this all formed the pretext for a raid on Mar-a-Lago. Step 1: send Trump's documents home to him. Step 2: allege possession of classified documents. When the FBI arrived, on orders from Merrick Garland, agents brought in "cover sheets" with various "classified" markings and staged photos. The whole charade was meant to deceive the public into believing Donald Trump knowingly held documents with these top secret labels.

If that wasn't enough, Jack Smith's team later admitted that the documents were mishandled during and after the raid. Here is their damning explanation in legalese: "In many but not all instances, the FBI was able to determine which document with classification markings corresponded to a particular placeholder sheet."[43]

Translation: We disorganized the documents, planted a few, took pretty pictures, and distributed them to the world in the hopes of putting a former president in jail and crushing a movement.

When our legal team sought access to internal documents from Smith and his team, they sought to block their access.[44]

My verdict: First they disputed President Trump's authority as chief executive to declassify documents. They conspired with the White House to trap him. They authorized the FBI agents to use deadly force in the raid. They would not allow our attorney on site the day of the raid. Then they tampered with evidence, and almost certainly planted evidence. It was all a trap.

And yes, Jack Smith even tried, unsuccessfully, to impose a gag order on Donald Trump. Where have we seen that before—it was par for the course.[45]

In case you don't think this case could get any more Soviet, according to reports, Jay Bratt even threatened the attorney of one of our employees, telling him that unless his client cooperated, the attorney would risk losing a potential judgeship.[46] [47]

THE JUDGE AND THE CONSTITUTION

I appreciate Judge Aileen Cannon's decisions to unseal so many unredacted documents that show how involved the Biden administration was in this entire "classified documents" case. The incompetence from Jack Smith and team stunk so much, the case was paused—before being dismissed.[48]

On July 15, 2024, her ruling came down. "Former President Trump's Motion to Dismiss Indictment Based on the Unlawful Appointment and Funding of Special Counsel Jack Smith is GRANTED in accordance with this Order." Another sham, finally over. Was it because U.S. AG Merrick Garland ignored the United States Constitution when he illegally appointed Smith? The Constitution clearly states that positions like this must be appointed by the president and confirmed by the U.S. Senate.[49]

Garland and Wray decided to stray from established protocol to injure President Trump."[50]

Swamp Creatures

MERRICK GARLAND

There is no question that Republicans blocked Merrick Gardland from serving on the U.S. Supreme Court in 2016 after Obama nominated him following the death of Justice Antonin Scalia. There is also no question that Garland has held a grudge to this day.

THE AUTOPEN

Of all the swamp creatures, this cyborg is the most mysterious. I really want to meet the people attached to the use of this powerful machine—preferably in a courtroom or congressional hearing. I believe we will eventually know who was actually running our executive branch for the past four years—and it is not the names that were on the top of the Democrat ticket. It's the people who were using the autopen on behalf of Joe Biden. Truly, the biggest political scandal of my lifetime.

The Supreme Court

In 2024, the U.S. Supreme Court delivered some remarkable rulings that restored my faith in our republic, and set the stage to constitutionally vaporize the lawfare against Donald J. Trump. Here are two cases that turned the tide.

PRESIDENTIAL IMMUNITY

In the July 1, 2024, ruling on *Trump v. United States*, Chief Justice John Roberts wrote: "Like everyone else, the President is subject to prosecution in his unofficial capacity. But unlike anyone else, the President is a branch of government, and the Constitution vests in him sweeping powers and duties. Accounting for that reality—and ensuring that the President may exercise those powers forcefully, as the Framers anticipated he would—does not place him above the law; it preserves the basic structure of the Constitution from which that law derives."

Indeed: the president is a branch of government.

Justice Clarence Thomas added, "No former President has faced criminal prosecution for his acts while in office in the more than 200 years since the founding of our country. And, that is so despite numerous past Presidents taking actions that many would argue constitute crimes. [. . .] [There] are serious questions whether the Attorney General has violated that structure by creating an office of the Special Counsel that has not been established by law."[51]

He is not wrong. The "crimes" were manufactured, and so was the prosecution. This ruling alone, confirming presidential immunity, unraveled most of the sham cases against Donald Trump. A defining victory for my father, our family, and America.

Their Playbook

When I say the lawfare in the array of cases against Donald Trump is "all connected" it's not a conspiracy theory.

They followed a similar playbook.

Search way back, even past statutes of limitations. Normally, felony cases in New York must be brought within five years. But the system leveraged COVID abnormalities to eliminate those restrictions and drag out the process. This "tolling" strategy was used in the Letitia James case and other cases against Donald Trump. Translation: If the rules get in the way, change the rules.[52] [53]

Go fishing. Dig deep, twist every law, and cobble together any case you can find, no matter how flimsy or desperate. For example, presidential immunity has never been scrutinized like it has for the 45th and 47th president of the United States. My father, our company, and I were on the receiving end of hundreds of subpoenas, resulting in millions of documents sent and tens of thousands of hours wasted. Thankfully, in April of 2024, the U.S. Supreme Court weighed in and chided them for these fishing expeditions. The message was clear: this reckless, endless hunt must stop—it's a dangerous abuse of power that threatens the very foundations of our democracy.[54]

Spy and use FISA (Foreign Intelligence Surveillance Act). "I'm not a big fan of FISA. . . . You know they spied on my campaign," my father famously said. It was used as a cover to spy on American citizens. And in April of 2024, former FBI deputy director Andrew McCabe finally admitted the obvious. "We now know there were many mistakes in that FISA. Those are all regrettable." The Privacy and Civil Liberties Oversight Board confirmed that there were approximately 5 million warrantless searches between 2019 and 2022 based on "little justification."[55] This goes way beyond Donald Trump.[56]

Coordinate with the swamp. The Biden White House, the D.C. swamp, and the media are all in this together. Every case against my father, my family, and our business was coordinated at some level with other players. And the media is a major player. In 2018, a Pulitzer Prize was given to "journalists" from the *Washington Post* and the *New York Times* for their reporting on the Russia hoax. (My father requested the awards be withdrawn based on proven fraud in the allegations, but they refused, of course. So we sued.) Of the 112 subpoenas I received, many were reported in the press before they arrived at my office. And isn't it interesting that the media often knew details of the New York cases before they were publicly released—and before our legal team was officially notified? The media was the swamp's delivery platform.

Find crooked pawns. This part is easy—there's no shortage of district attorneys and secretaries of state infected with Trump Derangement Syndrome. Alvin Bragg and Letitia James literally campaigned on a "get Trump" pledge. And secretaries of state in Colorado, Maine, and Illinois tried to "save democracy" by stripping Donald J. Trump from the ballot. Thankfully, in March 2024, the U.S. Supreme Court slammed the door on that scheme, ruling that states had no power to remove him.[57]

Find a suitable judge in a dark-blue jurisdiction. Have you noticed that all the cases against Donald Trump were brought in Washington, D.C., New York, and Fulton County (Atlanta), Georgia, were in districts that overwhelmingly vote Democrat? It's called judge shopping. The selection of judges in the Letitia James case and the Alvin Bragg case was surprisingly nonrandom, brought in front of a jury of "peers" in a district that overwhelmingly votes against you.

Threaten and intimidate. For over a decade, AGs have weaponized their offices to harass our clients, threaten our company, target our employees and their families—and even go

after members of our legal team. Judges have tried to intimidate attorneys, bully witnesses, and lean on Donald Trump
himself. They sanction, silence, and file bogus ethics complaints. Alina Habba was threatened with disbarment multiple
times—her "crime" being that she defended her client, and did
it so effectively in the media that it rattled the other side. They
wanted her gone because she refused to cower and had the guts
to say publicly what most lawyers only whisper.

Wound or kill. Even if their lawfare fails, the mission is the
same—drain our time, sap our energy, brand Donald J. Trump
and our company as criminals, and bleed us dry financially.
They fabricated lies in the Steele dossier to destroy a marriage,
and unleashed a barrage of subpoenas meant to grind people
down until they broke.

Break apart families. We have seen this firsthand, as vicious lies
are told about our family.

Deprive governmental resources. Robert F. Kennedy Jr.'s Secret
Service protection was pulled by the Biden administration.
Democrat lawmakers, led by Representative Bennie Thompson,
openly pushed to strip my father's detail in the middle of the
lawfare onslaught. How could any rational person not see this
for what it was—a calculated move to leave him vulnerable? And
sure enough, months later, the lack of resources nearly cost my
father his life.

Weaponize media. We saw this during the first term, when so-
called "journalists" parroted the "Russia hacked the election"
lie—over and over and over—until repetition blurred the line
between fiction and fact. They didn't just report the news; they
manufactured it, coordinated it, and force-fed it to the public
like propaganda. Night after night, headline after headline, the
goal wasn't truth—it was to delegitimize the presidency and poi-
son the minds of millions against my father before he even had a
chance to govern.

Censor, de-bank, and de-platform. This isn't just about my family or our business—it's a coordinated assault that has hit hundreds of thousands, if not tens of millions, of patriotic Americans. The goal is as clear as it is chilling: erase our voices from the public square, choke off our ability to make a living, and starve our movement of the oxygen it needs to survive.

The point of their coordinated siege is not to "right wrongs" or "seek justice." It's to crush political opponents by any means possible. When one attempt fails they will point their weapons at someone else, including you and me. They might be running for cover now, but they will never relent.

In July of 2024, the day after the U.S. Supreme Court's presidential immunity ruling, the *Washington Post* published another telling headline. "Justice Dept. Plans to Pursue Trump Cases Past Election Day, Even If He Wins." The article went on to say, "If Donald Trump is elected president, the finish line for federal prosecutors is Inauguration Day, not Election Day, people familiar with the discussions said."[58] It's a repeat of the headline they ran on Inauguration Day 2017: "The Campaign to Impeach President Trump Has Begun."[59]

They won't stop. And they won't stop with just Donald Trump. My father has been blessed with the notoriety and resources to fight back— and the loudest voice on the planet. But most Americans don't have either when they're unjustly persecuted or falsely accused. That reality weighed heavily on me throughout these battles and trials. The unintended consequence? These fights may ultimately restore some integrity to the Justice Department—and to this nation.

First, they aimed to take down Donald J. Trump because he dared to run for president. Now, they're panicked—shaken by our victory on November 5 and every day since.

It is all connected. And now, finally, it is all coming to light.

CHAPTER 11

NOT SENDING OUR BEST

"The most capable people are not necessarily running for political office, and that is a very sad commentary on the country."

—DONALD J. TRUMP, 1980[1]

Forty-five years ago, my father all but predicted Joe Biden's presidency. In a 1980 interview, he offered these words.

"Somebody with strong views, and somebody with the kind of views that are maybe a little bit unpopular, which may be right, but may be unpopular, wouldn't necessarily have a chance of getting elected against somebody with no great brain but a big smile."[2]

It is not an easy feat, but in 2021 our nation went from record-breaking economic growth, and record-breaking low unemployment to . . . Bidenomics.

Why? There are several reasons, but here's just one of countless clues from that administration. Jared Bernstein said in a May 2024 interview, "The U.S. government can't go bankrupt, because we can print our own money." He happened to be the chair of the White House Council of Economic Advisers. Why would Biden put him in that position? Maybe it's because of his bachelor's degree in music and doctorate in social work from Columbia University.[3]

That same month, then–Vice President Kamala Harris offered her wisdom on the issue of inflation. "Because of the Inflation Reduction Act—the infrastructure act—we are dropping trillions of dollars on the streets of America right now to build back up our roads and our bridges, our sidewalks, to invest in a clean energy economy, to deal with the climate crisis in a way that is about building up adaptation and resilience."[4]

If you did not understand that, neither did I, or anyone else for that matter. Typical BS—vocalization without meaning. Democrats talk about helping lower-income Americans, yet their policies only make the government bigger and a growing burden on citizens.[5]

We had a DEI transportation secretary who was a small-town mayor, and who never accomplished anything besides checking DEI boxes and spending $80 billion on DEI grants.[6] Amid a global supply chain crisis linked to the COVID-19 pandemic, Mayor Pete went on—you guessed it—"paternity leave," while hundreds of the largest cargo ships in the world waited for weeks outside of the Port of Los Angeles and shelves were empty across the country. He did almost nothing to help the people of East Palestine, Ohio, after the catastrophic train wreck. But this shouldn't be surprising. Pete Buttigieg backed the nomination of a Federal Aviation Administration director who didn't know the first thing about airplanes.[7]

We had Joint Chiefs of Staff chair General Mark Milley trying to understand "white rage" in the military, defending the study of critical race theory (CRT) and reportedly calling the Make America Great Again movement "fascist." These are the same people who advocate for battery-powered tanks, allow Chinese spy balloons to fly across our nation unchecked, and disgraced our great country in our disastrous withdrawal from Afghanistan—an astounding level of incompetence that left billions of dollars in U.S. military supplies, including helicopters, armored vehicles, sniper rifles, and night vision gear, in the hands of the Taliban. We wasted millions on absurdly renaming some of the world's most iconic military bases, like Fort Bragg—which was changed to Fort Liberty—a decision reversed in 2025, fulfilling a promise my father made during the 2024 campaign. I could go on and on, but you get the picture. Not the "most capable people."[8]

Donald Trump called it in 1980 and 2015, whether it's illegal immigration or elected officials, they're not sending their best.

He called it again in 2020.

DONALD J. TRUMP'S 2020 PREDICTIONS
ABOUT "SLEEPY JOE"

"He'll bury you in regulations, dismantle your police departments, dissolve our borders, confiscate your guns, terminate religious liberty, destroy your suburbs."
—PRESIDENT DONALD J. TRUMP[9]

Status: Accomplished.

"Your vote will decide whether we protect law-abiding Americans, or whether we give free rein to violent anarchists, agitators, and criminals who threaten our citizens."
—PRESIDENT DONALD J. TRUMP[10]

Status: Accomplished.

"But they want to dissolve your borders. They don't want borders. They want to have open borders, release criminal aliens, raise your taxes."
—PRESIDENT DONALD J. TRUMP[11] [12]

Status: Accomplished.

As a patriot who loves America, I wish these predictions had not come true. Whether it was outright malice or incompetence, or a twisted mix of both, not only was our family under siege, the Biden/autopen administration laid siege to America.

WHO'S IN YOUR WALLET?

After the sudden silence of the "loss" on November 3, 2020, things got a lot noisier. In January 2021, the knives were out for all things Trump. I became a target for the corporate cancel culture movement. Letter after letter, from dozens of institutions including Chase, First Republic, Capital One, Goldman Sachs, UBS, Signature Bank, Investors Savings Bank, Cushman & Wakefield, Aon Insurance, Professional Bank, Shopify, Barclays, and the list goes on.

One Trump-deranged bank's letter bore the headline "IMPORTANT: Closing our banking relationship," and gave us mere weeks to dissolve all corporate accounts.

I will never forget the notice from First Republic Bank. *Sorry, we're canceling all your accounts.* Except this time the CEO was a neighbor of mine. When my team brought me the letter, I said, "You gotta be kidding me! I'll call the CEO right now, he's a friend. Bet he doesn't even know, and this is coming from some woke staffer."

The CEO—my direct neighbor—a man who literally shared a wall with Lara and me in New York City. Like so many others during this time, he was a total disappointment. When I called him, he acted like a stranger, as if we'd never met. Then he told me it was out of his control.

"Out of your control?!" I responded. "You are the chairman of the bank. For what reason? We have been a perfect client."

Ironically, First Republic collapsed on May 1, 2023, just two years later, seized by California regulators and placed into FDIC receivership, marking one of the largest bank failures in U.S. history. While I never wish harm on anyone—especially their many employees—the irony is striking. The very bank that canceled us, closed our accounts, and shunned loyal customers and friends collapsed in total failure. Given what they tried to do to us, I can't say I was disappointed. This was one of the few times being canceled was a blessing, sparing me headaches and potential financial loss because of their downfall.

As they say, karma's never in a hurry, but when it arrives, it's worth the wait.

The most devastating surprise came from Capital One, after being a client for nearly twenty years.

"Eric, I just received notice via overnight mail terminating all our bank accounts, effective March 21, 2021."

The opening of the three-sentence letter read "Your account has been closed," and ended with this line: "If you have any questions, please get in touch."

I had questions.

Why? We had over 300 distinct accounts there, each connected to hundreds, possibly thousands, of tenant payments, employees, contractors, utilities—and loans. These were not political accounts, they were commercial buildings, golf properties, condo associations, restaurants, retail businesses, shopping centers, and more. How do you pay your employees, vendors, utilities, and real estate taxes? How about collecting rent, membership dues, common area maintenance, and revenue from hotels?

To make matters more complicated, most of these accounts were on auto pay—tenants who had been with us for years would have to be notified, wires changed, and ACH forms modified. Last but not least, these very accounts were subject to loan documents and lockbox loan provisions; the cancellation would be grounds for loan defaults. Our business was like a train without tracks—going nowhere. They were trying to rip those tracks out, and fast. I called all the big banks personally. For the first time in my life, their responses were slow, their tone cold and distant—completely different from just months before. For decades, banks had clamored for our business. Now, loyalty was nowhere to be found.

FINANCIAL SIEGE

The same siege came from some insurance carriers and other financial partners. Moreover, we lost our e-commerce platforms. Shopify sent a notice effectively saying, we're closing your accounts. When I decided to sell the Old Post Office (Trump International Hotel, Washington, D.C.), I was shocked—Cushman & Wakefield, CBRE, et al., denied the engagement.

They, as part of the establishment and the Left, wanted to see us fail. Humiliated. They wanted headlines. Bankrupt and gone.

And behind these stories is another story of regulators breathing down the necks of banks and insurance companies, whispering, "I see you're doing business with Trump. We're watching." More than one CEO of large financial institutions caved to that corruption. That didn't make them innocent, it made them complicit.

I heard this heartbreaking story from hundreds of Americans: "My bank suddenly refuses to finance me—and won't even give me a reason." But when they dug deeper, the truth was clear. It wasn't about money or risk. It was about politics, religion, their support for the Second Amendment, or simply a social media photo of them wearing a red MAGA hat. This was not just business—it was targeted punishment.

There was a domino effect. They abandoned me—but more importantly, they left our employees, tenants, and patrons in the dark. Their goal was clear: they wanted us to close up shop. Not only did our phones stop ringing, but our calls went unanswered. It echoed the isolation my father faced back in the early nineties. I wasn't fighting for a paycheck—I was fighting for our team, for my family, and for everything three generations of Trumps had built.

The careers of thousands depended on me. Sleepless nights blurred into long days spent away from my family, locked in the office. Like during COVID, my role shifted—from CEO to psychologist and crisis manager. I offered constant reassurance that we'd be okay, cracked jokes on the darkest days when all you wanted was to crawl under your desk. That intentional positivity—rooted in unwavering faith that justice would prevail—became the lifeblood that kept the entire organization moving forward.

The hits built warriors. Our team became hardened and resilient beyond words. They knew the siege was bullshit. They were offended that their hard work was being sabotaged by hateful forces. I was fighting for them and they were fighting for me. Our company has always been an extension of our family and we have the greatest team in the world.

Actions have consequences. When my father and our family lost our freedom of speech, we built Truth Social. When we lost our banking, we quickly became a leader in cryptocurrency. Banks should be in the business of investing, saving, and lending—not policing thought. Vernon Hill, founder of Commerce Bank, understood that. I'll always owe him a debt of gratitude. Thank you, my friend. I'll never forget you stepping forward when others stepped away.

It's actually cathartic. The good people you discover during the toughest times—you know they'll stand by you long after the storm passes. And there's a strange, almost surreal feeling when those who canceled you suddenly call back. "Hi, Eric. It's been a long time. We'd really like to rebuild the relationship and become great partners again with your incredible organization."

F— you.

At the time, and neck-deep in the chaos, I could not have imagined that, four years later, my father would address the World Economic Forum in Davos as president, look those de-bankers in the eye, and say, "I hope you start opening your bank to conservatives because many conservatives complain that the banks are not allowing them to do business within the bank and that included a place called Bank of America. [. . .] They don't take conservative business and I don't know if the regulators mandated that because of Biden or what but you and Jamie [Dimon] and everybody . . . I hope you open your banks to conservatives because what you're doing is wrong."[13] Faces went blank and jaws dropped. Exposed on the world stage.

Some claim "de-banking"—when financial institutions yank your accounts without warning or explanation—is just a myth. I can assure you it's very real. On March 7, 2025, I sued Capital One to prove it.

> Today, the Trump Organization filed a lawsuit in Miami-Dade County against @CapitalOne to hold the bank accountable for their egregious conduct in unjustifiably terminating over 300 of the company's bank accounts without cause, in 2021.
>
> The decision by Capital One to "debank" our company, after well over a decade, was a clear attack on free speech and free enterprise that flies in the face of the bedrock principles and freedoms that define our country. Moreover, the arbitrary closure of these accounts, without justifiable cause, reflects a broader effort to silence and undermine the success of the Trump Organization and those who dare to express their political views.
>
> By filing this lawsuit, we seek to hold Capital One accountable for the millions of dollars in damages they caused, not just to our company, but to the many dozens of properties, hundreds of tenants and thousands of Trump Organization employees who relied on these accounts for their livelihoods.
>
> Businesses should not be targeted or punished for their political affiliations. The actions taken by Capital One and other major financial institutions represents a dangerous precedent that could threaten the operations of countless businesses across the nation, particularly those with a strong and independent voice.

This lawsuit, and those that follow, are necessary steps to protect the integrity of American business practices and to ensure that no company or individual is unfairly targeted for their beliefs, affiliations, or business activities. We will not stand by while big banks misuse their power to stifle businesses and harm innocent Americans.[14]

"THREAT TO DEMOCRACY"

In a May 2024 interview, presidential candidate Robert F. Kennedy Jr. said the following about Biden.

I can make the argument that President Biden is a much worse threat to democracy, and the reason for that is President Biden is the first candidate in history, the first president in history that has used federal agencies to censor political speech.

The greatest threat to democracy is not somebody who questions election returns, but a president of the United States who uses the power of his office to force the social media companies—Facebook, Instagram, Twitter—to open a portal and give access to that portal to the FBI, to the CIA, to the IRS.[15]

How did we get to this terrible, un-American place in society? Slowly, but intentionally. The Left knows how to play the long game.

Soros knows that a half-million dollars is a drop in the bucket in a presidential campaign, but that same amount of money can flip a local race in his favor. This includes DAs, school boards, and judges. And guess who Alvin Bragg is beholden to? It's the same with Fani Willis and every Soros plant. When your puppet master says, "Jump," you jump. They would have done the same for Donald Trump before he entered the political arena. Those people are tools.

In May of 2024, the U.S. House of Representatives Committee on the Judiciary and the Select Subcommittee on the Weaponization of the Federal Government released an eight-hundred-page report detailing how the Biden administration worked with social media companies, Mark Zuckerberg, YouTube, and other players to block information and censor speech. Examples include removing posts and stories about the Wuhan COVID lab leak, posts critical of the vaccine, and Hunter's dirty laptop. As much as it was revealing to see it come out, this was nothing Americans did not already know.[16]

WHY DOES THE LEFT HATE YOU?

Plain and simple: the Left—which includes most Democrats—hates Donald Trump because no other president has pulled back the curtain to reveal just how corrupt Washington, D.C., really is. Think about it—anyone who thinks a $20 billion border wall is "too expensive" but sends $200 billion to Ukraine is completely out of touch with everyday Americans like you and me.[17]

Barack Obama went from community organizer to owning a $12 million estate on Martha's Vineyard. Bill and Hillary Clinton were basically broke at one point in their "career" and now they're worth eight figures. Nancy Pelosi and her husband somehow pick winners in the stock market that even Warren Buffett misses, and she repeatedly votes against insider trading restrictions for members of Congress.

People accuse my family of "profiting" off of politics. The truth is, our business has grown *despite* politics. And it cost us hundreds of millions in legal fees, and billions in untapped opportunities—not to mention almost $100 million spent financing his own campaign.

My father got out of business when he went to D.C. Joe and Hunter Biden got into business when Joe went to D.C.—and they're not the only ones.

WHY WE FIGHT

People often ask why my father fights—and why I stand firm alongside him. On a personal level, it comes down to two reasons. First, we have no choice. Surrendering to the chaos and madness simply isn't an option. And second, we genuinely care—deeply—about our family, our legacy, and the future of this country.

Believe me, our family could cut a deal with those attacking us in about three seconds. If we were willing to walk away, step out of politics, and quietly run a real estate business, the attacks on us and our company would stop immediately. It would be the easiest negotiation I've ever done. But the truth is—we truly love this country.

The fight costs us—money, time, and so much more. But I often think about what my Czech grandmother used to ask: "How many steaks can you eat?" Her point was simple—so long as you have enough to eat, what else truly matters? My family has been blessed with incredible fortune, and that places us in a unique position to be part of the solution. Which brings me right back to my first point.

We are stubborn as hell. Thankfully, millions of other Americans are wired the same way.

BACK TO THE BASICS

As a general rule, America certainly has not sent our best into elected office. Not even close. I hope that makes you angry. Maybe even pissed off enough to run for office.

Politicians have become increasingly filthy, and as a result, so has our politics. If we continue the way the Left wants, we'll see more filth and degradation. But it's not inevitable. We will change course. We will get back to the basics—back to doing what Americans do better than anybody: freedom and innovation.

The Left wants us to be distracted by trivial sideshows. They are smart, calculating, and patient. They have thirty-year plans, and they relentlessly execute on those plans.

The United States is the greatest force for good on the planet—but if we allow our influence to slip, we may never regain it. Losing the U.S. dollar's status as the world's reserve currency would be catastrophic. We'd hemorrhage foreign investment, the dollar's value would plummet, and other nations would rally behind the Chinese yuan. If that happens, it's the beginning of the end for this nation. Under no circumstances can we let it happen.

The same holds true with our rule of law. The reason the United States attracts capital, the reason people risk their lives to come here, is primarily because we have a system of justice that's fundamentally honest and unshakable. But it's being shaken right now, and the entire world can't believe what's happening. The weaponization of government is filthy. But we can stop it.

Yes, our government is full of corruption and it seems that so much of what comes out of D.C. is aimed at what we hold dear. Leftists keep chanting about what a terrible country this is. We can't buy their destructive propaganda.

If we let the Left tear down America's foundation, life will only get harder for every single one of us. But if we recommit to the principles that built this nation, life will improve for everyone—no exceptions. Donald J. Trump risked everything for this country. Now, it's on all of us to finish the fight and get America back on track. We won the White House. We are rallying the best and brightest to Make America Great Again—because this movement is unstoppable.

Now we need to win more state and local elections.

We need *capable* people, and I nominate you.

PART THREE

CRUSHING THE SIEGE

CHAPTER 12

PROUD OF THE FIGHT

"I want to start by, as always, thanking my family, my wife Melania.
My kids. They're not kids anymore, but they're kids as far as I'm concerned.
They'll always be my kids."
—DONALD TRUMP, AFTER WINNING THE 2016 INDIANA PRIMARY[1]

Honestly, in 2020 I didn't think the attacks could get any worse. I was wrong about that, but we were ready. The raid on Mar-a-Lago, the lawfare, the cancel culture commercial warfare, de-banking, and lies—by this time, nothing shocked me.

I often wondered, *How many lives do we have left?*

It took months to assemble the team we have in place today. We worked tirelessly to find new banks, insurance companies, platforms, and vendors. It was grueling, but our businesses never missed a beat. Our employees forged on. When Lara and I decided to move to Florida, the natural next step was to move our company headquarters. *But would anyone want to move? How would having teams in both New York and Florida work?*

When we announced we were moving to the Sunshine State, more than half the company raised their hand, and their trust and loyalty once again was overwhelming. Everyone was dedicated to the fight.

My mantra has always been "One team, one fight." It's not just some meaningless slogan, it's who we are and how I lead. No division. Full collaboration. No egos. Be the best at everything we do.

We began signing deals with partners for amazing projects overseas. These projects take years, not months, so anyone with an IQ greater than their age knows the projects we've announced in 2025 have nothing to do with the 2024 election win. Our successes are despite the siege—we truly have the greatest brand and hospitality company on earth.

Lara was doing fantastic in her career. My father was focused on endorsing candidates for primaries, while considering a second presidential run. In 2023, he called Lara and me. "I'm going for it." We knew exactly what he meant and knew what that would mean for us.

It was the White House or jail.

I knew it was the right call, but the majority of the weight, outside of Washington, D.C., would once again fall on me. My team and I had worked so hard the past three years to make the company bulletproof. Better than ever. Now we would face more hoaxes, more shams, and more lies. It was the Democrats' playbook 101—a playbook I knew better than anyone—and I knew they wouldn't be able to help themselves. *Would I jump back into the fray, or stay out of the spotlight?*

Maybe I had become a masochist, but there wasn't a second of indecision.

Within days we gathered at Mar-a-Lago with family and our campaign team. Just as my father had done in 2015, I knew that the fight for our nation was the most important cause of my lifetime. I would lead the company, lead my family, lead our defense against the lawfare, and do everything I could to see my father become president again.

I became the de facto patriarch for aspects of our family outside of D.C. If a comma was out of place, I knew I would be the one to pay the price. I'd seen the weaponization. I had been in the crosshairs. I was in those depositions, on the stand, and on those courthouse steps doing press conference after press conference.

Every week I commuted back and forth between New York and Florida. When I was away from home, I felty guilty for being away from Lara and our kids. When I was home, I worried about the court cases, the campaign, and our team in New York.

I'm sharing this for one reason: it's a joke to suggest politics ever benefited our family. It's an even bigger joke to suggest it served me.

Guiding the company through the onslaught, I learned next-level appreciation for the difference between being a leader and being the second-in-command. The difference is real. It gave me an even greater appreciation for my father and everything he had created, and for his comeback—in business and politics.

The cancel culture, COVID, "Russia," attacks on our employees, health inspectors from hell, thousands of leaked IRS tax returns, legal battles from local courts to the U.S. Supreme Court, millions of pages of discovery, censorship, mugshots, indictments, FBI "visits," spying, deceit, and packages of white powder delivered to our house (multiple times), just to name a few.

Just another day at the office, right? Too many sleepless nights and too many lost friendships.

But as we've also learned through the siege, there are always unintended consequences—some really good ones.

A TRIBUTE

Despite it all, my job was to hold a family and company together. By 2023 they had become one and the same.

As a too-brief but heartfelt tribute, thank you to Kim, Alan, Adam, Donna, Allen, Jeff, Larry, Ron, Mark, Deirdre, Deborah, Matt, Diana, Mike, Gia, and everyone from my team, both in our corporate offices and at the properties. They were incredible and they never took the bait. They are family. They fought through the impossible. They knew the truth. They became hardened warriors. Without them, the past ten years would have been unsurvivable.

The ridiculous hours. The frustration. As much as I tried to take off of their shoulders, they took even more off of mine. I made the difficult decisions; those decisions were on me and me alone, but they were relentless in terms of the execution. Behind that corporate team were tens of thousands of lives—families and kids. We were fighting for them.

I was also fighting for my family name, for the pride of a father and siblings. I hope my heart has come through on these pages—family, loyalty, country is my only motivation. Nepotism? Hell yes. The word means we bring what money can never buy—grit, determination, and the energy to fight for more than just a paycheck.

In a way, I think my father saw a 1990s version of himself in me the past five years. He was fighting to stay alive against crushing debt and mocking doubters. Like him thirty years earlier, I was fighting to stay alive in the worst political weaponization in history, trying to simultaneously navigate business, legal, and government. And we both won.

I didn't enjoy, nor was I energized by, the bravado of the cameras. I wanted to chart a direction, without making noise, and get to the finish line. I didn't need any pats on the back. That's never what motivated me. Winning the race has always been my aim.

And speaking of parallels, there are so many qualities Lara and my mother share: toughness, strength, athleticism, bold opinions, social grace, and crucial roles within the Trump family. My mom fought relentlessly by my father's side, in Atlantic City, the Plaza Hotel, and the beginnings of the real estate empire. She also fought tirelessly for her kids. Lara has excelled on all of those fronts, and so much more.

I'm not saying it's easy, but I'm committed to an atmosphere of confidence. While politics might be a game to Adam Schiff or Letitia James, it's not a game to Debe, or for Adam, Kim, Mickael, or Jodie. It's not a game for the thousands of employees in Florida, New York, and around the world. Lawfare and lies are not a game for the single mom caring for a handicapped child, the hostess who was recently engaged, or the overnight hotel employee who has worked in the Trump Organization for thirty years and relies on her income to support her family.

Our team has been unbreakable. To all of them (and you know exactly who you are), *I love you, appreciate you—you are a true family.* I am also humbled and grateful for my right hand, Kim. She has been beside me and Lara for so many years—endless flights, crazy hours, a trillion emails. Kim not only knows every detail of the company, she has become an expert on presidential campaigns, legal lawfare, and the madness of where those worlds collide. She was in the siege with us every day, and I can't imagine victory in any of these areas without her brilliance and dedication. *(Thank you, Kim!)*

We have a great company that's healthier than ever. Our properties have never been better, our teams have never been stronger, we have paid down virtually all of our debt, while doing some of our greatest real estate transactions this decade. We have gotten very little recognition, and a ton of abuse, but in terms of results there are few real estate companies in the world that come close.

When asked about all the lawfare, I always answered, "We will win, like we always do." Now I realize I sounded just like my father did thirty years ago. And he's never changed. Donald Trump has always been—or at least appeared to be—the least stressed-out person in the room, on the stage, or in the courthouse.

Flying in Trump Force One on the way to have his mug shot taken, I looked over at him as he launched a Starburst (red or pink only) in my direction—with a smile that meant a wild combination of "I love you," "It makes me feel less guilty if you eat one, too," and "This situation sucks, but let's have some fun and figure out how to win."

The avalanche effect is real. A snowball rolling downhill becomes bigger and heavier as it picks up speed. So does pessimism, sorrow, worry, and panic. So don't let the ball start rolling.

Donald Trump's confident demeanor, assertive speech, decisive body language, and unapologetic confidence projects true strength—and that's what snowballed during the siege, across our nation.

Unknowingly I was also doing the same with Lara. I hid so much of this aspect of life from her. I know it hurt her, especially when others were read in, where she was not. I wanted positivity in my house and around my family and children. I wanted a house of joy, a mother who could nurture two beautiful kids—free of subpoenas, indictments, and slime.

This gets back to a question I've been asked a thousand times. "Did your dad make every school or sporting event when you were growing up?" The simple answer is no. Was he there when it mattered? Always, yes. Do I make every event for my kids? I'm on a plane hundreds of days a year. The answer is no. Am I there for the moments that matter? Yes.

I work hard building the company for the good of my family—and to make them proud—but also for the good of our employees and their families.

It's the family, and the life, I was born to live.

FAME

I don't know what it's like to *not* have a famous father.

My kids have always seen their grandfather on television. They also see me, Lara, and other family members on TV daily. It is just normal for them. And there is an innocence to their perspective that I truly enjoy.

They'll be eating in the kitchen or playing in the living room, look up at the TV, and see Grandpa, Mom, or Dad on it—focus for about three seconds, then go right back to Hot Wheels, breakfast, or playing with the dogs. They see us and they smile, with no concept of the ugliness of politics or the battles we fight. "Dad, Fox News is *sooo* boring . . . can we watch *Peppa Pig*?"

It reminds me that if most politicians had even a trace of that innocence and kindness, the world would be a far better place. More often than not, politicians have been a detriment to the family unit in this country—the erosion of community and faith, the curriculum taught in schools, and bad economic policy pressuring parents to work long hours or multiple jobs. Turning that tide is a huge part of Make America Great Again.

FAITH AND FAMILY TOGETHER

In September of 2017, when Lara went into labor with Luke, the Secret Service whisked her into armored vehicles with flashing lights and sirens screaming across town to New York–Presbyterian Hospital. It was the same scene with Carolina two years later. As bizarre as it is to have guys with machine guns standing guard outside the delivery room, this is the world that has always surrounded them. Not only are they desensitized to it, they know nothing else. I grew up in a similar way, in a larger-than-life family, but without the political insanity and 24-7 security.

A White House historian told me that Luke and Carolina were among the first grandchildren to be baptized in the White House. Talk about worlds coming together—family, faith, and politics. They were baptized in the East Room right in front of the stunning fireplaces below the iconic portrait of Abraham Lincoln. For Lara and me, having Luke and Carolina baptized there just seemed natural. My father could leave the Chinese delegation, or whatever the meeting of the day, and Luke and Carolina could feel the beauty of a building, and a movement that was now engrained in their DNA.

After the baptism, my father picked up his new grandson and held him for a photo. Right on cue, and still dripping with water, Luke started to cry. Melania turned to him with a smile and took charge. "Donald, *you* run the country," she said as she gently took Luke and cradled him in her arms.

And speaking of a mother's care, there are few people more meaningful in my life than Dorothy, an Irish nanny turned second mother to Don, Ivanka, and me—who still works with our family four decades later. She taught me many valuable lessons. Perhaps the best one was the value of prayer. Both of my parents expressed faith in their own way, but Dorothy—or "Dot-Dot," as I called her from infancy—made sure I knew God in her perfectly Gaelic sort of way. I will always hear her voice.

Eric, let us pray.

Now I lay me down to sleep,
I pray the Lord my soul to keep.
If I should die before I wake,
I pray the Lord my soul to take.
Amen.

Followed by:

There are four corners to my bed,
Four angels overhead,
Matthew, Mark, Luke, and John,
God bless this bed that I lie on.
Amen.

Today, Luke and Carolina (whose middle name is Dorothy) do not go to bed until they say a combination of the Pledge of Allegiance, the Lord's Prayer, and Dot-Dot's two prayers. Usually, we'll ask the kids,

"What's one nice thing you did for somebody today?" "What's one nice thing someone did for you today?" And "What are you thankful for?"

It's remarkable to see their little vocabularies come to life, for them to comprehend and express thankfulness, appreciation, love, and grace. Often we pray for my father, and for good to triumph over evil. We pray for my mom in heaven to watch over us. This is one constant in our lives, and theirs. If I'm traveling, it's very rare that I won't be present on Face-Time, regardless of where in the world I am at that moment, or the time zone. Our routine has been a second "light switch," one usually preceded by wrestling, kisses, and giggles. After prayers, the day is over. The lights, and their lights, are officially off.

I'm not sure they appreciate that tradition as much as Lara and I do, but one day they will.

GRANDPA

Right now, Lara and I are grateful that our kids just know Grandpa as Grandpa—someone who loves them, and whose face lights up whenever he sees them.

They also know that Grandpa was, and is again, president of the United States. Every year they comprehend the significance more. As familiar as it is, it's hard not to realize something as extraordinary as walking up the red-carpeted stairs onto the incredible Boeing 747. "Welcome aboard Air Force One, sir," the pilot greets Luke, shaking his little hand. Or Carolina waving to hundreds of thousands of spectators at the Daytona 500, while setting the pace lap in a limo affectionately known as the Beast—with six inches of bulletproof glass and armor—as the Thunderbirds flew overhead and a pack of forty NASCAR machines roared behind in pursuit.

As much as Lara and I have worked to shield Luke and Carolina from indoctrination and media, we do influence them in our own ways. "Grandpa is a great president who loves America. He's tough as nails—like you are." I make sure they also know how proud they should be of their mother, and Lara tells them the same about me.

Our kids also know that we've stood together as a family, and we always will. One value I always reinforce to Luke and Carolina when we are all together is "You two *never* break apart. No matter what, you always stick together. Luke, always protect your sister." I've seen it so many times in political, and nonpolitical, families—kids who aren't proud of their parents, and who don't realize how much they sacrifice for them.

I could never imagine my kids not being proud of Lara and me, today or decades from now. It would be devastating, especially given how hard we have worked and the attacks we withstood. Every family is different, and everyone makes their own choices for their own reasons. But I can't help but say that I have never seen adult children of any other president both fight *and* take the arrows that I have. Of course, sometimes the kids are young, as in Barron's case and in the case of Malia and Sasha Obama, and should be kept out of the spotlight. I am grateful I was old enough, and responsible enough, to stand together through the siege with our father. In politics, that's a unicorn.

FLIPPING THE SWITCH

Everyone has good days and bad days at work, but I try not to bring those home with me.

"How was your day, Eric?"

"Well, my father's mug shot is trending. . . . They're trying to bankrupt our company and imprison our employees . . . and I was just barred from doing business in New York for three years, despite doing absolutely nothing wrong.[2] It was wonderful, thanks for asking!"

It's probably a protection mechanism. I'm not necessarily proud of this, but I've always had the ability to turn circumstances—and people—off.

Being able to "switch off" isn't about lacking emotion—it's about survival. When betrayal enters, emotional detachment becomes an asset, not a flaw. Some people self-destruct—they can't let it go. I'm usually unfazed. We've seen it all, from best friends to the strongest business relationship. Disappeared. Gone. You realize many aspects of life are fleeting, and some aren't worth fighting for. This mindset doesn't cheapen relationships—it refines them. If time is limited, then what you allow into your life should deserve to be there. I have enough friends.

That might sound cold, but it's not. Projects begin and end. And people come in and out of our lives. Time is our most valuable asset. Keeping this in the back of my mind actually helps me appreciate people *more*—and handle betrayal better.

I mentioned before how even people who shared our last name have betrayed us. Some were tempted by ten seconds of fame or an opportunity to monetize an election cycle. In the summer of 2025 I received a text from one of those family members. It read in part "You were right. I regret every day that I wrote that book."

Another person with a genuine love for helping kids in need, a person who I genuinely cared about and was honored to help . . . out of my life. Light switch off.

Mary Trump wrote a book, *Too Much and Never Enough: How My Family Created the World's Most Dangerous Man.* Give me an f-ing break. In my forty-one-year life, having virtually never missed a family meal with my father, I doubt I saw Mary more than five times, and only once that I recall during adulthood, when my father graciously invited her to the White House for my aunt's birthday dinner. I know the FedEx guy who delivers packages to my house substantially better than I know Mary Trump, and the same likely goes for my father and siblings.

People will always find a way to make a buck. I would later help spearhead a lawsuit and win a clear victory against her, but honestly, the whole charade impacted my father. He loved his brother, Mary's dad, a man he would always describe as the "best-looking guy you had ever seen." A man who, like my mom, would fall to alcoholism and crystallize my father's long aversion to drinking, drugs, and smoking.

Pick a team and have conviction—look at Michael Cohen, Anthony Scaramucci, Liz Cheney, John Bolton, and others. They now find themselves stranded in no-man's-land. Neither side sees them as allies, only as irrelevant relics. They lacked backbone and conviction. I can only imagine that's an awfully lonely world.

DESENSITIZED?

Lara and I want our kids to be happy, kind, *and tough.* For me, whether it was construction sites, the scrutiny of celebrity, the fray of my parents' public divorce, my mother's addiction, and spending summers in communist Czechoslovakia, the experiences gave me some—much needed—armor for life.

So many children of celebrities become basket cases because they've been coddled their entire lives. I'm not talking about young people with legitimate trauma or illness—I'm talking about those who were never made to work or learn a skill, who have been overly sheltered and thus can't compartmentalize real life. They have no internal strength to deal with adversity when it finally knocks on their door.

The recipe is hard, but Lara and I do what we can. Jujitsu? You better believe it. You never want to see your child get hurt, but you want to see him fight like hell on that mat, because that's life. Dirt bikes? I rode them my entire childhood, and I crashed. Often. It hurts. You bleed. It sucks in the moment, but again, that's life. Work? If you want something, go earn it. If you are good at it, you will succeed, if not you will fail. Then find something else to be good at. There are no free handouts.

Personally, I'm numb to all the nonsense. I compartmentalize it. My family all understands the game for exactly what it is. This lawfare and weaponization of government is . . . a game. It's not a fun game. It's not a nice game. It's higher stakes than any other political game in my lifetime. But it's a game.

Early in one of the many trials in New York, an attorney on our team, who the nation has come to know all too well, Alina Habba, called me. She had gotten her first negative story in the press *and* was parodied on *Saturday Night Live*. Alina was mortified and crying.

"Eric, did you see that story?"

Looking back, it was probably rude, but I just laughed.

"Habba, I'm the bubble boy on *Family Guy*, remember? I'm the 'dummy' with the fidget spinner every weekend on *Saturday Night Live*. Welcome to the major leagues, Alina. Politics are pretty simple. The more effective you are, the harder they hit. They see you on TV every night. You are out on those courthouse steps every day. You have developed an incredible voice and have ten times more backbone than any of your male counterparts, who never stood on those very steps—who never went in front of the camera. That's the swamp lashing out, trying to demean and exert control. Ignore them. You're doing great."

We are in this game because we are a threat to certain people, their pocketbooks, and their crazy ideas. Every time Adam Schiff says that we're Russian operatives, he's playing in his sick, political fantasy world. He knows damn well that Don, nor anyone else in our family, is a Russian operative, but there are people out there who actually believe him. In any other situation, where he didn't have congressional protections under the Speech or Debate Clause of the Constitution, Schiff would be sued for defamation. It's another variation of an October surprise—create a false, vicious story, spread it like wildfire, and by the time it's debunked, the damage has been done—the election is over and you have lost.

When we were little, Don used to push me to the ground, sit on me, and punch my arm over and over until it was black and blue. Don and I were inseparable, but we fought like animals. I remember going for my annual physical. Dr. Davis asked me to pull off my shirt, then gasped. "Oh my God, Eric, what happened to you?"

"That's from my older brother, Don."

"Eric, I know your brother, he's a wonderful boy, he wouldn't do that." Even back then Don had them all fooled.

But after a few months of being pinned and bruised, something happened. It stopped hurting. No more bruising. Maybe it was nerve damage, or maybe it was the realization that the more I let it bother me, the more he pounded. The same is true with the media, with social media, with campaigns, with politicians, with crooked lawyers and judges. It's inconvenient, it's insane, but over time, with the right attitude, you can become numb to the insanity.

Once I was taller than him, Don's pounding mysteriously stopped. And fighting back helps, too. Watching Don pick .177-caliber BBs out of his leg didn't make my arm hurt less, but it sure was satisfying.

The Art of the Deal: Have Fun
"I don't kid myself. Life is very fragile, and success doesn't change that. If anything, success makes it more fragile. Anything can change, without warning, and that's why I try not to take any of what's happened too seriously." —DJT[3]

PROUD OF OUR COMPANY

For the past ten years, much of my time has been invested in people—the thousands of great, hardworking men and women at the Trump Organization who do hospitality better than any company on the planet.

The Left's goal was not only to crush a political movement, they tried their best to shake us down and put us out of business. I saw wonderful employees—wonderful *people*—being subpoenaed and threatened, over and over, simply because they work for a company founded by Donald Trump. It was cruel.

I was in court in 2024 and a woman who has worked with our organization for decades was called to testify. She's strong, sweet, and motherly. When I first started working with the company, my cubicle was right outside her office. She had the office candy bowl on her desk. She walked into the courtroom, grabbed my hand, and blew a kiss. She does not have a dishonest bone in her body, and has never done anything wrong. But that's not the point. It's a game, remember? She didn't want to be there and I didn't want her to have to be there. She didn't sign up for any of this and didn't give a damn about politics. Yet she's one of hundreds of people in our company who've been harassed and pressured, despite doing absolutely nothing wrong. She was an absolute rock.

We have had countless employees threatened by far-left attorney generals and district attorneys. The messages, spoken and unspoken, were clear: "If you don't tell us something about Donald Trump, you are our target and you are going to jail."

Throughout the siege and especially in 2023 and 2024, I can't count the number of people who have come to me, tears in their eyes, asking if they should be concerned about losing their job. As one example that I often think about, late one Saturday evening I got a call from a wonderful woman and longtime member of our team. "Eric, I'm reading the headlines. I love you and this family, and no matter what, I am always here for you. But, please, if I'm going to lose my job, make sure I hear about it from *you* and not on TV."

As a kid I worked for her late husband, Vinny, on construction sites. I attended their wedding, they watched me grow, and I watched their son grow. I actually lived in their house for a summer while working at Seven

Springs. Later, I was the first one to get the call when Vinny collapsed while working on one of our construction sites. And I was there when she buried a father-like figure, a man whom I cared about deeply. The Trump Organization is not Marriott, we are not IBM—our employees are family. I know most of them well, including their kids and their spouses. I've officiated their weddings, and I have spoken at their funerals. I carry immense responsibility for them and their families.

When it comes to appreciating the emotional toll *they've* gone through, and still face, I flip that switch. *On.*

PROUD OF MY FAMILY

Despite the persistent attacks on our father, our family never broke, and that is remarkable. In fact, Don, Ivanka, and I just spoke before I began work on this chapter.

From hunting trips in the Arctic, sleeping on rocks and in the snow, catching salmon in zero-degree weather, and sitting in trees in the northeast with our bows, my camaraderie with Don and our mutual love of the outdoors is umatched. Don loves the fight and it's what he does best. His sense of humor knows no bounds, and lacks any perceivable filter.

Ivanka is a brilliant, caring person. She takes motherhood seriously. As polished as she is—never fumbling a word, carrying herself with tremendous poise—she is funny as hell (within trusted circles), which most will never see. She's a protector and I respect that. Similarly, her husband, Jared Kushner, has been a rock. More times than I can count, he has raised his hand to run into a fire for me. In politics you learn very quickly who shows up and who goes missing. Jared, and his father, are truly first-class people.

Tiffany is a beautiful person, and I would say she's the nicest of us all. She has a compassionate heart and it has been fun to be there in some really important moments of her life—as a brother, friend, and even a mentor a time or two, who could see the land mines and the viciousness of the world approaching. She is the first to roll her eyes at nonsense, and has always been present when it matters. At just twenty-two years old, Tiffany displayed remarkable courage by taking the stage at the 2016

RNC in Cleveland, confidently delivering her first political speech on one of the largest stages in the world. Eight years later she was at my side at the 2024 Republican National Convention as I cast the final ballot as a Florida delegate, which made our father the Republican candidate for president of the United States.

Melania has always done a remarkable job shielding Barron from the spotlight and unnecessary noise. School was always his focus in a world too often dominated by candidates parading their young children around for attention. Today, it's harder to shield his six-foot-nine frame and big personality. By the time he turned fifteen I was no longer the tallest in our family. I have a tremendous amount of respect for Barron and the young man he has turned out to be. He's respectful, funny, and smart, and I treasure our relationship.

I could imagine some families not being nearly as close, considering our unique blending. It was never forced. We genuinely love and care about each other. There are no "problem children." No drugs, no laptops from hell. Manners, loyalty, and respect run deep—as does work ethic.

I suppose we were all mutually desensitized to the madness, in a good way. I remember when Don, Ivanka, and I all started doing TV interviews, we would call or text each other with high-five emojis. "Great job. You rocked it!" But after a while it became normal, almost routine. I can't tell you the last time I got one of those calls.

Most of all, today, we love and respect and appreciate each other for who we are. We have all charted our own paths. We have all followed our own hearts, dreams, and desires. We've all created our own families, but we are still inseparable and remain unbreakable a decade later—despite being under siege.

WHY THIS BOOK?

Speaking of headlines, I'm certainly not looking for more media exposure.

Then why the hell are you writing this book, Eric?

First, despite all the news coverage around my father, I really don't believe most Americans grasp the extent of the corruption and hate that's been aimed at him, and those around him. Most people understandably tune out negativity and fake news. There's been so many attacks, including indictments and court cases, it's almost a full-time job to keep track.

Second, in the history of the Nation, I don't believe there has ever been someone who has been in the position I've been in: a thirty-three-year-old tasked with running a multibillion-dollar empire for the commander in chief—with thousands of employees, vendors, members, hotels, golf courses, residential buildings, commercial buildings, and tenants across the globe. I have navigated unthinkable attacks, COVID lockdowns, cancel culture, weaponization of our intelligence agencies—through over one hundred subpoenas, multiple Supreme Court cases, slanderous Russian smears, paid-for fictional dossiers, and foreign threats both personally and against our businesses.

Third, I owe it to the company, and the people who work so hard in the Trump Organization. Everyone associated with the company—including our excellent network of suppliers and contractors—has gone through hell because of the attacks. Whether they faced personal intimidation, or wondered if they would have a job because of the legal and financial setbacks, everyone held together. Whenever you hear about lawfare against my family and my company, I hope you'll consider how much it affects our wonderful family of employees.

Jimmy Carter had a peanut farm, and I'm pretty sure no Republicans ever tried to ruin his company. I have lived at the intersection of business and politics for the past ten years—running a great organization that shaped skylines across the world. No one in our nation's history has had to figure out how to walk the line between the executive branch and capitalism. It is my greatest hope that more businesspeople are elected to the White House—people who have built and created—not people dependent on government paychecks their entire career—and we need to fix the system so no future president is put through the same vengeful lawfare.

That's why we have stood before the Supreme Court time and again—fighting battles over executive privilege, statute of limitations, legal lawfare, the emoluments clause, campaign finance, and even the most basic rights to privacy.

Fourth, this book is for my kids, my siblings' kids, and future generations of our family. No family in history has gone through the combination of political, personal, and business attacks.

Luke and Carolina, your mom and I are fighting for you. Every day and night I wasn't home, I was working to build a stronger company for you. And your whole family was fighting to build a stronger country for you. We're Trumps—when something matters, we don't back down, we build, we fight, and we win. That's what we do.

I'm writing these stories because I'm proud of my family. Leading the Trump Organization through the siege was uncharted territory, and I hope this book does a good job charting the depths.

LARA

My wife amazes me every single day—always in ways I never see coming. I couldn't ask for a more amazing partner. As a mom, she miraculously juggles family, politics, business, her own media platform—all while on the Trump roller coaster, never missing our kids' soccer game or school play.

She stepped into Republican National Committee leadership with unmatched class. Under her watch, they cleaned house and multiplied fundraising. She zeroed in on four priorities: turning out low-propensity voters early, cracking down on voter fraud, raising record sums, and making every dollar count.

Early on, I talked with her about the job. "Listen, honey. This is a crappy position, to tell you the truth. This is being an NFL kicker—you'll either be a hero or a zero and there's nothing in between." She didn't need the job—she didn't have to step up—but thank God she did.

Lara has guts, she has backbone, and she truly did an amazing job.

Alex Floyd and the Democratic National Committee's rapid response team put out this shameless hit: "Her new nepo title only ensures that the RNC will keep putting up disastrous fundraising numbers and continue to underperform in election after election."[4]

On election night 2024, I would have been posting F— Yous to all the haters and doubters. "Record fundraising, overperforming in every state, winning every swing state, and crushing the Democrats in a popular-vote landslide." But Lara carried herself with far more grace.

She and Michael Whatley brought articulate leadership and relentless focus on election integrity, making sure the 2024 election was "too big to rig." Their team of poll watchers, voter registration volunteers, and attorneys made a huge difference. Lara was also the biggest proponent of early voting—a controversial subject among Republicans who treasure voting on Election Day. Lara and the RNC moved millions of people to the polls before that Tuesday. Aside from the candidate, it was the single greatest strategic change that would rewrite the GOP playbook—reshaping the party's ground game and closing the early-vote gap that had long favored Democrats. Donald Trump's campaign proved that with the right focus and tactics, the Republican Party could compete—and win—where it had previously struggled.

Donald Trump won the 2024 election, but Lara Trump and team got out the vote and kept it from being stolen. I am extremely proud of her.

LOYALTY ALWAYS WINS

I am in this fight, not because I *have* to be, but because I *want* to be.

When I was a kid, a friend shared a story about his grandmother. She gathered all her grandchildren and handed the youngest a bundle of pencils tied tightly together. She asked each of them to try breaking the bundle—and one by one, they failed. Then she untied the pencils and gave each child a single pencil to break, which they did with ease. That simple lesson stuck with me. It's why we stand strong—and why we stick together.

Just like those pencils, the same principle holds true for us as citizens. Alone, we can be broken or held back—but together, united as a movement, we are unbreakable. I want America to win. I want America to be first. We should be the best—absolutely unstoppable in everything we do. This is how we will Make America Great Again!

I truly hope Lara and I can instill in our children the same fight, the same passion, the same loyalty my family has shown. Nothing would make me more proud than to have them by my side, on the same stage—celebrating wins, supporting me in challenging times, and being unwavering in their convictions. That would be the ultimate achievement as a father.

I am proud of my family, not because we won. But because of how we fought.

CHAPTER 13

FIGHT, FIGHT, FIGHT

"Absolutely nothing changes."
—MY FATHER, TO ME, JULY 14, 2024

I wasn't there in Butler, Pennsylvania, on July 13, 2024. It was the Saturday before the Republican National Convention and I had gone home in hopes of getting my life together before what would inevitably be a sleepless week ahead.

Lara and I were watching the rally on TV with Luke and Carolina on our laps. I was mid-email, watching the rally out of the corner of my eye, when the crack of gunshots caught my attention. To me, that sound is unmistakable, one I've heard millions of times. I saw my father grab his ear and crouch in pain as all hell broke loose. We instantly turned our kids away from the screen as Lara grabbed them and ran them out of the room.

In that moment, I was in two places at once—at home trying to protect my kids, and there in Butler, right beside my father. I saw the blood. *Oh God! There's blood running down his face. Where is he shot? His head? His torso?* He was wearing his signature dark suit and it would be impossible to see a chest wound through the dark fabric. In an instant, he was down on the platform, covered by Secret Service agents. I was terrified, and powerless.

The bullet came from about 130 yards away. A chip shot for a rifle with modern-day optics. On a *whim*, my father decided to go off script and say something about immigration. He turned his head to look at the large screen on his right, which displayed a chart detailing invasion at our southern border. In that instant, the bullet hit his ear. Had he not done so—had there been even a momentary gust of wind—American history would have changed forever.

The huge American flag that hung over the crowd twisted into the form of an angel. Time stood still. Every aspect, still being broadcast to the world in high resolution.

My phone exploded with calls and texts, a nonstop tidal wave of worry and chaos. I was reeling, standing inches from the screen, trying to wrap my head around the scene and attempting to see if there was a noticeable wound.

One text stood out, from a dear friend, Tony from Pittsburgh, "ET, You need to get here. Are you in Westchester? My plane is on the way. It will be there in an hour to pick you up." I'll never forget that message that was true friendship.

I knew everyone in the political apparatus, almost everyone in those vehicles, and every agent on that stage. And I knew that every moment they lay there increased the chances that I would never see him stand back up.

For what felt like an eternity, the Secret Service swarmed, their Counter Assault team charged onto the stage in full ballistic gear, rarely seen publicly, while the crowd was frozen in a haze of fear and disbelief.

Finally, the swarm of bodies around my father rose. *He's standing! Thank God.*

But in a flash, amid twisted bodies and the dark blue suits of the Secret Service, I saw blood on his face and hand. The pain was real, but so was his determination—unyielding and fierce. Then, in one of the most heroic moments in political history—a moment that would forever define him and his American spirit—he stood tall, bloodied, pumped his fist in the air, and shouted, "Fight! Fight! Fight!" A powerful display of strength that brought our family and the nation to tears.

Emerging from the silence, I could hear an entire nation jump up and cheer. "USA! USA! USA!"

They just tried to kill him, and they failed.

Months earlier, in several TV interviews, I had expressed my fear that once they ran out of dirty tricks they would stop at nothing. "It wouldn't surprised me if they tried physical harm." I was written off as an alarmist, but the progression of the attacks was clear. They smeared him, they impeached him twice, they weaponized law enforcement against him, they spied on him, they tried to bankrupt him, they removed his right of free speech, they took his name off ballots, and they charged him ninety-one times, threatening jail time for bogus crimes. Then, they tried to kill him.

Unfortunately my intuition had, once again, been correct.

I took a deep breath as I watched the door close on the heavily armored Chevrolet Suburban; trucks our family had become so accustomed to, reinforced with heavy steel, bulletproof glass, run-flat tires, all designed to withstand the heaviest attacks. I knew that he was in a vessel of protection. We still didn't know the severity of his injuries as he was transported eleven miles to Butler Memorial Hospital.

I called Walt, a friend, a United States Navy veteran, and the person who served as my father's personal aide and valet—someone I knew would be calm in the chaos.

"Eric, he's hit, but he's going to be okay. I'll call you from the hospital."

Forty-five minutes later, my father called me from the ICU. He was remarkably calm, as he always is in the most horrible circumstances, and made one of his signature comments about having "one hell of an earache."

I was relieved, but enraged. I still am.

I chose the title of this book long before that horrible day, not knowing how fitting it would be more than a year later. A siege is where a person or group is targeted, surrounded, and attacked with the goal of total submission or destruction. Butler, Pennsylvania, was just the next step in the escalation. The attempt was exactly what they always wanted: his total and final removal.

But divine intervention kept my father alive. That perfect American flag, rolled up like an angel right above his head. In that moment of gratitude, I realized something else. I knew we had just won the 2024 presidential election.

> "Thank you to everyone for your thoughts and prayers yesterday, as it was God alone who prevented the unthinkable from happening. We will FEAR NOT, but instead remain resilient in our Faith and Defiant in the face of Wickedness. Our love goes out to the other victims and their families. We pray for the recovery of those who were wounded, and hold in our hearts the memory of the citizen who was so horribly killed."
> —DONALD J. TRUMP, JULY 14, 2024, THE MORNING AFTER
> THE ATTEMPTED ASSASSINATION

SECRETS?

After hearing his voice, the shock wore off and the rage took over.

The Secret Service agents on that stage are fantastic people. I know every single one of them personally; and privately, all would call Lara and me more than protectees. We're friends. The female agent, who heroically shielded my father on that stage in the infamous photo, was on my detail for three years. She's one of the greatest, most professional people you'll ever meet, and seeing her attacked—a person who ran into a wall of fire—was beyond infuriating. (Side note: she could outshoot all the guys on my former detail, which always put a smile on my face.)

I trust very few people with a 202 phone number—the area code for Washington, D.C.—but Sean Curran, my father's longtime detail leader and now twenty-eighth director of the United States Secret Service, had been with my father through thick and thin and genuinely loves our family. The feeling is mutual.

The two agents on his rear flank, let's just say are both well known to Lara and me, in very personal ways. They have been by my side all across the country and all around the world. I won't use their names, but every single one of those heroic agents behind the podium would have taken a bullet for my father that day. And they almost did.

These are individuals with spouses, young kids, and their own dreams and aspirations. Yet they ran into the fire, with disregard for their lives and personal protection. At the same time, I knew, and they knew, that the very agency they worked for almost got my father, and all of them, killed that day.

It breaks my heart to say this, but the eighth floor of the Secret Service became as political as any other agency in the years leading up to 2024.

Let me clear up the smoke screen about "requests for additional protection." Personally, I had several conversations with the agency in 2024 to raise the alarm. Moreover, the most senior managers of our campaign, who were as passionate and concerned as I was, had several "heart-to-hearts" with leaders in the Secret Service. The writing was on the wall. "He is the biggest target in the world and these people will stop at nothing," I said on multiple occasions. "It takes one guy, moderately capable of shooting a rifle at a golf course. . . ." How right I would be.

Those requests were ignored. No changes were made, to the bewilderment of the agents assigned to my father.

U.S. Secret Service director Kimberly Cheatle's claim that "no requests" were denied was a flat-out lie.[1] I know this because I made many of those requests personally.

Another lie that Cheatle would go on to offer was that no agents were stationed on the roof of the ARG International Inc. research building, located just outside the secure perimeter of the rally at the Butler Farm Show Grounds, from which Thomas Matthew Crooks fired, because of its "sloped" roof, which posed a "safety factor." *Seriously?* My little kids would have had no problem walking around on that roof. The Counter Sniper team was on a nearby roof that had a substantially steeper slope, yet this is the "explanation" she gave to Congress.

I'll stop short of getting into the role of DEI. We all know what this was: incompetence. The backlash, coupled with a July 22, 2024, House Oversight Committee hearing, led to bipartisan calls for Cheatle's resignation. She stepped down the next day.

The day after the attempted assassination, I did dozens of media interviews, trying to somehow balance on the tightrope of defending incredibly brave people in an organization that I loved—while knowing that Secret Service leadership failures and failure to secure the site were beyond negligent. They led to the death of an amazing man, Corey Comperatore, who died protecting his family from the gunfire, and two others found themselves in critical condition.

All of it, including the bureaucratic response, is unforgivable.

SHOOTING STRAIGHT

At a very young age, my grandfather Dedo (which means "Grandfather" in Czech) got Don and me into the outdoors. Like real estate and golf on my father's side, the love of hunting, shooting, fishing, and the wilderness was ingrained from our mother. My first rifle, like so many kids in our country, was a simple Ruger 10/22 with an iron sight. We were hooked.

A "brick" of .22-LR ammo was the best gift either Don or I could have received. The shooting sports shaped me, taught me discipline, responsibility, and focus, and has been my greatest passion and hobby my entire life—as unconventional as that may be for a "city boy" born and raised in a golden skyscraper.

In the years that followed, I competed in—or simply immersed myself in—every aspect of the shooting sports: shotgun, skeet, trap, and sporting clays; benchrest, small bore, service rifle, pistol, and bow; and just about anything else that would fly through the air at high speed. My true passion, however, lies in the art and science of precision long-range rifle—shooting targets well over a thousand yards away, building rifles from scratch, perfecting load development, and mastering the complex dance of wind, environmental conditions, and ballistics. My friends will tell you, if I'm not working, I'm shooting.

Tiger Woods will make a twelve-inch putt, a thousand out of a thousand times. Those are the same odds as a competent marksman shooting a modern rifle at an adult-size silhouette, lying prone from 130 yards away. It's a chip shot. It almost can't be missed. *Almost.*

The fact that an agency with a $3 billion budget allowed someone on the roof of a building—in plain sight—130 yards from Donald Trump defies explanation. As does the fact that the shooter *missed* from that range.

You would think this is Protection 101: *Keep people with range finders and rifles off roofs—and away from innocent crowds and away from the 45th president and front-runner to be the 47th president of the United States.*

A SOLEMN THANK-YOU

On behalf of myself, my family, and our great nation, I extend my deepest gratitude to the U.S. Secret Service Counter Sniper Teams—especially the agent who took that lone, decisive shot. I've had the privilege of shooting alongside them, running their final qualification course with their newest cadets, and I'm truly honored to call several of them friends.

In the world of precision marksmanship, the Secret Service Counter Sniper teams are unparalleled. Their skill was proven beyond a doubt with a snap headshot that neutralized a threat and saved countless lives in Butler.

To those heroes that day, you know who you are. *Thank you.* You are the best of the agency—the very ones who should be on that once-politicized eighth floor.

I know that you are as pissed, so am I. You were given no apology. Worse, you were told to bite your tongues while they watched a DEI hire talk "sloped roof" bullshit. Your professionalism allowed you to keep a unified front. You, and the agents on that stage, are heroes.

To the lone female agent, you are as good as anyone in the Secret Service, and everyone who matters knows this.

And to the family of Corey Comperatore: our family thinks about your loss every time we think about Butler, which happens to be every day.

We love you all.

EVERYTHING HIDDEN WILL BE REVEALED

The truth will come out. Like the raid on Mar-a-Lago, this is intensely personal. Even as I write this, we know more about a deported gang member from El Salvador than we do about the man who tried to kill Donald Trump. They managed to break into the phones of every innocent January 6 protester, but couldn't figure out who the guy was who tried to kill a president? My father has publicly expressed his "satisfaction" with the explanation, fully aware of the complex web of implications involved—including, most likely, national security concerns. In light of what happened, he has shown remarkable calm and grace, a quality I deeply admire. This is one of the very few times I have found myself in respectful disagreement—not with him, but with the situation. I am not satisfied, and neither is this nation. A twenty-year-old, armed with multiple cell phones, attempted to kill my father—the father of the greatest political movement in American history—from an unmanned, unprotected rooftop. I remain totally unsatisfied.

But in July 2024 there was no time to process all the events and revelations. We had a campaign to run, rallies to hold, an election to win, and a convention was just a day away.

NOTHING CHANGES

The original plan was for our whole family to go to Milwaukee for the Republican National Convention at 3 p.m. on Sunday. Between media interviews, I called my father that morning.

"Are you *okay*? Why don't you just fly out tomorrow?"

"Nothing changes, honey. Let's go as planned," he said, as if *nothing* had happened.

After we landed in Wisconsin, I rode in the Beast with him as we watched thousands of people along the route, waving flags and expressing their love. The next day at the convention, as the lead delegate from Florida, I had the honor of announcing my vote that secured Donald J. Trump's nomination as the Republican Candidate for 47th President of the United States. Forty-eight hours earlier, I didn't know if he was alive.

Life can change in the blink of an eye. Everything can flip in a moment, and when it does, it leaves no part of you untouched. I have been in hundreds of big rallies with my father, but the volume, and emotion, in the cheers that day was like nothing I've ever heard. A few hours later, he entered the arena, greeted by even more deafening applause, cheers, and tears—and hundreds of people wearing white patches on their right ear.

And I noticed something different about my father. He was somber and resolute.

"I wasn't supposed to be here," he said in his speech later that week. To which the crowd immediately answered, "Yes you are! Yes you are!"

Prior to July 13, 2024, I thought we had seen it all as a family. And through it all, I watched my father remain steadfast and determined. After a bullet came within a half inch of ending his life, I watched him stand up and yell, "Fight! Fight! Fight!"

This was not just a defining moment in the campaign, but a defining moment in American history. No matter what challenges he faces, his resolve never wavers, his spirit never breaks, and his commitment to this country remains unshakable.

"I wanted to keep speaking, but I just got shot."
—DJT[2]

VICE PRESIDENT VANCE

The Monday morning of the convention, I met with my father at his hotel, the Pfister, in Milwaukee. I hadn't gone there to talk about the vice presidential pick—but it was the obvious elephant in the room. The final three names were North Dakota Governor Doug Burgum, Florida senator Marco Rubio, and Ohio senator J.D. Vance. Contrary to popular belief, those choices were still being debated in Milwaukee.

"Who do you think it should be?" my father asked me.

I didn't answer his question, but instead voiced my annoyance and frustration over the "lobbying" from special interest groups and their handlers. Every day our phones were blowing up with messages of "Hey, just called to see how you're doing. . . . By the way, you should really consider . . ." People shamelessly pressed their agendas, and I found the opinions both interesting and amusing, especially coming from certain individuals who had previously "pushed" candidacies like Nikki Haley against my father in the primaries.

"So who do you like?"

"I want whoever *you* want. They are all incredible people who would do a great job. But this person will be by your side day and night. Who do you enjoy being around the most? Who has the strength and vision to carry the torch forward for the next four years? Trust your instincts—that's the choice that truly matters."

"J.D.," he replied. "Let's write up the post." It was déjà vu of the scene in Indianapolis, eight years prior, where I sat with my father in Indianapolis the night he chose Mike Pence.

There were no focus groups or polling. No pandering to various demographics. What J.D. brought to the table in terms of qualifications and appeal are simply a bonus, not the reason for the choice. My father never makes decisions based on politics. He never played the DEI game; he picked who he thought would be best for the job, agnostic of social pressures and influence.

Now it was time to focus on my speech.

TRUMP-A-MANIA

Thursday night—the electrifying finale of the RNC Convention in Milwaukee—was nothing short of wild. Hulk Hogan owned the stage and the crowd loved it. Then he ripped off his shirt.

"Let Trump-a-mania run wild, brother! Let Trump-a-mania rule again! Let Trump-a-mania make America great again!"

I grew up watching Hulk on WWE, *Saturday Night's Main Event*, battling icons like André the Giant, Randy "Macho Man" Savage, and Sgt. Slaughter. He was a childhood hero. Standing backstage with him before I went on, all I could think was, *How did I land on a stage with Hulk Hogan? How the hell do I follow this steroid-fueled show?* I laughed to myself, in my perfectly pressed suit.

At the last minute, my silent prayer was answered. They put in Franklin Graham, son of the late Billy Graham, to do the invocation—the perfect buffer between the wild show and the seriousness of a son's words that would follow.

> The whole world saw your strength as you stood up, wiped the blood off your face, put your fist in the air—and in a moment that will be remembered as one of the most courageous acts in the history of American politics—shouted, "FIGHT, FIGHT, FIGHT!"
>
> I am honored to be your son! I'm honored to speak to our great Nation tonight.
>
> You are a true leader. You epitomize strength.
>
> Our country loves you! Our country appreciates you! Our country misses you!
>
> And on November 5th, our country will re-elect you as the 47th President of the United States of America!
>
> Good night Milwaukee! God bless you all!

I have had the honor of speaking at three conventions, but that evening was by far the most meaningful. Just days earlier, we had come within a breath of losing him. Now, I was the family member standing before the nation, speaking just before my father took the stage. The moment was charged with meaning—it was time for victory.

OUR PARTY WAS READY TO WIN

We understand the system, the corruption, what works and what doesn't. When we first stepped out on those stairs overlooking Arlington National Cemetery in 2017, we didn't fully comprehend what was in front of us.

We do now. So do you.

And so did the Republican National Committee. Finally. On March 8, 2024, when Lara Trump and Michael Whatley were elected as co-chairs, they fought to win. Within weeks they announced one of many important initiatives to make sure the 2024 election was dramatically more secure and accurate. "Every ballot. Every precinct. Every processing center. Every county. Every battleground state. We will be there," said co-chair Lara Trump in the RNC's announcement. "The RNC is hiring hundreds of election integrity staff across the map—more than ever before because our Party will be recruiting thousands of more observers to protect the vote in 2024."[3]

In my totally unbiased opinion, the new Republican leadership did a legendary job in 2024. Republicans, and all Americans, needed to have their eyes wide open regarding election integrity. A month after the RNC announced plans to monitor the vote, the Department of Justice released a revealing statement.

"Today, Attorney General [Merrick] Garland convened a meeting of the Election Threats Task Force, underscoring the Department's #ElectionSecurity efforts to safeguard election workers—whether elected, appointed, or volunteer—from threats and intimidation."[4]

Any guesses about why the Biden DOJ didn't like the idea of increased scrutiny, and were ready to conflate "observation" with "intimidation"?

SEPTEMBER SURPRISE

On September 15, 2024, my father was playing a round of golf at the Trump International Golf Club in West Palm Beach, Florida—a course I know all too well. As he approached the sixth hole, a sharp-eyed Secret Service agent spotted the lunatic hiding in the bushes, rifle in hand.

I was shooting a few miles north on I-95 with a dear friend, a Palm Beach County Sheriff SWAT officer. We had just packed up for the day and he got a head start back home. Ten minutes later, he called me.

"Hey, this just came across the radio. Someone just tried to take another shot at Pops."

Not again. "I'm heading there now," I said, and jumped into my truck.

I didn't have much time to process any emotion. I wanted to get on the road and figure out what was happening, but all I could think was, *He's running out of lives.*

A few minutes later Austin called back. "The gunman is northbound on I-95. I just did a U-turn and I'm waiting for him."

On the side of the highway, Austin had pulled his M4 duty rifle from the back of his truck, spotted the vehicle, and pursued the suspect. In conjunction with officers from Martin County, one of my closest friends, and a person I was with minutes earlier, would be the officer who arrested the man who was accused of planning to kill my father.

Minutes later, I drove by the scene, helicopters hovering just overhead, the suspect's hands out the window, dozens of long guns pointed at every inch of him. For anyone who knows Martin County, those boys don't play games. The would-be assassin was out of chances, and I was less than fifty yards away. It took every ounce of strength to not drive across the median and ram his car at full speed, in a scene that in my head would have been reminiscent of Michael Douglas's movie *Falling Down*.

A few months later, I proudly presented my friend with an "Officer of the Year" award with the Palm Beach County Sheriff's Office. A full-circle moment that defies all odds.

STILL SEARCHING

We still don't know much about either accused attempted assassin. What we do know (or do we?) is that the Butler shooter was cremated a few days after his death, and the "steep" roof of that building was carefully cleaned off by law enforcement. I'm not a conspiracy theorist, but that doesn't seem like the normal protocol for a case of this magnitude.

All I can say is that there appear to be many who have no real interest in uncovering the truth about either of these individuals. Everybody lawyered up and the information was locked down. It raises the question: Why? The FBI spent years piecing together cases against civilians taking pictures in the Capitol on January 6, yet we have almost no photos of the shooters? No real effort has been made. No message has been communicated. No phones were "infiltrated."

This leaves the entire country, and world, once again questioning the very law enforcement agencies that were once so revered and respected. I hope those who care will get to the bottom of this, and other facets of the siege.

SHOCK AND AWE

As with every campaign—and every business endeavor before it—my father was ahead of the curve in 2024. Recognizing the growing influence of long-form podcasts and the deep bias of the mainstream media, he shifted focus and placed major emphasis on direct-to-audience conversations that bypassed the filters of the press. Theo Von, Mark Calaway ("the Undertaker"), Andrew Schulz on *Flagrant*, Adin Ross, *Bussin' with the Boys*, Lex Fridman, *Nelk Boys*, Logan Paul, *All-In Podcast*, Shawn Ryan, *Full Send Podcast*, Dan Bongino, the Patrick Bet-David podcast, Tyrus, and ultimately, Joe Rogan. Even though YouTube appeared to blatantly shadow ban the full Rogan interview, it received over 50 million views, in addition to tens of millions of views on other platforms and clips. All this unfolded while Kamala was reportedly paying podcasters and celebrities to boost her appearances, and shows like *60 Minutes* scrambled to piece together a coherent twenty-minute segment for her.[5][6]

I still smile when I think about my father at McDonald's, and how he became the first presidential candidate to "work" there—an opportunity to rightfully mock Kamala's false claim that she had once been employed by the fast-food giant. My father loves McDonald's and happens to know the menu as well as any. So why not jump in with those who work so hard?

After Joe Biden dismissed our supporters as "garbage," Donald Trump seized the moment—holding a press conference from the cab of a garbage truck and speaking to a sold-out rally wearing a bright orange safety vest. It was another opportunity to show Americans that he stands with them, while humorously ridiculing career politicians and their elitist attitudes. The campaign relentlessly broke every rule, in the best way possible. All the fundraising in the world couldn't pay for the earned media from those stops. McDonald's would say it was the most viral moment in their company's history.

But for me, the defining moment of October was our return to Butler, Pennsylvania—where I had the honor of standing alongside Lara and
speaking to a massive, fired-up crowd—84 days after the event that
nearly cost my father his life. It was more than a rally; it was a homecoming filled with love, emotion, and unmistakable momentum.

"This isn't politics . . . this is a movement of absolute love, of hundreds of millions of people who want to save the United States, who
want to keep our country number one at absolutely everything we do.
And that's why we're gonna reelect Donald Trump as the 47th president
of the United States." The reaction to my words from the crowd was
overwhelming.

My father was eager to return to Butler. That place represented more
than a rally location, it was a moment in history—a message to supporters, staff, family, and even to himself. "They cannot break us."

Car windows all across the parking lots were adorned with a cartoon
image of my father, defiantly raising a middle finger, with the words "You
missed."

To say I was proud is an understatement. The crowd was endless—a
sea of people that must have approached a hundred thousand. Lara and I
sat in the front row with the wife and daughters of Corey Comperatore,
and we barely held back tears as Donald J. Trump walked out on that
stage once again.

Months earlier, Corey's widow, Helen, told us about what he said to
her on the morning of July 13, 2024. "My husband kept saying, 'He's
gonna call me up onstage. You're gonna hear him. He's gonna say, "Corey,
get on up here!"'" Days later at the RNC, when my father had his fire-
fighter uniform placed on the stage as a tribute, and as he offered heartfelt words of support and consolation, she realized, "There's his moment.
He's up on stage."[7]

There were many unforgettable moments that summer and during
the convention, but that one was among the most moving and profound.

And then—true to form—Donald Trump did what only he can do.
In the face of all that had happened, just when no one expected it, he
brought levity. It was the same instinct he had when we were kids—me,
Don, and Ivanka—and the same one that surfaced moments after he was
shot three months earlier.

He smiled, looked at the crowd and opened his speech, "As I was saying . . ." The crowd erupted: "USA! USA! USA!"

This was the fighter America needed. The man would not be held down. In my mind, the election had been won.

WHY WE FIGHT

Just a few nights before the election, as we knelt beside our children's beds to say our prayers, our five-year-old daughter, Carolina, looked up at Lara and me with tired eyes and asked a question that stopped us cold: "Mom, Dad . . . when is this election over? I just want my parents back." It felt like a knife to the heart—pure, innocent truth cutting through the whirlwind we had been living in.

In that single sentence, she said what families feel but rarely say. She missed us—not the version of us always on the road or behind a podium, but just Mom and Dad. And in that moment, we were reminded why we do any of this at all. Our children—Carolina and her brother, Luke—are the reason we fight. For their future. For their freedom. For a country worthy of their dreams.

But this time, they weren't just watching us fight. They were part of it. They carried the weight in their own little ways—the missed dinners, the long goodbyes, the whispered prayers when we were gone. This election wasn't just ours. It belonged to them, too. And they felt it—deeply.

CHAPTER 14

SUCCESS AS REVENGE

"I don't care about the revenge thing.
I know they usually use the word revenge.
Will there be revenge?
My revenge will be success."
—DONALD J. TRUMP, FEBRUARY 2024[1]

I was extremely confident going into Election Day—but then again, I didn't think we could "lose" in 2020. Everything pointed to another resounding victory, yet we were both aware and numb to the system, to the games, the mail-in ballots, and the numerical discrepancies witnessed four years earlier.

My father led *four* rallies on November 4 and into the early morning of Election Day. When every other political candidate would have hung it up—he was taking the stage. Yes, he was campaigning for votes, but in many ways this was a thank-you tour to the Americans who had fought with him. No political candidate has ever fought harder. He was a machine. He was unrelenting.

"This is the end of an era," I said to Lara. In the past nine years I had done hundreds and hundreds of rallies, thousands of TV and radio appearances, countless fundraisers, robo calls, visited every victory office, relentlessly campaigned in every swing state, and appeared on almost every podcast my schedule allowed. Win or lose, we had nothing left to give.

Not only was the pressure on for my father—it was on for Lara, too. If there was ever a person whose professional reputation would rise or fall based on the outcome of that night, it was Lara, as co-chair of the Republican National Committee. Unlike 2016 and 2020, it wasn't just about my father winning—it was about my wife winning as well. It was about redemption. Karma for all they had done to him, and to me. His legacy, and ours, was deeply tied to the fight at hand. It was the ultimate referendum.

My father took the stage in Grand Rapids at 12:12 a.m.—walking the red carpet with Lee Greenwood's famous "God Bless the USA" blaring. As the navy-blue curtains opened, tens of thousands of supporters in the Van Andel Arena watched him walk onto that stage for the last time. The crowd went crazy. This was it. In mere hours, people would show up to the polls by the millions all across the nation. This would be the last campaign rally for Donald J. Trump.

At 2:05 a.m. he called us up onstage with him.

"My great children—Don, Eric, Tiffany, Lara . . . This group here, they are so committed—they didn't have to do this—I guess we all didn't have to do it—but they want to see our country be so great and so strong . . ."

He turned to me and asked, "Would you like to say a few words?"

I stepped forward, took the mic. "Good morning, Michigan," I began.

Who else could have this many people at 2:00 a.m.—only Donald Trump! I have watched the hell they have put him through over the past ten years, the fake impeachments, the dossiers, the Russia hoax, going after his Supreme Court justices, censoring him, taking away his First Amendment right, trying to take him off the ballots in states across the country, raiding his home, and yet he comes out every single day and he fights, and he fights and he fights. And when other candidates have packed it in for the night, you know who is standing on the stage at 2 a.m.—Donald Trump.

America, it is time for us to pick our fighter and it's that man right there—and I can tell you as a son, as a family, we have never been more proud of a person in our life. I have never been more proud to stand on a stage with somebody in my life. He is the most remarkable man I know. And I promise you I will be on

this stage with you until the end of earth because I truly believe
in you, I believe in what you are doing for this country and what
you are doing for our children and you are going to save democracy in the United States and you are going to keep peace in the
world and I love you. And we are proud of you. Let's Make America Great Again.

At 3:30 a.m., we got on Trump Force One for the ride back to Florida. None of us slept. He played iPad DJ during the entire flight—Sinéad
O'Connor, Pavarotti, and everything in between. When "November
Rain" by Guns N' Roses started blasting throughout the cabin, I flashed
back to Ivanka's teen years. She had a signed Axl Rose poster in her room
in Trump Tower—her first crush, with tattoos, the trademark bandanna
tied around his head, ripped jeans, and leather jacket.

We touched down in Palm Beach at 5:29 a.m. We'd left everything on
the field. Now we waited as America would head to the polls.

ELECTION NIGHT

Exhausted, we gathered at Mar-a-Lago to watch the results. The scene
was a surreal combination of a club I ran, a political movement I had
fought for, and the father I adored.

The campaign team sat in the offices above the Mar-a-Lago ballroom, where the partygoers were sipping champagne. It was a small
group. We had purposely kept it that way, telling very few people, not
wanting the inevitable distraction and fanfare.

Susie Wiles was a brilliant campaign manager—a great operator
who, unlike everyone else in politics, never wanted credit, notoriety, or
publicity. She brought a trademark calm to the room.

By the way, isn't it ironic that a presidential candidate repeatedly
accused of "sexism" and "never being seen around strong, intelligent
women"—as Mark Cuban foolishly claimed on ABC's *The View* in October 2024—actually made history by having not one, but two female
campaign managers: Susie Wiles and her predecessor, Kellyanne Conway, the first women ever to hold that role in a U.S. presidential campaign? All that slander is a complete fabrication. Susie and Kellyanne

are icons, trailblazers, and winners, through and through. The same is true for the many amazing female general managers running our golf properties—so uncommon in the golf and hospitality industries, but not in our company.

The mood was a cautious optimism. Every indicator was promising . . . but we had been burned before.

As we watched the evening's reporting, we braced ourselves for the early voting counts—a tactic that Lara had worked so effectively on promoting and implementing. In the past two elections, our opponents had always crushed us in these mail-in ballots. But this time was different. As we started seeing early vote tallies in the swing states I turned to Lara and gave her a look filled with quiet gratitude. "You did it." She faced relentless pushback on early voting—from Republicans clinging stubbornly to outdated strategies from the 1990s. But she never wavered. Not for a second.

Most of the night I went back and forth between the ballroom and the campaign room on the second floor. "How's Pennsylvania?" was my constant question. Everything hinged on a state that I love despite its questionable history of election reporting. I hated that feeling.

An entire book could be written about the battles waged and won in the state of Pennsylvania that day. In Allegheny County, a judge finally ordered Democrat "poll watchers" to remove their deceptive "Voter Protection" badges. Investigations into potentially fraudulent voter registration forms emerged in Lancaster, Monroe, and York Counties, with Lancaster County District Attorney Heather Adams confirming her office was actively probing suspicious registrations—and so many other attempts—to corrupt the vote.[2]

As Lara had pointed out to the media, in Pennsylvania, there were eight counties that tried to prevent Republican poll watchers from entering buildings.[3]

A few days after the election, as Bucks County was *still* counting ballots, the Democratic county commissioner had this to say about illegal ballots: "People violate laws any time they want. [. . .] So, for me, if I violate this law it's because I want a court to pay attention."[4] If this is what they say and do in broad daylight, imagine what they've done in the shadows. Speaking of darkness, there's a really *interesting* parallel between states Democrats usually win and states that don't require photo ID to vote.[5]

* * *

They began calling states for Donald Trump soon after polls closed. Indiana was the first, projected for Trump at approximately 7:07 p.m. ET, followed within minutes by Kentucky. By 8:01 p.m. ET, Florida was called—a state we fled to based on the oppression of New York. We won big.

At 11:43 p.m. they called North Carolina, Lara's home state. The Mar-a-Lago ballroom erupted in cheers—not just because of the victory, not just because of the sixteen electoral votes, but because of Lara, who had become synonymous with the state. Lara waved to accept congratulations on this must-win state—all under the Swarovski chandeliers in the very ballroom we had gotten married in years earlier.

I went back upstairs to check the latest numbers.

We were looking at the raw vote totals coming in from each of the precincts—the same numbers being displayed on cable news outlets, but being tabulated second by second. We could see where we were compared to 2016, 2020, low-propensity voters, the shift to the right and to the left, county by county. All indicators were in our favor. For the first time, the Democrats had no commanding lead in early voting.

Finally, James Blair looked at the team and said, "Based on the early vote and what's left to come in across the state, we just won Pennsylvania."

"I'll let him know." I walked downstairs and whispered to my father, "Congratulations. You just won Pennsylvania."

He kept his expression neutral, but the question cut through the air. "How do you know? They don't have enough outstanding votes to make up the difference."

Moments later, Elon looked up from his phone and said, "Sir, it looks like we just won Pennsylvania."

We watched and waited for the official call from the networks. *Why does it take them so long?* First, for the legacy media, announcing a Republican win is devastating. We have all seen the tears, the frowns, and the meltdowns. Second, election night is one of the biggest ratings opportunities of the year. It can be an infuriating game. When you are winning by hundreds of thousands of votes, and only have a small fraction of those votes outstanding: call the race.

Forty-five minutes later they called Pennsylvania. A roar of cheers erupted and shook the ballroom.

State by state, we were witnessing landslides. Lara turned to me, eyes wide with disbelief, and said, "We won Miami-Dade County!" This county had been solidly blue for decades—even in 2016 and 2020. For the first time in 36 years, a Republican carried Miami-Dade, and we won it by an astonishing 11-point margin. It was an overwhelming victory in our home state of Florida. We had made gains with every demographic in every county—race, veterans, party affiliation, gender, age groups, urban, suburban, rural, religion, and education.[6]

It was time to prepare another speech and head to the official watch party at the West Palm Beach County convention center. I had been with him while writing the 2016 election night victory speech, but this one was my favorite. Call it superstition, or just plain wisdom, but as I've mentioned, he never wrote them beforehand. While others might be wordsmithing victory speeches days in advance, my father was on a stage at two in the morning trying to win Michigan. He didn't give a shit about the pageantry. He cared about victory.

At 2:06 a.m., while the former and future president read through his draft and prepared to address the crowd, I snapped a photo and posted it on X.[7]

The battles of 2024 felt like a fusion of the best parts of our previous two campaigns. We brought the raw energy and scrappy spirit of 2016, combined with the strategic precision and data-driven focus we had sharpened in 2020. Back then, we were learning as we went—outsiders disrupting the system. By 2020, we had the infrastructure, but the soul of the campaign got diluted in the stale, rented office space in Arlington—too close to the D.C. swamp. This time, we returned to our roots. We ran it from Florida, far from the bureaucrats and political lifers. It had the urgency of a start-up, but with the experience of a seasoned operation. It was, without question, the best of both worlds.

NOVEMBER 6

I called my father early in the morning after the election with two things to tell him. First: a congratulations. "I'm *so* proud of you."

Second: "Dad, I'm officially retiring from politics."

I wanted to get back to full focus on my family, employees, our properties. Most of all, I wanted to get back to Luke and Carolina.

"We won the Super Bowl and it's been the greatest honor of my life to stand on that stage for over a decade," I said. "There are no more plays for me to run. I'll make our family proud, you go make our country proud."

He does every single day.

THE PHONES STARTED RINGING

Within minutes of victory, everything changed—both in our world and around the world. The phones lit up—a far cry from the silence after the 2020 election, when some people in the West Wing scattered like mice. A far cry from the months we spent in a courthouse, fighting not just for our company, but for our freedom and our lives.

Just like in 2016, people we hadn't heard from in years started reaching out. People who had deserted Donald Trump for the Nikki Haleys of the world called to "apologize" . . . and ask for jobs.

Some men only remember loyalty when they run out of options.

I'll never forget a contractor for LIV Golf—screaming at my staff during one of our tournaments, demanding that all MAGA hats immediately be pulled from our pro shop, barking orders and trying to sanitize any sign of support for my father. After the 2024 win, that same individual was now reaching out, all smiles and flattery, asking to be considered for secretary of the Air Force. It was one of those moments that perfectly captures Washington, D.C.

It wasn't just political operatives—world leaders were suddenly reaching out, too. The leaders of Mexico and Canada, who had spent the past four years dismissing Trump's tough stance on immigration and tariffs, were now scrambling to open lines of communication and tighten their borders. Virtually every world leader was trying to make contact with him—and their tones had all shifted dramatically. No longer dismissive or defiant, they approached with a new level of respect and urgency.

I even saw on his phone that New York Governor Kathy Hochul—that longtime ally of Letitia James—had tried calling him multiple times. When the president-elect finally picked up, her tone was a world apart from previous years—and even just months earlier, when she had publicly declared, "Donald Trump should be prosecuted to the fullest extent of the law." Now, faced with the new reality, she was forced to set aside the rhetoric and engage with the man she once sought to silence.

Like the others, she realized she'd need something for her state or be left behind—and the tune changed fast.

On a personal level, on election night and the days that followed, my phone wouldn't stop ringing and buzzing. Most of the calls and texts came from dear friends and loyal supporters—people who had given everything, worked tirelessly for the campaign, and never once backed down.

But the other people called, too. You know, ones we hadn't seen in years but who suddenly wanted to reconnect, get a certain title—or be in charge of a certain department. It wasn't that I took pleasure in saying no or steering our team away from certain names—but what I truly valued was the clarity we all shared this time around.

Life is a roller coaster of exhilarating highs and crushing lows—of loyalty and of betrayal—and I've lived both, sometimes in the same hour. The victories are unforgettable. But the lows—the moments where the walls felt like they were closing in—taught me more than any win ever could. They forced me to grow a thicker skin—to harden. It's a powerful shield that, a decade later, all of us carry with us.

I truly believe that it is the full ride that shapes you—not just the moments when everyone's cheering, but also the silence after the crowd walks away. Those dark chapters taught me who I am, and more important, who others are when it counts.

As an EVP of the Trump Orginization, I've learned that loyalty, grit, and the ability to stand tall when the storm hits aren't optional—they're everything. The people who can weather both the peaks and valleys with you are the ones who belong in the next chapter.

THE DYING ECHO

The 2024 election rendered the "mainstream" media obsolete, reshaped the Republican Party, canceled celebrity "influencers," and pummeled the bought-and-paid-for pollsters. The meltdown was all around—and honestly, I couldn't have enjoyed it more.

Dismiss the outdated media. It's time to stop giving weight to what these lunatics say. Don't celebrate Bill Maher or anyone like him when they accidentally agree with us—remember, they oppose our values 99 percent of the time.

Ridiculing these people and their networks was necessary. Now it's time to let their influence die by simply tuning them out. No one cares what editorial pages publish anymore. The worst fate these people can imagine is irrelevance.

Exhibit A: Joe and Mika went from ranting, "He will imprison, he will execute whoever he is allowed to imprison" *before* the election, to begging to meet at their old stomping grounds of Mar-a-Lago.[8] Joe defended himself by saying, "For those asking why we would speak to the president-elect during such fraught times, [...] I guess I would ask back, 'Why wouldn't we?'"[9]

For eight years, Joe Scarborough and Mika Brzezinski had built their brand on sneering contempt for Donald Trump—only to come knocking after 2024, hoping to "reset" the very relationship they torched. How do you have the audacity to essentially label someone Hitler 2.0, call days after they win an election, and then go to Mar-a-Lago to reopen lines of communication?

Donald Trump is much better than I am at handling betrayal. He never forgets who someone is or what they've done, but he has an uncanny ability to be graceful, reset relationships, and keep moving forward when it serves a greater purpose. I can't do it—I'm more of a light switch: when it's off, it's off. That instinct isn't always right, especially in the game of politics, where alliances shift constantly. Still, for me, some of these people are just impossible to respect—watching them flip, spin, and come crawling back tests every bit of my patience.

And as a son, I reserve the strongest reaction when disloyalty is directed at him.

MAKE AMERICA EXCELLENT AGAIN

Donald Trump's real estate career can be summed up in one mission: to build and operate the greatest projects on earth. When our company acquires a property, we don't just slap on a fresh coat of paint—we transform it completely. If a building is beyond repair, we tear it down to its steel and concrete bones and rebuild from the ground up, turning every project into a masterpiece. I am proud to carry that legacy forward—and to expand it even further.

That same relentless approach defines my father's presidency. His first term was just the beginning. Despite the lunacy, relentless attacks, impeachments, lawfare, and intentional smoke screens, he made it all look easy—guided by uncommon common sense and unwavering determination.

How do we get rid of inflation? We lower energy costs, again.

How do we reduce unemployment and unlock more opportunity? By bringing critical manufacturing back home. We must produce our own steel, automobiles, power, medicines, and computer chips—rebuilding the backbone of American industry and independence.

My father brought America back to the basics—back to the steel, concrete, and core. Stop with the DEI and transgender bathrooms, and get back to the realities of the world. Get criminals off the streets, secure the border, offer our kids the highest-quality learning environments, and put America first. Slash the federal bureaucracy until it's been transformed into something that actually serves and protects Americans. We must stay the course, and never stop fighting.

WE'LL SEE

There's an old story of a Chinese farmer and his son who had a beloved work horse. One day, the horse ran away, and the neighbors brought him the news, "Your horse ran away, what terrible luck!"

"Maybe so, maybe not. We'll see," the farmer replied.

Days later, the horse returned, leading several wild horses back to the farm as well. "Your horse has returned, and brought several horses home with him," his neighbors shouted. "What great luck!"

The farmer replied, "Maybe so, maybe not. We'll see."

The next week, the farmer's son tried to break one of the new horses and was thrown to the ground, breaking his leg. The neighbors moaned, "Your son broke his leg, what terrible luck!"

"Maybe so, maybe not," the farmer replied. "We'll see."

A few weeks later, soldiers from the national army marched through town, recruiting all boys for the military. They did not take the farmer's son because he had a broken leg. The neighbors whispered, "Your boy is spared, what tremendous luck!"

The farmer replied, "Maybe so, maybe not. We'll see."

We can't script our lives. And we shouldn't be too quick to judge life by its daily ups and downs. The here and now is important, but we're also playing the long game. I suppose it's a lot like real estate. If there's one lesson that I've learned—from the past ten years and that Chinese proverb— is that what seems like the worst news possible can turn out for the best.

This approach is exactly how I have come to lead the Trump Organization, making it the strongest it's ever been despite the challenges of COVID, relentless lawfare, and constant siege. It's the same resilience that carried us through a difficult political journey—and why the stakes in the 2026 and 2028 elections are higher than ever before.

LEMONS INTO LEMONADE

Both impeachment efforts were meant to politically destroy my father. Instead, Donald Trump used them to energize his base, raise record-breaking donations, and turn legal persecution into a narrative of political martyrdom—fueling a comeback campaign that shocked the establishment and the world.

The loss in 2020 could have been the end. But Trump flipped it into a movement, reshaping the GOP into his bold, America-first vision, and building momentum that carried him back to the top.

Every hit piece, every smear campaign, every late-night joke only amplified his visibility. Trump mastered the art of using media outrage as validation—*They're all coming after me because I'm fighting for you.*

When the events of January 6 became a political bludgeon, Trump pivoted to frame the aftermath as proof of a two-tiered justice system and an attack on First Amendment rights. He used it to galvanize a movement centered around government overreach and political targeting.

Getting banned from Twitter and Facebook was meant to silence him. Instead, it led to the creation of Truth Social—his own platform that not only gave him an uncensored voice but also symbolized independence from Big Tech's control.

What was meant to break him—investigations, indictments, and court battles—became the bedrock of his 2024 campaign. Trump turned personal legal adversity into a political identity: *If they can do this to me, they can do it to you.* It resonated deeply, especially with voters who felt forgotten or were targeted themselves.

Roll in the rallies in New Jersey and the Bronx—during the sham New York trials—and you start to see why New York went redder than it has in decades. I'd call it a success.

In the end, the lawfare and "irregularities" of 2020 actually *helped* Donald J. Trump become president again. By now you know that I'm not necessarily an optimist. I'm certainly not a pessimist. But I absolutely have come to believe in the wonder of "unintended consequences."

What if a company that was relentlessly attacked, at great cost—personally and financially—actually emerged stronger than it was ten years ago? We Are!

What if a family grew closer the more others tried to tear them apart? We Did!

What if a former president was wrongly charged in a series of sham trials, became Chief Executive of the United States of America—again? It Happened!

WORTH IT?

People often ask me about the past ten years and the pressure it brought to my family and our business. "Is it worth it?"

"And what about the fact that your father came close to being murdered—at least twice?"

Looking back, it was an endless game of Russian roulette that we somehow managed to survive, against all odds.

Winning the 2024 election was even more fulfilling—and satisfying—than winning 2016 and 2020 back-to-back could have been. It was the sweetest victory in political history—a perfect blend of *The Art of the Deal* and *The Art of the Comeback.*

My father has always believed in common sense and practical solutions that bring the country together. As he famously said, "Success will be my revenge."

Speaking of revenge, January 6 is one of the most important dates in my life, for reasons you might not know. On that day, I came into this world. And in 2025, my birthday present was seeing Kamala Harris certify my father as the duly elected president of the United States.

INAUGURATION 2.0

Going back to Arlington National Cemetery on Sunday, January 19, 2025—the day before the inauguration—felt like déjà vu, an echo of history. The solemn quiet was still there, but it was raining. And this time Lara and I had our children with us. I remember the way Luke stood tall, and seeing Carolina standing on the wet steps in her little ballerina slippers.

Our kids were remarkably disciplined in the freezing cold for over an hour—too innocent to understand those hallowed grounds or the gravity of the moment for us as a family—but undoubtedly feeling the magnitude of the moment. Their small hands clutched ours, their eyes wide with what I can only imagine was countless unspoken questions, sensing the weight of sacrifice etched into every stone, and the soon-to-appear grandfather, who would lay a wreath at the Tomb of the Unknown Solider.

In that sacred silence, beneath the gray sky, we stood united once again. The only sound was the soldiers' footsteps on the granite. I noticed the solemn inscription on the Tomb: "Here Rests in Honored Glory an American Soldier Known but to God."

I will never forget the silence at Arlington in 2017, but this was a silence of hard-fought redemption.

The following day, the inauguration was moved to the Capitol because of the bitter cold. As I looked across the room, I knew almost everyone there with us. I did miss the massive expanse of the ceremony eight years earlier, but the intimacy of this gathering was even more fitting for the moment.

President Donald J. Trump's speech set a new standard for straight talk, courage, and positivity.

After he was sworn in I spent time talking with people who were seated around us. Mark Zuckerberg was right behind me—I had never met him until that day. Looking back, he might have been the only person in the room I did not know.

Weeks earlier he had been one of the first to call and congratulate my father. I shook his hand.

"Let's fucking go!" he said. I'm not naïve, but he appeared genuinely happy about the election. Maybe so, maybe not . . . we'll see.

Same with Sundar Pichai, CEO of Google, who couldn't have been nicer as I sat next to him at lunch in Statuary Hall. But I'll never forget googling "Trump assassination attempt," "Hunter Biden Laptop," "Donate to Trump" and finding only links and glowing stories about the *other* campaign—not to mention the widespread censorship of an entire movement and party across their YouTube platform. But maybe I should be more like my father and let people back into the fold—even people who may not deserve it.[10]

Some believe that holding on to anger only corrodes the soul. They are probably right. Maybe grace is what's needed now—or maybe it's exactly what those who were part of the siege count on. Unfortunately, after living in a system where they tried to imprison, bankrupt, and kill us, I don't have much of it in me.

THANK YOU

Thanks to our voters, volunteers, true leaders, amazing team, and brave voices. Not only did we win in a landslide on November 5, all fifty states shifted Republican.[11]

You know what I'd call that?

A good start.

EPILOGUE

SO MUCH WINNING

"I'm draining the Swamp, and the Swamp is trying to fight back.
Don't worry, we will win."
—PRESIDENT DONALD J. TRUMP

Speaking of unintended consequences, "losing" in 2020 was the best thing that ever happened to Donald Trump and the MAGA movement. It gave the Democrats all the time they needed to show the country and world their true colors, and gave my father the ability to recalibrate, reassemble a team, and have a clearer view of Washington, D.C.

Today, we have a president who returns to Washington not as a newcomer, but as a seasoned leader—battle-tested, clear-eyed, and more prepared than ever to confront the swamp. This time, he's surrounded by a cabinet of unmatched strength and appointees ready to deliver lasting, transformational change across government. The BS-tolerance level is set to zero in this administration. We have the House, we have the Senate, we have a six-three majority on the Supreme Court. We won all seven swing states and the popular vote. The mainstream media is all but dead, distrusted by all and replaced by independent podcasts and free-speech platforms like X and Truth Social. And the RINOs (Republicans in Name Only), they are virtually extinct.

Donald Trump was never afraid to flick the hornet's nest, but now he fires stinger missiles—throwing so much "lead in the air" it's almost impossible for the Left to keep up.

Trump 2.0 isn't just working harder than ever—he's driving the mission with renewed purpose and unmistakable energy. But this time, he's doing it on his terms, and he's having more fun than ever doing it. The Republican Party has been reborn. It's no longer the party of cautious consultants and stale talking points—it's the party of America First, unapologetically committed to Americans first. This is a movement with backbone, grit, and vision—and it's only just beginning.

NO TIME FOR WHISPERS

A few years ago, Kerry, a wonderful woman who runs Trump Winery in Charlottesville, Virginia, shared this insight. "Eric, there's something going on out there. I go to every wine show in the country, every festival—and I've had *thousands* of people come up to me and whisper, 'Hey, we're a hundred percent behind your boss.' I always laugh and ask them, 'Why are you whispering?'"

In 2016, Donald Trump had massive support—some of it loud, but much of it quiet. That silent backing made the polls painfully unreliable.

But during the 2024 campaign, a flight attendant walked up next to me on the plane and said, "I'm from New York. Your father is our last hope." She wasn't whispering. In fact, it felt like the entire cabin turned and looked at us. She could probably tell that I just wanted to blend in, but continued in an even louder voice. "I just don't care what people think anymore. The Biden administration is destroying my country. Tell your father I love him and hope he wins. We're all behind him."

A few minutes later she gave me three envelopes: one for Donald Trump, one for Melania, and one for me. Each contained a handwritten, heartfelt note—almost apologetic in terms of admitting she had been too quiet the past two elections. But now she was all in.

THEN YOU WIN

First they ignore you, then they laugh at you, then they fight you, then you win. I've thought about this saying a lot over the years.

Barack scoffed at my father at the 2011 White House Correspondents Dinner. Less than six years later, Donald J. Trump was president.

In the lead-up to the 2016 election—and long after—Obama, Clinton, James Comey, James Clapper, and John Brennan spun and perpetuated a web of lies about so-called Russian "interference." Hillary's team was eventually caught, and fined for misrepresenting spending on "research."[1] There was zero evidence linking my father to Russia, and they knew it. Yet anyone who questioned the obvious falsehoods was mocked, censored, or worse.

In 2025, newly declassified documents seem to finally reveal what we've long suspected: Hillary Clinton approved a plan, backed by George Soros's network, to fabricate a story linking Donald Trump to Russian hackers—explicitly to distract from her own missing emails. One internal message reportedly read, "HRC approved Julia's idea about Trump and Russian hackers hampering U.S. elections. That should distract people from her own missing email." Another Clinton associate wrote, "Later the FBI will put more oil into the fire."[2]

Why were these reports hidden for years? And why were many of these documents hidden in burn bags?

In May of 2020, my father said it plainly: "This was all Obama. This was all Biden. These people were corrupt. The whole thing was corrupt. And we caught them. We caught them." He added, "It was impossible for it to happen without the man that sits right in that chair in the Oval Office. He knew everything."[3]

And now, it's clear to me from these documents that President Obama directly intervened to alter the intelligence findings—shielding his allies and perpetuating a lie that divided the country for years.

Biden accused my father of being a crook, and today no one can deny that Joe and Hunter were in an apparent pay-to-play scheme.

Fani Willis failed, both legally and personally. She made going after Donald Trump her singular mission. In December 2024, she was disqualified from the case.[4]

Alvin Bragg and his political allies stitched together a case from thirty-four non-crimes. Two weeks after the election, he was still begging the courts to "pause" the case—until 2029, when Donald Trump would leave office. Transparently desperate.[5][6]

Jack Smith's cases evaporated in the light of day after November 6, 2024. He went from demanding lightning-speed trials to stalling and, eventually, surrendering. His partisan crusade cost taxpayers over $50 million—only to end in failure.[7]

Letitia James fully exposed herself as a vengeful operative masquerading as an attorney general. Her mission was never justice, it was pure political retribution. Even after the election, she continued her baseless attacks.[89] Had we not won, she could have become the attorney general of the United States. Thankfully, we also learned about her own mortgage arrangements under investigation—eerily similar to the very accusations she threw at Donald Trump.

Kamala Harris knew Joe Biden wasn't capable of doing the job—likely from the moment they first campaigned together. Yet she played along, covered for him, and helped deceive the American people. That deception is now one of the most underreported political scandals in American history.

And the winning continues.

Woke is dead.

The border is finally secure—for the first time in decades, maybe ever.

The Democratic Party is shattered—or, more accurately, their corruption and hypocrisy have been fully exposed and publicly rejected.

My father, along with our family and millions of other patriots, was silenced on social media. Today, Donald J. Trump has the loudest voice in the world.

Was there ever a siege so relentless?

And has there ever been such complete and undeniable vindication?

First it was slander and economic warfare.

Next it was relentless lawfare.

They invaded his home.

Then, they tried to kill him.

And then we won.

UNDER SIEGE—BUT NEVER BROKEN

There were moments—many of them—when the night seemed endless, the noise deafening, and the weight of history unbearable. We didn't ask for the battle that was brought to our doorstep. We didn't choose the persecution or the hatred that tried to divide not only our family, but this great country. But we never ran from it, either.

Over the past ten years, we stood tall—not just as individuals, but as a family. A family that refused to bend, refused to retreat into the background, and refused to let the soul of America be rewritten. For the first time in American political history, it wasn't just one man running for office—it was a family effort. Not because we wanted it that way, but because we had no other choice. Because at the end of the day, we only had each other.

And through it all, through every firestorm and every late-night war room, we held on to three things: our love for God, our love for this country, and our love for the Constitution. These were our compass. These are still our guides.

There's a strange symmetry in life. My father wrote *The Art of the Deal* when he was on top of the world—rising, building, blazing new trails. He followed it with *The Art of the Comeback* when everything was stacked against him and he had to fight tooth and nail to survive—and win. I've lived both of those stories. I've walked through the fire just as he did in the early 1990s—watching empires shake, legacies threatened, friends vanish, and enemies circle.

At thirty-three years old, I stepped into a role I never expected as a younger man. I became a patriarch of sorts—not only to our company, but in some ways to my own family. It wasn't just about business—it was about pride of family, about giving my father the ability to do the unthinkable: to try and save this nation. I hope that by holding the line, I gave him the space to do what he was born to do, and what God spared his life to do.

There was no playbook for this journey, no map for the uncharted territory we crossed. We wrote our own. And by the grace of God, and by the will of the American people, we won.

We won because we stood, relentlessly, for something greater than ourselves. We won because we loved this country more than we loved our comfort. We sacrificed it all—time, privacy, money, business, friendships, reputation—not for glory, but for the future of our children, for your children, and for the America we *know* still exists, buried under bureaucracy and corruption.

I am honored—truly—to have stood on that stage every single day beside a man I love.

To those who stood beside us: thank you. To those who prayed for us: we felt every one. And to those still fighting—don't stop. Because what we built together wasn't just a campaign. It was a cause. A calling. A rebirth of something American to its core. A movement to Make America Great Again!

We stood under siege. But we never broke. And now we rise. Stronger. Freer. Unafraid.

God bless you. God bless the American family. And may God forever bless the United States of America.

ACKNOWLEDGMENTS

To my incredible wife, Lara. Your love has never been passive. It's a force—steady, fierce, and unshakable. For seventeen years, you've stood beside me, not behind me. You've carried weight few people ever see and made it look effortless.

You're the anchor of our family, both publicly and privately, and are the heart and soul of our home. Watching you raise our children with integrity, strength, and compassion is one of the greatest joys of my life. You excel in absolutely everything you do.

I've faced battles, but I've never faced them alone—not with you by my side. You balance the world with compassion and determination, and I am endlessly inspired by your work ethic, resilience, and warmth. I'm proud of the life we've built together, and I am forever grateful for your love.

To my siblings, Don, Ivanka, Tiffany, and Barron. I couldn't be prouder to walk through life as part of this family, and even more honored to walk beside each of you.

Don and Ivanka, growing up together was its own adventure. The memories of childhood vacations, the family trips, the laughter around the dinner table, and the victories we've shared both personally and professionally are etched into who I am. From the early days to building the company side by side, it's been a remarkable journey—one marked by drive, loyalty, and unshakable unity.

Tiffany, it's been such a joy watching you grow into the graceful, grounded woman you are today. You radiate a quiet strength and kindness that this world needs more of, and I'm so proud of the beautiful life you and Michael have built together.

Barron, you're stepping into the world with poise beyond your years.

Your humor, sharp mind, and sensibility, and, yes, our shared love of crypto, continue to impress me. It's been fun watching you come into your own and find your place on the global stage.

They tried to break us—all five of us. They tried to divide, discredit, and distract. But they failed. They underestimated the bond we share and the strength of the women who raised us. Our mothers stood firm with courage and conviction, and we did too. Together, we've been one unit. And one unit fighting together is always unstoppable.

I'm proud of each of you, for the lives you've built, the grace with which you've carried yourselves, and the way you've represented our family with strength and elegance.

We are Trumps. And we don't break.

To Kim. There are few people in life who show up every single day with quiet strength, endless loyalty, and a heart full of purpose. You are one of those people. For more than ten years, you've been by my side—through the long days, the hard decisions, the moments few ever see. You've stood with me in the toughest times, and you've celebrated the best ones with equal heart.

You don't just work tirelessly for me—you show the same care and dedication to my family, to our children, and to everyone who is part of our world. Your commitment is beyond a job; it's personal. It's loyal. It's rare.

You've carried so much on your shoulders, often without recognition, and I want you to know how deeply I see and appreciate everything you do. I trust you implicitly, and I can't imagine navigating this journey without you.

I am forever grateful for you—not just for what you do, but for who you are.

To my incredible team at the Trump Organization (you know exactly who you are). The chapters of this book exist because of you! Every challenge we've faced, every victory we've earned—none of it would have been possible without your unwavering dedication, relentless work ethic, and unshakable loyalty.

You stood tall—day after day. Through good times and bad, you never wavered. You believed in this company, in our mission, and in one another. And together, we pushed back against an onslaught of corruption, noise, and distractions.

But beyond the hard work, the long hours, and the wins, I want you to understand this: you are part of something far bigger than you may even realize.

This isn't just a company. It's a *movement*—a mission to save America. And every one of you has played a critical role in that fight.

There's no substitute for grit. No replacement for heart. You're not just employees—you're family.

From the bottom of my heart, thank you. I am honored. I am humbled. And I am forever grateful.

To my mother—Ivana Trump. Wow, were you tough as nails. But you were also stunning, fearless, fun, wild, and absolutely unforgettable.

You were an athlete through and through—competitive, driven, strong. Thank you for putting skis on our feet before we could walk, for dragging us through airports with trunks heavier than we were, and for teaching us that sitting still was never an option.

You were a force of nature—equal parts elegance and grit. You could beat any man on the slopes and outshine any model on the runway. You ruled with an iron fist and a heart of gold. When we gave you hell, you gave it right back, and usually far worse.

You had that old-world discipline, that glamorous Eastern European flair, and a presence that couldn't be ignored. That accent, that hair, that confidence—you were so many things at once. Fierce. Loyal. Proud. Sharp. Strong. Beautiful. Uncomfortably direct. Hilarious in ways you probably didn't even realize.

You showed us the world. You instilled in us a work ethic that won't quit and a fire that won't go out.

You were the embodiment of the American Dream, without ever letting go of your European roots. And you were a fiercely proud mother who raised us with strength, sarcasm, and relentless love.

You battled your demons and unfortunately, we lost you far too soon. But I am so lucky to be your son. Lucky to be shaped by your fire. We miss you every single day.

Until we meet again, Mom. You were truly one of a kind.

To Dorothy Curry. For more than forty years, you've been the steady Irish rock in our lives. Your accent, your grace, our nighttime prayers, your constant presence at my mother's side—every memory etched into my heart. You have seen it all. You've stood by me through childhood, through chaos, through moments we treasure and moments we would rather forget. You have given more of yourself than anyone could ever ask. You've sacrificed so much of your personal life for mine, and I love you more than words could ever express. You shaped the man I am. I was honored to name my daughter *Carolina Dorothy Trump* in your name. You gave me my warmth and my kindness—qualities I promise never to lose.

To Paige. You are one of my longest and dearest friends, and your loyalty and heart have meant the world to me. Through every chapter—especially the difficult ones—you never flinched. When the noise got loud, you stayed focused. You were one of the few who raised your hand without hesitation, something I'll never forget.

Your unwavering dedication to our shared mission—the fight against childhood cancer—is nothing short of extraordinary. I see the tireless hours, the passion, the personal sacrifices. You don't just run an organization—you breathe life into it. You are the visible heart and soul of everything we dreamed this mission would be.

The children at St. Jude, and so many others who will never know your name, are better off because of you.

Thank you for fighting for the kids. Thank you for fighting for me. You are an incredible human being, Paige. I'm honored to call you my friend—and forever proud of all that we've built together.

To Natasha Simons and Jennifer Long. You are both truly remarkable. When I first heard "Simon & Schuster," my reaction was somewhere between disbelief and "no f-ing way." But from our very first conversations—that dinner at Mar-a-Lago—I knew I was in amazing hands.

I've never considered myself a writer—I'm the guy who builds the places where others write. But this process has been unexpectedly cathartic, and you made it not only meaningful, but genuinely fun. What started as a project quickly became something more personal, and you've taken a far deeper role in that journey than I ever imagined.

Thank you for your brilliance, your tenacity, and your belief in the story.

To Clara Linhoff. Your countless emails, late nights, and meticulous edits helped bring this book to life. Your commitment and precision shaped every page, and I'm endlessly grateful.

To Mike Loomis and Tom Winters. Thank you both for your wisdom and guidance throughout this journey. Mike, your talent and insight helped bring these stories to life in a way I never could have imagined. Tom, your steady counsel has been invaluable every step of the way. I'm deeply grateful to have had both of you by my side through this process.

To the American Patriots. From the depths of my heart—thank you.

You are the reason we fight. The reason we don't back down. The reason this movement is alive and stronger than ever.

Through every smear, every attack, every crooked headline and weaponized agency—you never blinked. You stood tall. You stood proud. And you stood with us.

You are the backbone of this nation—the forgotten men and women who never asked for credit but deserve all of it. You wake up early, work hard, raise your families, honor God, love this country, and never take a single freedom for granted.

Your patriotism is fierce. Your courage is unmatched. And your loyalty—to the truth, to our flag, to the ideals that built this nation—is what keeps America from falling into darkness.

You've had every reason to give up. But you never did. Instead, you rose louder, stood firmer, and fought harder.

You are not just supporters—you are warriors. And make no mistake, we are shoulder to shoulder with you in this battle for the soul of America.

Thank you for believing in my father. Thank you for believing in our family. But most of all, thank you for believing in *America*.

We will never stop fighting for you. We will never stop fighting *with* you. And we will never, ever let this country fall.

NOTES

INTRODUCTION: UNDER SIEGE

1. "Eric Trump: They Don't Want Trump to Win Again in 2024," Fox News, August 8, 2022, https://www.foxnews.com/media/eric-trump-they-dont-want-trump-win -again-2024.
2. Allie Griffin, "Eric Trump Alerted His Dad to FBI Raid, Said Agents 'Ransacked' the Ex-President's Office," *New York Post*, August 9, 2022, https://ny post.com/2022/08/09/eric-trump-alerted-his-dad-to-the-mar-a-lago-raid.
3. Donald J. Trump, "Statement by Donald J. Trump, 45th President of the United States of America," *Politico*, August 8, 2022, https://www.politico.com /f/?id=00000182-80d4-dd9f-a7ea-a9f47f2e0000.
4. Catherine Herridge et al., "Special Counsel Finds Biden 'Willfully' Disclosed Classified Documents, but No Criminal Charges Warranted," CBS News, February 8, 2024, https://www.cbsnews.com/news/biden-special-counsel-report-hand ling-classified-documents.
5. Kathryn Watson, "Biden Says He Has 'No Regrets' on Handling of Classified Documents Since Discovery," CBS News, January 19, 2023, https://www .cbsnews.com/news/joe-biden-classified-documents-handling-no-regrets.
6. Herridge et al., "Special Counsel Finds Biden 'Willfully' Disclosed Classified Documents, but No Criminal Charges Warranted."
7. Miranda Devine, "America Is Tired of Joe and Hunter Biden 'Weaponizing Addiction' as a Get-Out-of-Jail-Free Card," *New York Post*, November 5, 2023, https://nypost.com/2023/11/05/news/america-is-tired-of-joe-and-hunter -biden-weaponizing-addiction-as-a-get-out-of-jail-free-card.
8. Brooke Singman, "Trump Highlights Biden Admin Authorizing 'Deadly Use of Force' in Mar-a-Lago Raid," Fox News, updated May 22, 2024, https:// www.foxnews.com/politics/biden-administration-authorized-use-of-deadly -force-mar-a-lago-raid; Julie Kelly (@julie_kelly2), "Tons of new unsealed filings on classified docs case [. . .]," X, May 21, 2024, https://x.com/julie_kelly2 /status/1792969008657948733.
9. Josh Gerstein and Kyle Cheney, "Prosecutors: Docs in Boxes Seized from Mar-a-Lago Were Inadvertently Jumbled," *Politico*, May 3, 2024, https://www.politico .com/news/2024/05/03/mar-a-lago-trump-classified-documents-00156124.
10. Michael Lee, "Biden Administration Officials Were Reportedly Involved in Mar-a-Lago Raid Despite Claiming Otherwise," Fox News, April 11, 2023,

https://www.foxnews.com/politics/biden-white-house-officials-involved -mar-a-lago-raid-despite-claiming-otherwise-report.

11. Eric Trump (@EricTrump), "Breaking: DonaldJTrump.com is shattering all fundraising records [. . .]," X, August 9, 2022, https://x.com/EricTrump/status /1557180062440505344.

12. Brandon Gillespie and Brooke Singman, "Treasury Confirms Terms like 'MAGA,' 'Trump,' 'Kamala,' 'Biden' Used in Private Bank Transaction Searches," Fox News, February 9, 2024, https://www.foxnews.com/politics/biden-admin-confirms-ter ms-maga-trump-kamala-private-bank-transaction-searches.

13. Brooke Singman, "Feds Conducted 'Broad' and 'Unjustified' Surveillance of Americans' Private Financial Data: House Judiciary," Fox News, March 6, 2024, https://www.foxnews.com/politics/feds-conducted-broad-unjustified-sur veillance-americans-private-financial-data-house-judiciary.

14. Bradley A. Smith, "The Unresolved IRS Scandal," *Wall Street Journal*, May 9, 2018, https://www.wsj.com/articles/the-unresolved-irs-scandal-1525905500; "IRS Scandal Fast Facts," CNN U.S., September 26, 2022, https://www.cnn .com/2014/07/18/politics/irs-scandal-fast-facts/index.html.

15. "Siege," Merriam-Webster, https://www.merriam-webster.com/dictionary/siege.

CHAPTER 1: MY FATHER THE FIGHTER

1. Donald J. Trump and Kate Bohner, *Trump: The Art of the Comeback* (Times Books, 1997).

2. Guinness World Records (@GWR), "Hi Jonathan, Mr. Trump did appear in our 1999 and 2000 editions. [. . .]," X, May 22, 2019, https://x.com/GWR /status/1131205196921675776.

CHAPTER 2: FAMILY BUSINESS

1. Trump and Bohner, *Trump: The Art of the Comeback*.

CHAPTER 3: THE APPRENTICES

1. "Obama Says Trump Won't Be President: 'It's Not Hosting a Talk Show,'" ABC News, February 16, 2016, https://abcnews.go.com/Politics/obama-hits-trump-re ality-show-past-win-presidency/story?id=36986828.

2. "The Apprentice," Trump Organization, https://www.trump.com/lifestyle/the -apprentice.

3. Trump and Bohner, *Trump: The Art of the Comeback*.

4. Caitlyn Oprysko, "The Most Cringeworthy Lines from the Third Demo-crat Debate," *Politico*, September 13, 2019, https://web.archive.org/web/2022 1226013900/https://www.politico.com/story/2019/09/13/cringe-debate -2020-moments-1494494

5. Gabriel Hays, "The Most Awkward and Embarrassing Kamala Harris 'Word Salads' of 2022," Fox News, December 31, 2022, https://www.foxnews.com /media/most-awkward-embarrassing-kamala-harris-word-salads-2022.

6. Rebecca Klar, "Trump Hits MSNBC's Donny Deutsch over New TV Show," *The Hill*, August 11, 2019, https://thehill.com/homenews/administration/457 043-trump-hits-msnbcs-donny-deutsch-over-new-tv-show.

7. Harold Hutchison, "MSNBC Analyst Lays Out Biden's Path to Victory: 'Scare the Sh*t out of People,'" *Daily Caller*, March 1, 2024, https://dailycallernews foundation.org/2024/03/01/msnbc-analyst-lays-out-bidens-path-to-victory -scare-the-shit-out-of-people.

8. "*Variety*'s Ramin Setoodeh to Write Book About Donald Trump's *The Apprentice*," *Variety*, March 23, 2021, https://variety.com/2021/tv/news/the-appren tice-book-donald-trump-1234936339.

9. Michael Hein, "Chris Wallace's Dad Mike Once Grilled Donald Trump's Politics on '60 Minutes,'" PopCulture.com, July 19, 2020, https://popculture.com/trending /news/chris-wallace-dad-mike-once-grilled-donald-trump-politics-60-minutes.

10. Magnolia Pictures & Magnet Releasing (@magnoliapictures), "Mike Wallace Is Here - Exclusive Clip - Donald Trump," YouTube, July 25, 2019, https://www .youtube.com/watch?v=mrdgShrFznw.

11. Kori Schulman, "'The President's Speech' at the White House Correspondents' Dinner," Obama White House, May 1, 2011, https://obamawhitehouse.archives .gov/blog/2011/05/01/president-s-speech-white-house-correspondents-dinner.

12. "Inside America's Missile Fields," CBS News, April 25, 2014, https://www .cbsnews.com/news/nuclear-missile-crews-burdened-by-old-phone-system.

13. Cleve R. Wootson Jr., "Oprah Winfrey's Weirdly Revealing Donald Trump Interview—from 1988," *Washington Post*, January 8, 2018, https://www.wash ingtonpost.com/news/retropolis/wp/2018/01/08/oprah-winfreys-weird ly-revealing-donald-trump-interview-from-1988; OWN (@OWN), "Donald Trump Teases a President Bid During a 1988 Oprah Show | The Oprah Winfrey Show | OWN," YouTube, June 25, 2015, https://www.youtube.com /watch?v=SEPs17_AkTI.

14. George F. Will, "Donald Trump Is a Counterfeit Republican," *Washington Post*, August 12, 2015, https://www.washingtonpost.com/opinions/a-counterfeit-re publican/2015/08/12/c8c2968-4052-11e5-bfe3-ff1d8549bfd2_story.html.

15. "Read the Transcript of Donald Trump's Speech at the Al Smith Dinner," *Time*, October 21, 2016, https://time.com/4539981/read-the-transcript-don ald-trump-speech-al-smith-dinner.

16. Donald J. Trump and Tony Schwartz, *Trump: The Art of the Deal* (Random House, 1987).

CHAPTER 4: 2016

1. The New York Times (@nytimes), "Our presidential forecast, updated," X, October 20, 2016, https://x.com/nytimes/status/789083772205600768.

2. Eli Stokols, "Jeb's Shock-and-Awe Number," *Politico*, July 9, 2015, https:// www.politico.com/story/2015/07/jeb-bush-2016-fundraising-11-million-in -16-days-119908.

3. "Who's Winning? CNN Delegate Estimate," CNN Politics, accessed July 25, 2025, https://www.cnn.com/election/2016/primaries.

4. Trump and Schwartz, *Trump: The Art of the Deal*.

5. "Nevada Caucus Results," NBC News, accessed July 25, 2025, https://www.nbcnews.com/politics/2016-election/primaries/nv.

6. CNN (@CNN), "Eric Trump Downplays Fund Raising Gap with Clinton," YouTube, June 22, 2016, https://www.youtube.com/watch?v=89PNmyjexSE.

7. "President Obama Says Trump Doesn't Have 'Preparation,' 'Temperament' and 'Values,'" ABC News, September 27, 2016, https://abcnews.go.com/Politics/president-obama-trump-preparation-temperament-values/story?id=42399292.

8. Colin Campbell, "Chris Christie: Donald Trump Doesn't Have the 'Temperament' to Be President," *Business Insider*, August 14, 2015, https://www.businessinsider.com/chris-christie-donald-trump-temperament-president-2015-8.

9. MJ Lee, "Tears and Shock at Clinton's Election Night Party," CNN Politics, November 9, 2016, https://www.cnn.com/2016/11/09/politics/hillary-clinton-shock-election-party/index.html.

10. Kelly O'Donnell, "Uncertain Trump Team Prepared 2 Speeches on Election Night: Sources," NBC News, November 9, 2016, https://www.nbcnews.com/storyline/2016-election-day/uncertain-trump-team-prepared-2-speeches-election-night-sources-n681511.

11. "Here's the Full Text of Donald Trump's Victory Speech," CNN Politics, November 9, 2016, https://www.cnn.com/2016/11/09/politics/donald-trump-victory-speech/index.html.

CHAPTER 5: SEPARATION OF COMPANY AND STATE

1. Mark Moore, "Donald Trump Reveals Plan for His Business," *New York Post*, updated January 12, 2017, https://nypost.com/2017/01/11/donald-trump-reveals-plan-for-his-business.

2. "Campaign 2016: President-Elect Donald Trump News Conference," C-SPAN, January 11, 2017, https://www.c-span.org/video/?421482-1/president-elect-donald-trump-news-conference.

3. "Swalwell Introduces Bill to Stop Trump from Using the Presidency to Enrich Himself and His Family," Congressman Eric Swalwell, July 23, 2018, https://swalwell.house.gov/media-center/press-releases/swalwell-introduces-bill-stop-trump-using-presidency-enrich-himself-and.

4. Donald J. Trump (@realDonaldTrump), "France just put a digital tax on our great American technology companies. [. . .]," X, July 26, 2019, https://x.com/realDonaldTrump/status/1154791664625606657.

5. Georgi Gotev, "Macron Backs Down on Digital Tax Following Trump's Tariff Threats," *Euractiv*, January 21, 2020, https://www.euractiv.com/section/global-europe/news/macron-backs-down-on-digital-tax-following-trumps-tariff-threats.

6. Kate Sullivan, "Trump Reverses Course and Says His Florida Resort Won't Be Used for G7 Summit," CNN Politics, October 20, 2019, https://www.cnn.com/2019/10/19/politics/trump-property-no-longer-considered-for-g7-summit/index.html.

7. Dareh Gregorian, "Trump Organization Completes $375 Million Sale of D.C. Hotel," NBC News, May 11, 2022, https://www.nbcnews.com/politics/donald-trump/trump-organization-completes-375-million-sale-dc-hotel-rcna28428.

8. Trump and Schwartz, *Trump: The Art of the Deal*.

CHAPTER 6: WELCOME TO WASHINGTON

1. Mallory Shelbourne, "Schumer: Trump 'Really Dumb' for Attacking Intelligence Agencies," *The Hill*, January 3, 2017, https://thehill.com/homenews /administration/312605-schumer-trump-being-really-dumb-by-going-af ter-intelligence-community.

2. Matea Gold, "The Campaign to Impeach President Trump Has Begun," *Washington Post*, January 20, 2017, https://www.washingtonpost.com/news /post-politics/wp/2017/01/20/the-campaign-to-impeach-president-trump -has-begun.

3. Phil Wahba, "Macy's CEO Says Dumping Donald Trump's Line Was Still the Right Move," *Fortune*, November 10, 2016, https://fortune.com/2016/11/10 /macys-ceo-says-dumping-donald-trumps-line-was-still-the-right-move.

4. Mary Frances Schjonberg, "Trump Inaugural Events End in Prayer at National Cathedral," *Episcopal News Service*, January 21, 2017, https://www.episcopal newsservice.org/2017/01/21/trump-inaugural-events-end-in-prayer-at-na tional-cathedral.

5. "The Inaugural Address," National Archives, Trump White House, January 20, 2017, https://trumpwhitehouse.archives.gov/briefings-statements/the-inaugural -address.

6. Christopher Leonard, "Lockheed Martin's $1.7 Trillion F-35 Fighter Jet Is 10 Years Late and 80% over Budget—and It Could Be One of the Pentagon's Biggest Success Stories," *Fortune*, August 2, 2023, https://fortune.com/longform /lockheed-martin-f-35-fighter-jet.

7. Zachary Cohen, "Trump: I've Saved U.S. Billions on F-35 Fighters," CNN Politics, April 25, 2017, https://www.cnn.com/2017/04/25/politics/f-35-trump -gao-annual-review/index.html.

8. Dan Mangan and Leslie Josephs, "Boeing Lost $1.1 Billion on Trump Air Force One Contract; CEO Regrets Deal," CNBC, April 27, 2022, https://www .cnbc.com/2022/04/27/boeing-lost-billion-dollars-on-trump-air-force-one -plane-deal.html.

9. Morgan Phillips, "Boeing Bungled $3.9B Air Force One Project, Blew Past Deadline and Opened Door for Qatari Jet Offer," Fox Business, May 16, 2025, https://www.foxbusiness.com/politics/boeing-bungled-3-9-billion-air-force -one-project-blew-past-deadline-opened-door-qatari-jet-offer.

10. "FBI Probing Attempted Hack of Trump Organization, Officials Say," ABC News, May 26, 2017, https://www.abcnews.go.com/Politics/fbi-probing-at tempted-hack-trump-organization-officials/story?id=47652150.

11. Lesley Stahl, "The *60 Minutes* Interview That President Trump Cut Short," CBS News, October 26, 2020, https://www.cbsnews.com/news/president -trump-60-minutes-interview-lesley-stahl.

12. Ken Dilanian, "Two of 4 Warrants Letting FBI Spy on Ex-Trump Aide Carter Page Were Not Valid, Says DOJ," NBC News, January 23, 2020, https://www .nbcnews.com/politics/national-security/two-4-warrants-letting-fbi-spy-ex -trump-aide-carter-n1121406.

13. "Fact Sheet: President Donald J. Trump Addresses Risks from Perkins Coie LLP," The White House, March 6, 2025, https://www.whitehouse.gov/fact

-sheets/2025/03/fact-sheet-president-donald-j-trump-adresses-risks-from -perkins-coie-llp.

14. Callie Patteson, "Hillary Clinton Pushed Trump-Russia Theory at Center of Durham Case," *New York Post*, updated February 18, 2022, https://nypost.com/2022/02/14/hillary-clinton-pushed-trump-russia-theory-in-2016.

15. U.S. House Committee on the Judiciary, *Examining the Inspector General's Findings on FISA Applications* (hearing, H. Jud. Comm., December 4, 2019), HHRG-116-JU00-20191204-SD1284, https://www.congress.gov/116/meeting/house/110281/documents/HHRG-116-JU00-20191204-SD1284.pdf.

16. Victor Nava, "CIA and Foreign Intelligence Agencies Illegally Targeted 26 Trump Associates Before 2016 Russia Collusion Claims: Report," *New York Post*, February 13, 2024, https://nypost.com/2024/02/13/news/cia-and-foreign-intelligence-agencies-illegally-targeted-26-trump-associates-before-2016-russia-collusion-claims-report.

17. *Crossfire Hurricane Binder 1*, *Federalist*, Scribd, April 9, 2025, https://www.scribd.com/document/848636280/Crossfire-Hurricane-Binder-1.

18. Zachary Cohen et al., "Special Counsel John Durham Concludes FBI Never Should Have Launched Full Trump-Russia Probe," CNN Politics, updated May 16, 2023, https://www.cnn.com/2023/05/15/politics/john-durham-report-fbi-trump-released/index.html.

19. Samantha Raphelson, "FBI Apologizes to Court for Mishandling Surveillance of Trump Campaign Adviser," NPR, January 11, 2020, https://www.npr.org/2020/01/11/795566486/fbi-apologizes-to-court-for-mishandling-surveillance-of-trump-campaign-adviser.

20. Eric Tucker and Lindsay Whitehurst, "Special Prosecutor Ends Trump-Russia Investigation, Saying FBI Acted Hastily," Associated Press, May 16, 2023, https://apnews.com/article/durham-trump-russia-probe-7e84f94ca9cf7905cbc5eddc108575b3.

21. Victor Nava, "CIA and Foreign Intelligence Agencies Illegally Targeted 26 Trump Associates Before 2016 Russia Collusion Claims: Report."

22. Chuck Grassley, "Justice Dept. Admitted It Lacked Probable Cause in Carter Page FISAs," January 23, 2020, https://www.grassley.senate.gov/news/news-releases/justice-dept-admitted-it-lacked-probable-cause-carter-page-fisas.

23. "Donald Trump Says His Money Drew Hillary Clinton to His Wedding," ABC News, August 7, 2015, https://www.abcnews.go.com/Politics/trump-money-drew-hillary-clinton-wedding/story?id=32936868; "Donald Trump's Surprisingly Honest Lessons About Big Money in Politics," ABC News, August 11, 2015, https://abcnews.go.com/Politics/donald-trumps-surprisingly-honest-lessons-big-money-politics/story?id=32993736.

24. Trump and Schwartz, *Trump: The Art of the Deal*.

CHAPTER 7: NO GOOD DEED

1. "Trump Says He Will Dissolve Foundation amid Investigation," CBS News, December 24, 2016, https://www.cbsnews.com/texas/news/trump-says-he-will-dissolve-foundation-amid-ny-investigation.

2. "U.S. Childhood Cancer Statistics," American Childhood Cancer Organization, accessed June 29, 2025, https://www.acco.org/us-childhood-cancer-statistics.

3. "Families Never Pay St. Jude for Anything," St. Jude Children's Research Hospital, 2020, https://www.stjude.org/about-st-jude/why-support-st-jude/no-bills.html.

4. "The Pediatric Cancer Genome Project: Era of Discovery," St. Jude Children's Research Hospital, accessed July 25, 2025, https://www.stjude.org/about-st -jude/stories/promise-magazine/pcgp-2020/pediatric-cancer-genome-proj ect-era-of-discovery.html.

5. Trump and Schwartz, *Trump: The Art of the Deal.*

6. Jake Lahut, "N.Y. AG Schneiderman Examining Eric Trump Foundation," *Politico*, June 9, 2017, https://www.politico.com/story/2017/06/09/eric-trump-foun dation-new-york-attorney-general-eric-schneiderman-239358.

7. Geoff Earle, "Bill Clinton Foundation Has Spent More than $50M on Travel Expenses," *New York Post*, August 20, 2013, https://nypost.com/2013/08/20 /bill-clinton-foundation-has-spent-more-than-50m-on-travel-expenses.

8. Kenneth P. Vogel and Katy O'Donnell, "Clinton Foundation to Lay Off Dozens of Staff," *Politico*, September 20, 2016, https://www.politico.com/story /2016/09/clinton-foundation-layoffs-228443.

9. Dan Alexander, "New York Attorney General Looking into Eric Trump Foundation," *Forbes*, updated June 10, 2017, https://www.forbes.com/sites /danalexander/2017/06/09/new-york-attorney-general-looking-into-eric -trump-foundation; Dan Alexander, "New Filings Show Donations to Eric Trump's Foundation Plunged amid Scandal," *Forbes*, January 8, 2019, https:// www.forbes.com/sites/danalexander/2019/01/08/donations-to-eric-trumps -foundation-plunged-amid-scandal.

10. "Eric Trump Funneled Cancer Charity Money to His Businesses, Associates: Report," ABC News, June 7, 2017, https://abcnews.go.com/Politics/eric-trump-fun neled-cancer-charity-money-businesses-associates/story?id=47878610.

11. Sophie Tatum, "New York AG Eric Schneiderman Resigns over Assault Allegations," CNN Politics, May 8, 2018, https://www.cnn.com/2018/05/07/poli tics/eric-schneiderman-violence-allegations/index.html.

12. Isabel Vincent, "Tax Filings Reveal Biden Cancer Charity Spent Millions on Salaries, Zero on Research," *New York Post*, updated November 16, 2020, https:// nypost.com/2020/11/14/biden-cancer-initiative-spent-millions-on-payroll -zero-on-research-report/.

13. Trump and Bohner, *Trump: The Art of the Comeback.*

CHAPTER 8: DEFEAT BY A THOUSAND CUTS

1. Jack Rosenthal, "A Terrible Thing to Waste," *New York Times Magazine*, July 31, 2009, https://www.nytimes.com/2009/08/02/magazine/02FOB-onlanguage-t.html.

2. Stephanie Ebbs and Benjamin Siegel, "Police Did Not Clear Lafayette Square So Trump Could Hold 'Bible' Photo Op: Watchdog," ABC News, June 10, 2021, https://abcnews.go.com/Politics/police-clear-lafayette-park-area-trump-hold -bible/story?id=78171712.

3. Jeremy Gorner et al., "Mayor Imposes Curfew After Chaotic Scenes Unfold in Loop, near North Side as Protesters Clash with Police During Demonstration

over Death of George Floyd in Minneapolis," *Chicago Tribune*, May 31, 2020, https://www.chicagotribune.com/2020/05/31/mayor-imposes-curfew-after-chaotic-scenes-unfold-in-loop-near-north-side-as-protesters-clash-with-police-during-demonstration-over-death-of-george-floyd-in-minneapolis.

4. Joseph Wulfsohn, "CNN Panned for On-Air Graphic Reading 'Fiery but Mostly Peaceful Protest' in Front of Kenosha Fire," Fox News, August 27, 2020, https://www.foxnews.com/media/cnn-panned-for-on-air-graphic-reading-fiery-but-mostly-peaceful-protest-in-front-of-kenosha-fire.

5. The Wall Street Journal (@wsj), "Rahm Emanuel on the Opportunities of Crisis," YouTube, November 19, 2008, https://www.youtube.com/watch?v=_mzcbXi1Tkk.

6. Maneesh Arora, "How the Coronavirus Pandemic Helped the Floyd Protests Become the Biggest in U.S. History," *Washington Post*, August 5, 2020, https://www.washingtonpost.com/politics/2020/08/05/how-coronavirus-pandemic-helped-floyd-protests-become-biggest-us-history.

7. Olivia Land, "Tim Walz's Wife, Gwen, Said She Kept Windows Open During George Floyd Riots to Smell 'Burning Tires,'" *New York Post*, August 7, 2024, https://nypost.com/2024/08/07/us-news/gwen-walz-said-she-kept-windows-open-during-george-floyd-riots-to-smell-burning-tires.

8. Larry Buchanan et al., "Black Lives Matter May Be the Largest Movement in U.S. History," *New York Times*, July 3, 2020, https://www.nytimes.com/interactive/2020/07/03/us/george-floyd-protests-crowd-size.html.

9. Dan Diamond, "Suddenly, Public Health Officials Say Social Justice Matters More than Social Distance," *Politico*, June 4, 2020, https://www.politico.com/news/magazine/2020/06/04/public-health-protests-301534.

10. Luis Ferré-Sadurní, "Health Agency Under Cuomo 'Misled the Public' on Nursing Home Deaths," *New York Times*, March 15, 2022, https://www.nytimes.com/2022/03/15/nyregion/nursing-home-deaths-cuomo-covid.html.

11. Bernard Condon and Jennifer Peltz, "AP: Over 9,000 Virus Patients Sent into NY Nursing Homes," Associated Press, February 11, 2021, https://apnews.com/article/new-york-andrew-cuomo-us-news-coronavirus-pandemic-nursing-homes-512cae0abb55a55f375b3192f2cdd6b5.

12. Andrew Cuomo, *American Crisis: Leadership Lessons from the COVID-19 Pandemic* (Crown, 2020).

13. Sergio Martínez-Beltrán and Jonathan Oosting, "Michigan Gov. Whitmer Draws Fire for Out-of-State Trip Before She Was Vaccinated," *Bridge Michigan*, April 19, 2021, https://www.bridgemi.com/michigan-government/michigan-gov-whitmer-draws-fire-out-state-trip-she-was-vaccinated.

14. Ben Popken and Andrew W. Lehren, "Release of PPP Loan Recipients' Data Reveals Troubling Patterns," NBC News, December 2, 2020, https://www.nbcnews.com/business/business-news/release-ppp-loan-recipients-data-reveals-troubling-patterns-n1249629.

15. "New York State Emblems," Department of State, New York State, https://dos.ny.gov/new-york-state-emblems.

16. Joe Concha, "Hunter Biden, the Protected Third Rail of Journalism," *The Hill*, March 23, 2022, https://thehill.com/opinion/campaign/599245-hunter-biden-the-protected-third-rail-of-journalism; Uri Berliner, "I've Been at NPR for

25 Years. Here's How We Lost America's Trust," *Free Press*, April 9, 2024, https://www.thefp.com/p/npr-editor-how-npr-lost-americas-trust.

17. Noah Manskar, "Jack Dorsey Says Blocking *Post*'s Hunter Biden Story Was 'Total Mistake'—but Won't Say Who Made It," *New York Post*, March 25, 2021, https://nypost.com/2021/03/25/dorsey-says-blocking-posts-hunter-biden -story-was-total-mistake.

18. David Molloy, "Zuckerberg Tells Rogan FBI Warning Prompted Biden Laptop Story Censorship," BBC News, August 26, 2022, https://www.bbc.com/news /world-us-canada-62688532.

19. Steven Nelson and Bruce Golding, "Zuckerberg's Election Spending Was 'Carefully Orchestrated' to Influence 2020 Vote: Ex-FEC Member," *New York Post*, October 14, 2021, https://nypost.com/2021/10/14/zuckerberg-election -spending-was-orchestrated-to-influence-2020-vote.

20. Natasha Bertrand, "Hunter Biden Story Is Russian Disinfo, Dozens of Former Intel Officials Say," *Politico*, October 19, 2020, https://www.politico.com /news/2020/10/19/hunter-biden-story-russian-disinfo-430276.

21. "The Intelligence Community 51: How CIA Contractors Colluded with the Biden Campaign to Mislead American Voters," Select Subcommittee on the Weaponization of the Federal Government, and Permanent Select Committee on Intelligence, Committee on the Judiciary, U.S. House of Representatives, June 25, 2024, https://intelligence.house.gov/uploadedfiles/the_intelligence _community_51-_how_cia_contractors_colluded_with_the_biden_cam paign_to_mislead_american_voters.pdf.

22. "Protecting Speech from Government Interference and Social Media Bias, Part I: Twitter's Role in Suppressing the Biden Laptop Story," Hearing Before the Committee on Oversight and Accountability, House of Representatives, One Hundred Eighteenth Congress, First Session, U.S. Government Publishing Office, February 8, 2023, https://www.govinfo.gov/content/pkg/CHRG-1 18hhrg50898/html/CHRG-118hhrg50898.htm.

23. Tom Winter et al., "Analysis of Hunter Biden's Hard Drive Shows He, His Firm Took in About $11 Million from 2013 to 2018, Spent It Fast," NBC News, May 19, 2022, https://www.nbcnews.com/politics/national-security/analysis -hunter-bidens-hard-drive-shows-firm-took-11-million-2013-2018-rcna 29462.

24. Tom Winter, "Records Released by House Republicans Show That Joe Biden Repeatedly Emailed Hunter Biden's Business Associate in 2014," NBC News, December 21, 2023, https://www.nbcnews.com/news/records-released-house -republicans-show-joe-biden-repeatedly-emailed-h-rcna130682; Jeff Mordock, "FBI Agent Confirms Authenticity of Hunter Biden's Laptop," *Washington Times*, June 4, 2024, https://www.washingtontimes.com/news/2024/jun/4/erika-jensen -confirms-authenticity-of-hunter-biden; "The Bidens' Influence Peddling Timeline," Committee on Oversight and Accountability, accessed July 26, 2025, https://oversight.house.gov/the-bidens-influence-peddling-timeline; "Comer Releases Direct Monthly Payments to Joe Biden from Hunter Biden's Business Entity," Committee on Oversight and Government Reform, December 4, 2023, https://oversight.house.gov/release/comer-releases-direct-monthly-payments -to-joe-biden-from-hunter-bidens-business-entity.

25. Jake Tapper, "Jake Tapper Presses Lara Trump in Heated Interview," *State of the Union*, CNN Politics, October 18, 2020, https://www.cnn.com/videos/poli tics/2020/10/18/sotu-lara-trump-full.cnn; transcript available here: https://tran scripts.cnn.com/show/sotu/date/2020-10-18/segment/01.

26. Donald Trump, "Remarks by President Trump in Press Briefing | August 10, 2020," Trump White House, August 11, 2020, https://trumpwhitehouse.archi ves.gov/briefings-statements/remarks-president-trump-press-briefing-au gust-10-2020.

27. Randy DeSoto, "Election Integrity Win in Georgia: Election Board Reprimands Fulton County, Will Appoint Monitor for 2024," *Western Journal*, May 9, 2024, https://www.westernjournal.com/election-integrity-win-geor gia-election-board-reprimands-fulton-county-will-appoint-monitor-2024.

28. Domenico Montanaro, "President-Elect Joe Biden Hits 80 Million Votes in Year of Record Turnout," NPR, November 25, 2020, https://www.npr.org/2020/11 /25/937248659/president-elect-biden-hits-80-million-votes-in-year-of-record -turnout.

29. Mollie Hemingway, "Written Testimony to the House Administration Committee Rep. Bryan Steil, Chairman," Congress, February 7, 2024, https://www .congress.gov/118/meeting/house/116804/witnesses/HHRG-118-HA00 -Wstate-HemingwayM-20240207-U1.pdf.

30. Josh Christenson, "How Non-Citizens Are Getting Voter Registration Forms Across the U.S.—and How Republicans Are Trying to Stop It," *New York Post*, updated July 10, 2024, https://nypost.com/2024/06/14/us-news/how-non-citi zens-are-getting-voter-registration-forms-across-the-us-and-how-republicans -are-trying-to-stop-it.

31. Bradford Betz, "AG Garland Pledges to Fight Voter ID Laws, Election Integrity Measures," Fox News, March 3, 2024, https://www.foxnews.com/politics /ag-garland-pledges-fight-voter-id-laws-election-integrity-measures.

32. Devon Link, "Fact Check: Joe Biden Misspoke About His Campaign's Voter Protection Efforts," *USA Today*, October 29, 2020, https://www.usatoday.com /story/news/factcheck/2020/10/29/fact-check-joe-biden-misspoke-cam paigns-voter-protections/6061563002.

33. "Statistics," American Presidency Project, UC Santa Barbara, https://www .presidency.ucsb.edu/statistics/elections/2024.

34. "2024 Election Results," Fox News, updated July 24, 2025, https://www.foxnews .com/elections.

35. "2024 National Popular Vote Tracker," *Cook Political Report with Amy Walter*, accessed June 29, 2025, https://www.cookpolitical.com/vote-tracker/2024 /electoral-college.

36. "Was Trump Right All Along? 2024 Results Revive Doubts About 2020," *tippinsights*, November 21, 2024, https://tippinsights.com/was-trump-right-all -along-2024-results-revive-doubts-about-2020.

37. Natalie Colarossi, "Donald Trump's 73.6 Million Popular Votes Is over 7 Million More than Any Sitting President in History," *Newsweek*, November 19, 2020, https://www.newsweek.com/donald-trumps-736-million-popular -votes-over-7-million-more-any-sitting-president-history-1548742.

38. "Fact Check: Vote Spikes in Wisconsin, Michigan and Pennsylvania Do Not Prove Election Fraud," Reuters, November 10, 2020, https://www.reuters.com

/article/world/fact-check-vote-spikes-in-wisconsin-michigan-and-pennsyl
vania-do-not-prove-ele-idUSKBN27Q304.

39. Ryan King, "FBI Delivers Intel to Congress on Alleged Chinese Plot to Interfere in 2020 Election," *New York Post*, June 17, 2025, https://nypost.com
/2025/06/17/us-news/fbi-delivers-intel-to-congress-on-alleged-chinese-plot
-to-interfere-in-2020-election.

40. Trump and Bohner, *Trump: The Art of the Comeback.*

41. Matthew Impelli, "Read the Full Text of Donald Trump's Final Farewell Speech at
Joint Base Andrews," *Newsweek*, January 20, 2021, https://www.newsweek.com
/read-full-text-donald-trumps-final-farewell-speech-joint-base-andrews-1563052.

CHAPTER 9: SHOW ME THE CRIME

1. Michael Henry, "Show Me the Man and I'll Show You the Crime," *Oxford
Eagle*, May 9, 2018, https://www.oxfordeagle.com/2018/05/09/show-me-the
-man-and-ill-show-you-the-crime.

2. Erin Durkin, "Tish James Just Sued Trump—but They've Been at It for Years,"
Politico, September 21, 2022, https://www.politico.com/news/2022/09/21
/james-lawsuit-trump-longstanding-battle-00058128.

3. Kristine Phillips, "New York's Next Attorney General Targeted Slumlords. Now
She's Going After Trump," *Washington Post*, December 19, 2018, https://www
.washingtonpost.com/politics/2018/12/19/new-yorks-next-attorney-general
-targeted-slumlords-now-shes-going-after-trump.

4. Dan Mangan, "Manhattan DA Vance 'Still Fishing for Ways to Justify' Harassment of Trump over Tax Records, Lawyers Claim," CNBC, August 10, 2020,
https://www.cnbc.com/2020/08/10/trump-defends-challenge-to-tax-rec
ords-subpoena-by-manhattan-da-cyrus-vance.html.

5. Chief Justice John G. Roberts Jr., opinion of the Court in *Trump v. Vance*,
No. 19-635, slip op. (U.S. Supreme Court, July 9, 2020), https://www.supreme
court.gov/opinions/19pdf/19-635_o7jq.pdf.

6. Joe Marino and Melissa Klein, "NYC Tourist Shot over Six-Figure Watch Is
Crypto Expert and 'Lifestyle Guru,'" *New York Post*, March 19, 2022, https://ny
post.com/2022/03/19/nyc-tourist-shot-over-six-figure-watch-is-crypto-expert.

7. Natalie Duddridge and Nick Caloway, "Police: Customer Shot When Armed
Robbers Target Outdoor Dining at Philipe Restaurant on Upper East Side,"
CBS News, September 17, 2021, https://www.cbsnews.com/newyork/news
/upper-east-side-restaurant-shooting.

8. Aaron Katersky, "Manhattan DA Cy Vance Will Not Seek Reelection, Trump
Case Pending," ABC News, March 12, 2021, https://abcnews.go.com/US/man
hattan-da-cy-vance-seek-reelection-trump-case/story?id=76411417.

9. Tom Kertscher, "In Context: What NY Attorney General Letitia James Said
About Trump That Trump's Video Left Out," PolitiFact, August 12, 2022, https://
www.politifact.com/article/2022/aug/12/context-what-ny-attorney-general-le
titia-james-sai.

10. Eric Trump (@EricTrump), "As my father sits for a deposition in front of the
most corrupt Attorney General in the United States (Letitia James)[. . .]," X,
August 10, 2022, https://x.com/EricTrump/status/1557341592515747841.

11. Natalie Venegas, "Eric Trump Could Open Himself Up to Criminal Charge, Ex-Prosecutor Warns," *Newsweek*, updated November 6, 2023, https://www.newsweek.com/glenn-kirschner-warns-eric-trump-charged-perjury-1840987.

12. Erik Larson, "Eric Trump Invoked Fifth Amendment About 500 Times, N.Y. AG Says," *Bloomberg*, January 19, 2022, https://www.bloomberg.com/news/articles/2022-01-19/eric-trump-invoked-fifth-amendment-about-500-times-n-y-ag-says.

13. Ari Melber, "Eric Trump Takes 5th in New York Probe into Trump Org. Finances," *The Beat with Ari Melber*, MSNBC, August 24, 2020, https://www.msnbc.com/the-beat-with-ari/watch/eric-trump-takes-5th-in-new-york-probe-into-trump-org-finances-90571845585.

14. Tal Axelrod, "Trump Says He Changed His Mind About Taking the Fifth, Which He Once Said Was for 'the Mob,'" ABC News, August 10, 2022, https://abcnews.go.com/Politics/trump-changed-mind-taking-claimed-mob/story?id=88211107.

15. Ayana Archie, "Andrew Cuomo Files a Complaint Against Letitia James for Her Sexual Harassment Report," NPR, September 14, 2022, https://www.npr.org/2022/09/14/1122894632/andrew-cuomo-letitia-james-new-york.

16. Cristina Laila, "New: Letitia James Visited Joe Biden White House Several Times amid Trump Witch Hunt," *Gateway Pundit*, January 10, 2024, https://www.thegatewaypundit.com/2024/01/new-letitia-james-visited-joe-biden-white-house.

17. "Trump Levels Unsubstantiated Claims of Collusion Against New York AG as Civil Fraud Trial Wraps Up," *U.S. News & World Report*, January 12, 2024, https://www.usnews.com/news/best-states/new-york/articles/2024-01-12/trump-levels-unsubstantiated-claims-of-collusion-against-new-york-ag-as-civil-fraud-trial-wraps-up.

18. Jonathan Turley, "The $335M Trump Crazy Civil Court Decision Has All Kinds of Unexpected Consequences," Fox News, February 20, 2024, https://www.foxnews.com/opinion/355m-trump-crazy-civil-court-decision-kinds-unexpected-consequences.

19. "Boeing Charged with 737 Max Fraud Conspiracy and Agrees to Pay over $2.5 Billion," U.S. Department of Justice, January 7, 2021, https://www.justice.gov/archives/opa/pr/boeing-charged-737-max-fraud-conspiracy-and-agrees-pay-over-25-billion.

20. Nick Robertson, "Kevin O'Leary: 'Rogue Judge' Handed Down Trump Fraud Verdict," *The Hill*, February 21, 2024, https://thehill.com/regulation/court-battles/4481795-kevin-oleary-rogue-judge-handed-down-trump-fraud-verdict.

21. Kristen Altus, "Billionaire CEO, Real Estate Investor on Impact of Trump Verdict: 'Nobody Wants to Do Business' in NYC," Fox Business, May 31, 2024, https://www.foxbusiness.com/media/billionaire-ceo-real-estate-investor-impact-trump-verdict-nobody-wants-do-business-nyc.

22. Kristen Altus, "Real Estate Investor to 'Immediately Discontinue' Working in NYC over Trump Verdict, Eyeing Florida, Texas," Fox Business, February 21, 2024, https://www.foxbusiness.com/real-estate/real-estate-investor-immediately-discontinue-working-nyc-trump-verdict-florida-texas.

23. Lauren Irwin, "Hochul Tells NY Businesses Not to Fear About Trump Verdict: 'Nothing to Worry About,'" *The Hill*, February 18, 2024, https://thehill.com

/homenews/state-watch/4474774-hochul-tells-ny-businesses-not-to-fear
-about-trump-verdict-nothing-to-worry-about.

24. Brooke Singman, "Trump Says He Has Nearly $500M in Cash, Suggests He Could Afford Bond in New York AG Case, Slams 'Hack' Judge," Fox News, March 22, 2024, https://www.foxnews.com/politics/trump-says-he-has-nearly -500m-cash-suggests-could-afford-bond-new-york-ag-case-slams-hack-judge.

25. The New York Times (@nytimes), "Donald Trump owes $454 million by Monday [. . .]," X, March 24, 2024, https://x.com/nytimes/status/1771989117 548577119.

26. NY AG James (@NewYorkStateAG), "+$114,553.04," X, February 24, 2024, https://x.com/NewYorkStateAG/status/1761457522395750576.

27. Harold Hutchinson, "'They Are Lunatics': Trump Blasts Letitia James, Judge After Civil Fraud Case Ruling," *Daily Caller*, February 16, 2024, https://daily caller.com/2024/02/16/lunatics-trump-blasts-letitia-james-judge-civil-fraud.

28. Trump and Schwartz, *Trump: The Art of the Deal*.

29. Harold Hutchison, "Andrew Cuomo Says Trump Civil Fraud Case 'Should Have Never Been Brought,'" *Daily Caller*, June 22, 2024, https://dailycaller .com/2024/06/22/andrew-cuomo-trump-civil-fraud-case.

30. Susan Edelman and Rich Calder, "FDNY Boss Hunts Down Staffers Who Booed NY AG Letitia James, Cheered for Trump at Promotion Ceremony," *New York Post*, March 9, 2024, https://nypost.com/2024/03/09/us-news/fdny -boss-laura-kavanagh-hunts-down-staffers-who-booed-ny-ag-letitia-james -cheered-for-trump-at-promotion-ceremony.

31. Frieda Powers, "Fuming FDNY Officials Call All Firefighters Who Booed Letita [*sic*] James to 'Come Forward' for 'Education,'" *American Wire*, March 12, 2024, https://americanwirenews.com/fdny-officials-deny-hunting-down-firefighters -who-booed-letitia-james-but-still-demand-they-come-forward-report.

CHAPTER 10: IT'S ALL CONNECTED

1. "'The Real Verdict Is Going to Be November 5th by the People,'" C-SPAN, May 30, 2024, https://www.c-span.org/video/?c5119261/the-real-verdict-no vember-5th-people.

2. Graham Kates, "Prosecutors Threatened to Charge Trump Organization CFO's Son, Lawyers Say," CBS News, February 23, 2022, https://www.cbsnews.com /news/prosecutors-trump-organization-cfo-allen-weisselberg-son-barry.

3. *New York v. Allen Weisselberg*, New York State Unified Court System, March 4, 2024, https://www.nycourts.gov/LegacyPDFS/press/PDFs/SCI-03042024 100454.pdf.

4. Corinne Ramey, "Trump Case: New York Prosecutor Known for Aggressive Pursuit of Evidence," *Wall Street Journal*, May 28, 2021, https://www.wsj.com /politics/policy/trump-case-new-york-prosecutor-known-for-aggressive -pursuit-of-evidence-11622206821.

5. Michael R. Sisak and Philip Marcelo, "Former Trump Executive Allen Weis-selberg Sentenced to 5 Months in Jail for Lying," Associated Press, April 10, 2024, https://apnews.com/article/weisselberg-trump-perjury-new-york-b76c de56c6cb983ab8789f95d5a0c6c0.

6. Robin Levinson-King and Kayla Epstein, "Who Is Juan Merchan, the 'No-Nonsense' Judge Who Oversaw Trump's Hush-Money Case?" BBC News, May 31, 2024, https://www.bbc.com/news/world-us-canada-65182727.

7. Alvin L. Bragg Jr. to all staff, "Day-One Letter: Policies & Procedures," January 3, 2022, https://www.manhattanda.org/wp-content/uploads/2022/01/Day-One-Letter-Policies-1.03.2022.pdf.

8. Melissa Klein, "NYC Convictions Plummet, Downgraded Charges Surge Under Manhattan DA Bragg," New York Post, updated November 27, 2022, https://nypost.com/2022/11/26/convictions-plummet-downgraded-charges-surge-under-manhattan-da-bragg/.

9. Shayna Jacobs et al., "Prosecutor Who Resigned over Stalled Trump Probe Says Ex-President Committed Felonies," Washington Post, March 23, 2022, https://www.washingtonpost.com/national-security/2022/03/23/trump-pomerantz-resignation-guilty.

10. Mark Pomerantz, "Read the Full Text of Mark Pomerantz's Resignation Letter," New York Times, March 23, 2022, https://www.nytimes.com/2022/03/23/nyregion/mark-pomerantz-resignation-letter.html.

11. Jonah E. Bromwich, "Manhattan D.A. Hires Ex-Justice Official to Help Lead Trump Inquiry," New York Times, December 5, 2022, https://www.nytimes.com/2022/12/05/nyregion/alvin-bragg-trump-investigation.html.

12. Josh Christenson, "Trump Hush Money Prosecutor Matthew Colangelo Was Political Consultant for DNC, Ex-Obama Donor," New York Post, May 6, 2024, https://nypost.com/2024/05/06/us-news/trump-hush-money-prosecutor-matthew-colenagelo-was-political-consultant-for-dnc-ex-obama-donor.

13. Aaron Katersky and Peter Charalambous, "Timeline: Manhattan DA's Stormy Daniels Hush Money Case Against Donald Trump," ABC News, June 11, 2025, https://www.abcnews.go.com/Politics/timeline-manhattan-district-attorney-case-donald-trump/story?id=98389444.

14. Former Congressman Matt Gaetz (@FmrRepMattGaetz), "NEW VIDEO: Trump Prosecutor PLEADS FIFTH when asked if he BROKE THE LAW investigating Trump!," X, May 2, 2024, https://x.com/FmrRepMattGaetz/status/1786003646712270941.

15. Margot Cleveland, "Chuck Schumer's Brother Works for Law Firm Behind Bragg's Get-Trump Indictment," Federalist, June 4, 2024, https://thefederalist.com/2024/06/04/chuck-schumers-brother-works-for-law-firm-behind-braggs-get-trump-indictment.

16. "Robert B. Schumer," Paul, Weiss, accessed June 29, 2025, https://www.paulweiss.com/professionals/partners-and-counsel/robert-b-schumer.

17. "Robert B. Schumer," Lawdragon, accessed July 26, 2025, https://www.lawdragon.com/attorneys/robert-b-schumer.

18. Darren Samuelsohn, "Feds' Probe into Trump Hush Money Payments Is Over, Judge Says," Politico, July 17, 2019, https://www.politico.com/story/2019/07/17/trump-hush-money-payments-probe-over-1418074.

19. Glenn Thrush et al., "Why Was Trump Indicted by the Manhattan D.A. over Hush Money, but Not by the Justice Department?," New York Times, March 31, 2023, https://www.nytimes.com/2023/03/31/nyregion/justice-dept-trump-indictment-charges.html.

20. Aaron Blake, "The FEC's Inexplicable Punt on Trump's Hush-Money Payments," *Washington Post*, May 7, 2021, https://www.washingtonpost.com/politics/2021/05/07/trump-skates-past-legal-trouble-first-time-post-presidency.

21. "§30.10 Timeliness of Prosecutions; Periods of Limitation" (2010) New York Consolidated Laws, New York State Senate, accessed June 29, 2025, https://www.nysenate.gov/legislation/laws/CPL/30.10.

22. Devan Cole, "Who Is Juan Merchan? What to Know About the Judge in Trump's Hush Money Case," CNN Politics, April 15, 2024, https://www.cnn.com/2024/04/15/politics/juan-merchan-judge-nyc/index.html.

23. "Part 100: Judicial Conduct" (1972) New York State Unified Court System, accessed June 29, 2025, https://ww2.nycourts.gov/rules/chiefadmin/100.shtml.

24. Jon Levine and Rich Calder, "Dem Clients of Daughter of NY Judge in Trump Hush-Money Trial Raised $93M off the Case," *New York Post*, March 30, 2024, https://nypost.com/2024/03/30/us-news/dem-clients-of-daughter-of-judge-in-trump-trial-raised-90m-off-case.

25. "Stefanik Files Judicial Complaint Against Acting Supreme Court Justice Juan Merchan," Elise for Congress, May 21, 2024, https://eliseforcongress.com/2024/05/21/stefanik-files-judicial-complaint-against-acting-supreme-court-justice-juan-merchan.

26. Jesse McKinley and Jonah E. Bromwich, "Trump Trial Week 4: Testy and Explicit, Then Calm Before the Cohen Storm," *New York Times*, May 10, 2024, https://www.nytimes.com/2024/05/10/nyregion/trump-michael-cohen-trial.html.

27. Josh Gerstein, "Judge Limits Scope of Testimony from Trump's Planned Expert Witness," *Politico*, May 20, 2024, https://www.politico.com/live-updates/2024/05/20/trump-hush-money-criminal-trial/judge-limits-trumps-expert-00158857.

28. Andrew Mark Miller, "Jury Instructions Conclude in Trump's NYC Criminal Trial, Here's What the Jury Was Told," Fox News, May 29, 2024, https://www.foxnews.com/politics/jury-instructions-conclude-trumps-nyc-criminal-trial-heres-what-jury-told.

29. Jonathan Turley (@JonathanTurley), "Before the jury entered, the judge told the parties not to go into the law, 'that will be my job.' [. . .]," X, May 28, 2024, https://x.com/JonathanTurley/status/1795457475816083768.

30. Trump War Room (@TrumpWarRoom), "@EricTrump: While New Yorkers watch murders in the streets, women getting thrown in front of trains, and kids getting shot in Times Square [. . .]," X, May 28, 2024, https://x.com/TrumpWarRoom/status/1795512072119243197.

31. Joe Marino et al., "3 Suspects in Custody After Reported Machete Attack Injures 1 at Times Square McDonald's," *New York Post*, May 30, 2024, https://nypost.com/2024/05/30/us-news/1-injured-in-possible-machete-attack-at-times-square-mcdonalds.

32. Elon Musk (@elonmusk), "Indeed, great damage was done today to the public's faith in the American legal system. [. . .]," X, May 31, 2024, https://x.com/elonmusk/status/1796440638617244012.

33. Michael R. Sisak, "Prosecutors Want Donald Trump to Remain Under a Gag Order at Least Until He's Sentenced July 11," Associated Press, June 5, 2024,

https://apnews.com/article/donald-trump-gag-order-hush-money-juan-mer chan-795452fdd31fda3fedc086bd6c0fc94d.

34. Brooke Singman and Brandon Gillespie, "Fulton County Prosecutor, Fani Willis Romantic Partner, Met with Biden White House Twice Before Charging Trump," Fox News, January 9, 2024, https://www.foxnews.com/politics/fulton -county-prosecutor-fani-willis-romantic-partner-met-biden-white-house -twice-before-charging-trump.

35. Sean O'Driscoll, "Fani Willis Met with Kamala Harris Before Indicting Trump—Attorney," Newsweek, updated March 7, 2024, https://www.newsweek .com/fani-willis-kamala-harris-indict-donald-trump-attorney-ashleigh -merchant-1876573.

36. Katelynn Richardson, "Appeals Court Pauses Trump's Georgia Case Until Decision on Fani Willis," Daily Signal, June 5, 2024, https://www.dailysignal.com /2024/06/05/appeals-court-pauses-trumps-georgia-case-until-decision-on -fani-willis.

37. Katelynn Richardson, "Supreme Court Rules Trump 'Entitled to Immunity' from Prosecution for Official Acts," Daily Caller, July 1, 2024, https://daily caller.com/2024/07/01/supreme-court-rules-trump-has-immunity-for-offi cial-acts-in-appeal.

38. Jeff Mordock, "FBI Returns Property Seized from Trump During Mara-Lago Raids," Washington Times, February 28, 2025, https://www.wash ingtontimes.com/news/2025/feb/28/fbi-returns-property-seized-trump -mar-lago-raids.

39. Julie Kelly, "Unredactions Reveal Early White House Involvement in Trump Documents Case," RealClearInvestigations, May 2, 2024, https:// www.realclearinvestigations.com/articles/2024/05/02/unredactions_reveal _early_white_house_involvement_in_trump_documents_case_1028630.html.

40. Adam Carlson et al., "AG Merrick Garland Says He Signed Off on Trump Search, Denounces Attacks on Law Enforcement," ABC News, August 11, 2022, https:// www.abcnews.go.com/Politics/attorney-general-merrick-garland-set-speak /story?id=88252143.

41. Charlie Spiering, "Joe Biden Insists He Had 'Zero' Prior Notice of FBI Mar-a-Lago Raid," Breitbart, August 24, 2022, https://www.breitbart.com/politics/2022/08/24 /joe-biden-insists-he-had-zero-prior-notice-of-fbi-mar-a-lago-raid.

42. Amy Sherman, "Joe Biden Classified Documents Timeline: Where, When Were Files Found?," PolitiFact, January 25, 2023, https://www.politifact.com/article /2023/jan/25/i-have-no-regrets-tracking-the-joe-biden-classifie.

43. Gerstein and Cheney, "Prosecutors: Docs in Boxes Seized from Mar-a-Lago Were Inadvertently Jumbled."

44. United States District Court for the Southern District of Florida, case no. 23-80101-CR-CANNON(s) (docket no. 2:24-cv-14153-AMC), https://sto rage.courtlistener.com/recap/gov.uscourts.flsd.648652/gov.uscourts.flsd .648652.277.0.pdf.

45. Joy Pullmann, "Did Federal Agencies Plant Classified Documents to Frame Trump?," Federalist, May 9, 2024, https://thefederalist.com/2024/05/09/did -federal-agencies-plant-classified-documents-to-frame-trump.

46. Hannah Rabinowitz et al., "Florida Hearing in Trump Classified Documents Case Devolves into Shouting Match," CNN Politics, May 22, 2024, https://

www.cnn.com/2024/05/22/politics/trump-documents-case-judge-cannon
-hearing/index.html.

47. Dan Mangan, "Trump Valet's Lawyer Complains of Threats After Special Counsel Revealed Mar-a-Lago Worker Changed Story," CNBC, updated August 26,
2023, https://www.cnbc.com/2023/08/25/trump-valets-lawyer-received-threats
-after-special-counsel-bombshell.html.

48. Alan Feuer, "Clarence Thomas Raised Another Issue: Was Jack Smith Legally
Appointed?," *New York Times*, July 1, 2024, https://www.nytimes.com/2024
/07/01/us/politics/clarence-thomas-special-counsel-appointment.html.

49. Greg Norman, "Judge Dismisses Trump's Florida Classified Documents Case,"
Fox News, July 15, 2024, https://www.foxnews.com/politics/judge-dismiss
es-trumps-florida-classified-documents-case.

50. Brooke Singman, "Trump to Sue DOJ for $100M over Mar-a-Lago Raid, Alleg-
ing 'Political Persecution,'" Fox News, August 12, 2024, https://www.foxnews
.com/politics/trump-sue-doj-100m-over-mar-a-lago-raid-alleging-political
-persecution.

51. Greg Norman and Chris Pandolfo, "5 Key Lines from Supreme Court Trump
Immunity Decision," Fox News, July 2, 2024, https://www.foxnews.com/poli
tics/5-key-lines-from-supreme-court-trump-immunity-decision.

52. Chris Mueller, "After Conviction, Trump Questioned the New York Statute
of Limitations. Here Are the Facts," *USA Today*, June 5, 2024, https://www
.usatoday.com/story/news/factcheck/2024/06/05/trump-case-statute-of-lim
itations-explained/73983592007.

53. Priscilla DeGregory and Kyle Schnitzer, "Judge Pushes Back on Trump's 'Statute of Limitations' Claim at $250M Civil Fraud Trial," *New York Post*, October
3, 2023, https://nypost.com/2023/10/03/trumps-statute-of-limitations-claim
-at-civil-trial-explained.

54. Chief Justice John G. Roberts Jr., opinion of the Court in *Trump v. Vance*,
no. 19-635 (U.S. Supreme Court, July 9, 2020), https://www.supremecourt.gov
/opinions/19pdf/19-635_o7jq.pdf.

55. The Privacy and Civil Liberties Oversight Board, *Report on the Surveillance
Program Operated Pursuant to Section 702 of the Foreign Intelligence Surveillance Act*, September 28, 2023, https://documents.pclob.gov/prod/Docu
ments/OversightReport/054417e4-9d20-427a-9850-862a6f29ac42/2023%20
PCLOB%20702%20Report%20(002).pdf.

56. Jason Cohen, "Andrew McCabe Acknowledges 'Mistakes' in Trump Campaign Investigation as He Pushes Warrantless Surveillance Tool," *Daily Caller*,
April 11, 2024, https://dailycaller.com/2024/04/11/andrew-mccabe-acknowl
edges-mistakes-in-trump-campaign-investigation-as-he-pushes-warrant
less-surveillance-tool.

57. Zach Montellaro et al., "States Can't Kick Trump Off Ballot, Supreme Court
Says," *Politico*, March 4, 2024, https://www.politico.com/news/2024/03/04
/states-cant-remove-trump-from-ballot-supreme-court-says-00144673.

58. Devlin Barrett and Perry Stein, "Justice Dept. Plans to Pursue Trump Cases
Past Election Day, Even if He Wins," *Washington Post*, July 2, 2024, https://
www.washingtonpost.com/national-security/2024/07/02/justice-dept-trump
-prosecute-after-election.

59. Gold, "The Campaign to Impeach President Trump Has Begun."

CHAPTER 11: NOT SENDING OUR BEST

1. "This Is a Transcript of Rona Barrett's 1980 Interview of Donald Trump," *Washington Post*, May 2, 2025, https://www.washingtonpost.com/wp-stat /graphics/politics/trump-archive/docs/rona-barrett-1980-interview-of-don ald-trump.pdf.

2. Sky News Australia (@SkyNewsAustralia), "Young Donald Trump Predicts Joe Biden in 1980 Interview," YouTube, March 9, 2024, https://www.youtube.com /watch?v=QQDKekRg6B4.

3. "Jared Bernstein," Columbia School of Social Work, accessed June 12, 2025, https://socialwork.columbia.edu/content/jared-bernstein; "Jared Bernstein," Cen- ter for Immigration Studies, accessed June 12, 2025, https://cis.org/Jared-Bern stein.

4. Gabriel Hays, "VP Harris Grilled for Saying Inflation Reduction Act Is Work- ing via Gov't Giving Out 'Trillions of Dollars,'" Fox News, May 17, 2024, https:// www.foxnews.com/media/harris-grilled-saying-inflation-reduction-act -working-via-govt-giving-trillions-dollars.

5. Eric Revell, "White House Economic Adviser Struggles with Question on Monetary Policy," Fox Business, May 4, 2024, https://www.foxbusiness.com /politics/white-house-economic-adviser-struggles-with-question-on-mone tary-policy.

6. Josh Christenson, "Pete Buttigieg's DOT Spent $80 Billion on DEI Grants, Delayed Air Traffic Control Upgrades: Records, Industry Insiders," *New York Post*, July 21, 2025, https://nypost.com/2025/07/21/us-news/pete-buttigiegs -dot-spent-80-billion-on-dei-grants-delayed-air-traffic-control-upgrades -records-industry-insiders.

7. David Shepardson, "Exclusive: Biden Nominee to Head FAA Withdraws After Republican Criticism," Reuters, March 25, 2023, https://www.reuters.com /business/aerospace-defense/biden-nominee-head-faa-withdraws-after-re publican-attacks-sources-2023-03-26.

8. Michael Ruiz, "Milley Maintains Military Is 'Apolitical' After 'White Rage' Comment," Fox News, July 21, 2021, https://www.foxnews.com/politics/mil ley-maintains-military-is-apolitical-after-white-rage-comment.

9. Darlene Superville, "Trump Paints Apocalyptic Portrait of Life in U.S. Under Biden," Associated Press, October 29, 2020, https://apnews.com/article/elec tion-2020-joe-biden-donald-trump-police-economy-3082b995c1fd8912967 1b245797bc902.

10. "RNC 2020: Trump Warns Biden Will 'Demolish' American Dream," BBC News, August 28, 2020, https://www.bbc.com/news/election-us-2020-53942667.

11. Donald Trump, "Donald Trump Rally, Johnstown, PA, Transcript October 13," rev. October 13, 2020, https://www.rev.com/transcripts/donald-trump-rally -johnstown-pa-transcript-october-13.

12. Donald Trump, "President Trump Campaign Rally in Tucson, Arizona," C-SPAN, October 19, 2020, https://www.c-span.org/program/campaign-2020 /president-trump-campaign-rally-in-tucson-arizona/554925.

13. Amanda Gerut, "Trump Swings at Bank of America CEO Brian Moynihan and JPMorgan's Jamie Dimon at Davos: 'What You're Doing Is Wrong,'" *For- tune*, January 23, 2025, https://fortune.com/2025/01/23/trump-davos-bank-of

-america-brian-moynihan-jpmorgan-jamie-dimon-debanking-conservatives
-andreessen.

14. Eric Trump (@EricTrump), "Today, the Trump Organization filed a lawsuit in Miami-Dade County against @CapitalOne [. . .]," X, March 7, 2025, https://x.com/EricTrump/status/1898061264968204332.

15. CNN (@CNN), "RFK Jr. Says Biden Is Bigger Threat to Democracy than Trump," YouTube, April 1, 2024, https://www.youtube.com/watch?v=KAgQ2sfAjV0.

16. Committee on the Judiciary and Select Subcommittee on the Weaponization of the Federal Government, *The Censorship-Industrial Complex: How Top Biden White House Officials Coerced Big Tech to Censor Americans, True Information, and Critics of the Biden Administration*, appendix, U.S. House of Representatives, May 1, 2024, https://judiciary.house.gov/sites/evo-subsites/republicans-judiciary.house.gov/files/evo-media-document/Censorship-Industrial-Complex-WH-Report_Appendix.pdf.

17. Julia Edwards Ainsley, "Exclusive—Trump Border 'Wall' to Cost $21.6 Billion, Take 3.5 Years to Build: Homeland Security Internal Report," Reuters, February 9, 2017, https://www.reuters.com/article/idUSKBN15O2ZY.

CHAPTER 12: PROUD OF THE FIGHT

1. "Presidential Candidate Donald Trump Indiana Primary Night Speech," C-SPAN, May 3, 2016, https://www.c-span.org/video/?409020-1/presidential-candidate-donald-trump-indiana-primary-night-speech.

2. Ben Kochman, "Trump Temporarily Allowed to Run NY Company but Remains on Hook to Pay $454M Penalty," *New York Post*, February 28, 2024, https://nypost.com/2024/02/28/us-news/trump-temporarily-allowed-to-run-ny-company-but-remains-on-hook-to-pay-454m-penalty.

3. Trump and Schwartz, *Trump: The Art of the Deal*.

4. "DNC Statement on Lara Trump Being Elected Co-Chair of the RNC," Democratic National Committee, March 8, 2024, https://democrats.org/news/dnc-statement-on-lara-trump-being-elected-co-chair-of-the-rnc.

CHAPTER 13: FIGHT, FIGHT, FIGHT

1. Ivana Saric and Avery Lotz, "'Full of S**t': Secret Service Director Grilled over Trump Rally Shooting," *Axios*, July 22, 2024, https://www.axios.com/2024/07/22/kimberly-cheatle-secret-service-trump-hearing.

2. Byron York, "Trump: 'I'm Not Supposed to Be Here,'" *Washington Examiner*, July 14, 2024, https://www.washingtonexaminer.com/news/campaigns/presidential/3082224/trump-im-not-supposed-to-be-here.

3. "Trump Campaign and RNC Unveil Historic 100,000 Person Strong Election Integrity Program," Republican National Committee, April 19, 2024, https://gop.com/press-release/trump-campaign-and-rnc-unveil-historic-100000-person-strong-election-integrity-program.

4. U.S. Department of Justice (@TheJusticeDept), "Today, Attorney General Garland convened a meeting of the Election Threats Task Force [. . .]," X, May 13,

2024, https://x.com/TheJusticeDept/status/1790134573931626571; Merrick B. Garland, "Attorney General Merrick B. Garland Delivers Remarks at the Election Threats Task Force Meeting," U.S. Department of Justice, May 13, 2024, https://www.justice.gov/opa/speech/attorney-general-merrick-b-garland-delivers-remarks-election-threats-task-force-meeting.

5. Stephen Sorace, "Harris Campaign Costs for Star-Studded Events on Election Eve Ballooned to over $10M: Report," Fox News, November 18, 2024, https://www.foxnews.com/politics/harris-campaign-costs-star-studded-events-election-eve-ballooned-over-10m-report.

6. Brian Flood, "CBS News Statement on Controversial *60 Minutes* Edit Falls Flat on Social Media: 'Publish. The. Transcript,'" Fox News, October 22, 2024, https://www.foxnews.com/media/cbs-news-statement-controversial-60-minutes-edit-falls-flat-social-media-publish-the-transcript.

7. Audrey Conklin, "Trump Assassination Attempt Victim Corey Comperatore's Family Vows to Get Justice: 'Blood Is on Their Hands,'" Fox News, August 16, 2024, https://www.foxnews.com/us/trump-assassination-attempt-victim-corey-comperatore-family-vows-get-justice-blood-their-hands.

CHAPTER 14: SUCCESS AS REVENGE

1. "Trump: 'My Revenge Will Be Success,'" *The Ingraham Angle*, Fox News, February 20, 2024, https://www.foxnews.com/video/6347284833112.

2. Jim Hoft, "Judge Orders Democrat 'Poll Workers' to Remove Misleading 'Voter Protection' Badges After Voter Intimidation Complaints in Allegheny County," *Gateway Pundit*, November 5, 2024, https://www.thegatewaypundit.com/2024/11/judge-orders-democrat-poll-workers-remove-misleading-voter.

3. Greg Norman, "GOP Pennsylvania Poll Watchers Admitted After Initially Being Turned Away, RNC Says," Fox News, November 5, 2024, https://www.foxnews.com/politics/gop-pennsylvania-poll-watchers-admitted-after-initially-being-turned-away-rnc-says.

4. Louis Casiano, "Pennsylvania Dem Gov. Josh Shapiro Sides with State Supreme Court Ruling Not to Count Certain Mail-In Ballots," Fox News, November 18, 2024, https://www.foxnews.com/politics/pennsylvania-dem-gov-josh-shapiro-sides-state-supreme-court-ruling-not-count-certain-mail-in-ballots.

5. Amber Coakley, "What States Don't Require ID to Vote In-Person?" FOX 5 San Diego, November 3, 2024, https://fox5sandiego.com/election/what-states-dont-require-id-to-vote-in-person.

6. InteractivePolls (@IAPolls2022), "Pew Research: 2024 Presidential Election validated voters survey (swing from 2020 [. . .]," X, June 27, 2025, https://x.com/IAPolls2022/status/1938601443583226181; "2016–2024 Voter Demographics, Based on Validated Voters," Pew Research Center, accessed July 1, 2025, https://www.pewresearch.org/politics/2025/06/26/behind-trumps-2024-victory-a-more-racially-and-ethnically-diverse-voter-coalition/.

7. Eric Trump (@EricTrump), photograph of Donald Trump, X, November 6, 2024, https://x.com/EricTrump/status/1854057676612755608.

8. Joe Concha, "Where Are the Joes? Scarborough, Biden Lay Low after Embarrassing Debate," Fox News, July 1, 2024, https://www.foxnews.com/opinion/where-joes-scarborough-biden-lay-low-after-embarrassing-debate.

9. David Bauder, "'Kissing the Ring?' MSNBC *Morning Joe* Hosts Meet with Trump to Reopen Lines of Communication," Associated Press, November 18, 2024, https://apnews.com/article/morning-joe-trump-meeting-ring-cf4816dd28372a4c942d256df2e440ae.

10. Lauren Aratani, "Jeff Bezos, Mark Zuckerberg and Other Business Leaders Congratulate Trump," *Guardian*, November 6, 2024, https://www.theguardian.com/us-news/2024/nov/06/trump-election-win-billionaires.

11. America (@america), "All 50 States shifted more Republican from 2020 to 2024. [. . .]," X, November 27, 2024, https://x.com/america/status/1861889787298238708.

EPILOGUE: SO MUCH WINNING

1. Jill Colvin, "DNC, Clinton Campaign Agree to Steele Dossier Funding Fine," Associated Press, March 31, 2022, https://apnews.com/article/russia-ukraine-2022-midterm-elections-business-elections-presidential-elections-5468774d18e8c46f81b55e9260b13e93.

2. Brooke Singman, "Soros' Alleged Ties to Russiagate Exposed in Declassified Annex of Durham Report," Fox News, July 31, 2025, https://www.foxnews.com/politics/soros-alleged-ties-russiagate-exposed-declassified-annex-durham-report.

3. "Trump: Unmasking of Flynn Is 'Greatest Political Scam in History of Our Country,'" Fox News, May 17, 2020, https://www.foxnews.com/transcript/trump-unmasking-of-flynn-is-greatest-political-scam-in-history-of-our-country.

4. Sam Gringlas, "Georgia Court Blocks Fulton DA Willis from Trump Election Interference Case," NPR, December 19, 2024, https://www.npr.org/2024/12/19/nx-s1-5234059/georgia-trump-case-fani-willis-dismissal.

5. Brooke Singman, "Bragg Case 'Effectively Over' in 'Major Victory,' Trump Officials Say," Fox News, November 19, 2024, https://www.foxnews.com/politics/bragg-case-effectively-over-major-victory-trump-officials-say.

6. Brooke Singman, "Prosecutors Request Stay in Trump NY Case Until 2029 as Defense Plans Motion for Dismissal 'Once and for All,'" Fox News, November 19, 2024, https://www.foxnews.com/politics/ny-prosecutors-request-stay-trump-case-until-2029-defense-plans-motion-dismissal-once-all.

7. Brooke Singman et al., "Judge Grants Jack Smith Request to Dismiss Jan. 6 Charges Against Trump, Appeal Dropped in Florida Docs Case," Fox News, November 25, 2024, https://www.foxnews.com/politics/judge-grants-jack-smith-request-dismiss-jan-6-charges-against-trump-appeal-dropped-florida-docs-case.

8. "Jack Smith to Drop Trump Election Interference Case," *America Reports*, Fox News, November 25, 2024, https://www.foxnews.com/video/6365172468112.

9. "N.Y. AG James on New Trump Administration: 'We Are Prepared to Fight Back,'" NBC News, November 6, 2024, https://www.nbcnews.com/video/n-y-ag-james-says-her-office-is-prepared-to-fight-back-in-new-trump-presidency-223744069784.

ABOUT THE AUTHOR

Eric Trump is the Executive Vice President of the Trump Organization, where he oversees the company's vast global real estate portfolio and leads its strategic growth across luxury hospitality, commercial, and residential development; golf; and blockchain-based ventures. Based in Palm Beach, Florida, Eric plays a central role in all aspects of the business, including acquisitions, financing, design, construction, branding, and all hospitality operations.

Under Eric's leadership, the Trump Organization has expanded its global footprint and solidified its position as one of the world's most iconic private real estate brands. He has been instrumental in the rise of Trump Golf, growing it from just three properties in 2006 to nineteen world-class clubs across the United States, Europe, Asia, and the Middle East. He personally oversaw the £200 million restoration of Trump Turnberry in Scotland—host of four Open Championships—and the $250 million revitalization of Trump National Doral Miami, reestablishing both as international golf destinations, just to name a select few.

Eric played a founding role in the creation of Trump Hotels, the award-winning luxury hotel brand with flagship properties in New York, Chicago, Las Vegas, Miami, Virginia, Ireland, and Scotland. The brand has received top honors from Forbes Travel Guide, Tripadvisor, AAA, and *Condé Nast Traveler* under his leadership. He also oversees the Mar-a-Lago Club, a collection of exclusive private estates—including Le Château des Palmiers in Saint Martin—and one of the most exclusive portfolios of office, residential, and retail properties anywhere in the world, including Trump Tower, Trump 40 Wall Street, and Trump Park Avenue, just to name a few.

In 2022, Eric led the record-breaking sale of Trump International

Hotel in Washington, D.C., achieving the highest price-per-key ever recorded for a leasehold interest in U.S. history and earning Single Asset Transaction of the Year from Americas Lodging Investment Summit. He also directed some of the largest commercial real estate deals in New York, including long-term partnerships with Louis Vuitton, Gucci, and other global luxury brands on 5th Avenue. He facilitated the successful sale of Ferry Point in New York to Bally's Corporation, one of the largest golf transactions of its kind in United States history.

Eric leads the operations of Trump Winery in Charlottesville, Virginia—the largest vineyard on the East Coast and a recipient of multiple gold medals and international awards—and *Wine Enthusiast* magazine named him their Rising Star of the Year in 2013. Eric also oversees a pipeline of more than twenty major projects in development around the globe, including high-profile ventures in the Dominican Republic, Indonesia, the Philippines, the United Arab Emirates, Saudi Arabia, Oman, India, Uruguay, and other key international markets—further extending the Trump brand's reach and influence.

An early adopter of innovation, Eric has pushed into cryptocurrency and blockchain technology. He plays a key role in World Liberty Financial, a decentralized finance platform bridging traditional capital markets and blockchain applications. He is also a cofounder and the chief strategy officer of American Bitcoin, a U.S.-based initiative focused on domestic bitcoin mining and accumulation, underscoring his commitment to shaping the future of digital finance.

Eric appeared in seven seasons of NBC's hit television show *The Celebrity Apprentice*, where he served as a boardroom advisor. The show consistently drew millions of viewers and achieved some of the highest ratings of any show on network television.

Beyond business, Eric has a long-standing commitment to philanthropy. At the age of twenty-one, he founded the Eric Trump Foundation, which has since raised more than $50 million for St. Jude Children's Research Hospital. The hospital opened a state-of-the-art surgical ICU named in his honor, recognizing his efforts in the fight against pediatric cancer.

Eric has played a key role in his father's three presidential campaigns as a senior advisor and national surrogate. He crisscrossed the country to energize supporters, deliver the campaign's message, and represent the Trump family's values on the national stage. His discipline, communication skills, and relentless dedication have made him a trusted and highly visible figure in American politics.

Eric graduated with honors in finance and management from Georgetown University. He has a deep love for construction, skiing, the shooting sports, and the outdoors. He lives in Florida with his wife, Lara, and their two children, Luke and Carolina.

EricTrump.com